# Walking
## the Dream

*Ellen Wolfe 11/19/99*

### BY
# Ellen Wolfe

One Step Press
Cookeville, Tennessee
1999

For information address:
3623 Bartlett Drive
East Lake Estates Cookeville, TN 38506

e-mail:  ewolfe@usit.net

ISBN:
0-9675829-0-3

## On the Cover

Photo of Ellen Wolfe in front of Mt. Katahdin and at the
base of the Mt. Katahdin trail by Suellen Alfred

Photo of Mt. Katahdin with Jo Mary Lake in the foreground
by Ellen Wolfe.

Cover designed by Robin J. Choate

Printed by Anderson Performance Printing, Cookeville, Tennessee

I dedicate

# Walking the Dream

to:

My friend and colleague:
Laura LeCoultre Lawson
1962 - 1998

My grandmother:
Katharine S. Ordway
1902 - 1986

&

To All Women
who have lost their lives to breast cancer or who battle the disease.
A cure will be found.

# ACKNOWLEDGMENTS

Thank you Cookeville businesses, members of the community, and Cookeville and Knoxville Chapters of the American Cancer Society for supporting Hike for Healing.

Next, I thank my daughter, Kate Wolfe, for having the insight to know I needed her to walk with me for the first fifty miles. To Suellen Alfred, Judy Madonia, Jane Crooks, my son David, and the children's father Tom Wolfe, thank you for being with Kate and me on that gray drizzly day of March l, 1997, as we planted flowers in honor of breast cancer victims and began our journey.

For driving me to hot meals, clean sheets, and safe respites, my deepest thanks go to my slack pack providers: Suellen Alfred, Sue Pfaltz, Waverly Parker, Janet Ady, Helen Walker, Barbara Digiovanni, George Barboro, Gloria Priest, and Dot McDonald. To Suellen Alfred, Judy Flerl, Linda Brown, Susan Connolly, Dennie Kelley, Pat Perry, Bic Craven, Pam Scott, Gloria Priest, and George Barboro who drove many miles to offer support along the way, I thank you for keeping my focus northward and my dream alive. For mailing support letters, I thank Suellen Alfred, Gloria Priest, George Barboro, Judy Flerl, David Wolfe, my mother Ann Higgins, my sister Sue Westra, Linda Brown, Beth Urquhart, Kate Wolfe, Suzanne Benson, and Mr. and Mrs. Earl Nash, Kim Farmer, Donna Darden, Jane Crooks, Shirley Ulm, the Knoxville Chapter of the American Cancer Society, the Beach Gang, and Cumberland Career Equity Center. I especially thank Gloria Priest for Tic Tacs and Uncle George for wool socks and liners.

For the comradeship of my 1997 Appalachian Trail family community, I thank the following male companions: Stryder, OAB, Pilgrim, Broken Road, Tacet, Vagabond, Crash, Crazy, Luvtuhike, Cowpenski, Roy, Map Man, Rain, Snail, Preacher, veteran Highpocket, Daddy, Stick-in-Face, Buddha Jim, Lynx, Tacoma, Stork, Snake Eyes, Drifter, Peppi, Lorax, Ron Derby, Two Winds, Chief, and thru-hiker Lum of 1994 who flew back from Minnesota to hike Mahoosac Notch with me. To the women Pat Derby, Magot, Grasshopper, Phoenix, and section hikers, Dot, Barbara, Sylvia, Fairbairn, Whippoorwill, and Down Under, I needed each of you.

For a delightful celebration dinner at the Big Moose Inn on July 23d, I thank Suellen Alfred, Jen Hall, Jody Angotti, and Carol Coffin. Special appreciation goes to Jody for helping me edit my manuscript and for emailing support throughout the writing process. I thank Carol for giving me a beautiful color photograph of Mt. Katahdin and Jen for making the Big Moose Inn connection possible.

My deep appreciation goes to Ann D'Alessandro and Helen Rousseau for a wonderful rest in their home following the hike. To Ann I am very grateful for her commitment in taking on the laboriously long-distance task of editing my manuscript. Her professional eye and precise work made Suellen's task of polishing the final draft effortless. I also want to thank my mother Ann Higgins, my Aunt Sue Pfaltz, my daughter Kate Wolfe, and my stepmother Gloria Priest for editing assistance.

With much gratitude I thank Amy Haase, Heather Bailey, Gawaine Long, Troy McCord, Liesl McCord, Chris Stevens, Aaron Bibb as computer help desk workers at Tennessee Tech. University. Without their technical knowledge I might still being trying to figure how to save my manuscript. I thank Mendy Richards for technical assistance with my home computer enabling me to remove the green and red marks from the manuscript. A huge thank you to Cindie Miller of the Herald Citizen, Mandy Mullinix, and Marty Mouton for proof reading the last draft. I am especially grateful to Robin Choate for the professional creative manner in which she put the manuscript on

Pagemaker, scanned the pictures, and reassured me that she could get the manuscript ready for printing by Anderson Performance Printing, where Harvey Anderson was very helpful.

A special thank you goes to my dear Uncle George for hiking some of the roughest sections of the White Mountains with me, supervising my ice water foot soaking, (I still say boo boo pencils would have been a better remedy for swollen feet.), slack packing me in the White Mountains, and being the best friend my father, the late Pete Priest, could have had.

For helping me be aware that my the story of my success could help others follow their dreams, I thank Jesse McIntire, Matt Hawes and Orion Thompson.

Many people were significant to the success of my thru-hike, but steadfast support and encouragement came from my dear friend, Suellen Alfred. From suggesting breast cancer campaign contacts, sending notes in all the maildrop boxes, saying just the words I needed to hear each time I called, driving over a thousand miles to be with me for the last two and a half weeks, and for bringing me back to Tennessee; I could not have walked from Georgia to Maine without Suellen's commitment to my journey and belief that I would climb Katahdin.

To schedule your school or organization for a presentation, please contact:

Ellen Wolfe
3623 Bartlett Drive
East Lake Estates Cookeville, TN 38506
(931) 526-1974

Email:   ewolfe@usit.net

Web site: http://gemini.tntech.edu/~ewolfe

# Table of Contents

**Chapter One**     *"Mummy, why is there white paint on that tree?"*     1
**In the Beginning There was a Goal**

**Chapter Two**     *"Line up fellows, the Cancer Lady is here!"*     12
**A Goal with A Purpose**

**Chapter Three**     *"Guess what Mom, I have three weeks off!"*     20
**Springer Mountain, Georgia to Fontana Dam, North Carolina**

**Chapter Four**     *"Get off the ridge if it snows!"*     35
**Fontana Dam, North Carolina to Hot Springs, North Carolina**

**Chapter Five**     *"She needs to stay off her feet for at least two weeks!"*     46
**Hot Springs, North Carolina to Damascus, Virginia**

**Chapter Six**     *"Call me, I will come get you!"*     62
**(Southwest Virginia) Damascus to Pearisburg**

**Chapter Seven**     *"Thru-hikers add to the ambiance!"*     83
**(Central Virginia) Pearisburg to Waynesboro**

**Chapter Eight**     *"Follow me for water, right over this way!*     107
**Shenandoah National Park to Maryland**

**Chapter Nine**     *"Oh, my feet hurt!"*     124
**Pennsylvania**

**Chapter Ten**     *"Give me a call and I will come get you!"*     142
**New Jersey - New York**

**Chapter Eleven**     *"I can't stand the mosquitoes!"*     158
**Connecticut - Massachusetts**

**Chapter Twelve**     *"Keep those magic feet going!"*     177
**Vermont - New Hampshire**

**Chapter Thirteen**  *"I did it!"*  **194**
Mt. Katahdin, Maine

**Chapter Fourteen**  *"Goals are dreams with a deadline"*  **215**
Returning South

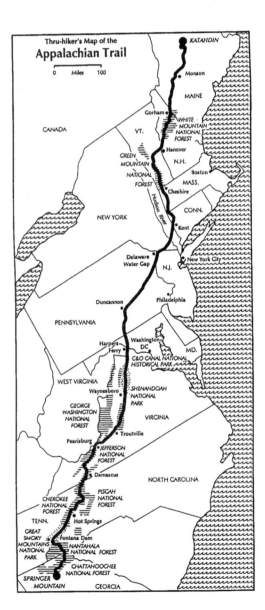

# Chapter 1

## *"Mummy, why is there white paint on that tree?"*

### In the Beginning There was a Goal

"This can't possibly be the Appalachian Trail? I must be lost." As I tripped over rhododendron branches and rotted tree roots, I knew I hadn't seen a white blaze in at least a quarter of a mile and there was a good chance I was off the Trail.

A wet world met my gaze as I peered from under my dripping hood for the hundredth time that afternoon. Still no blazes were in sight. Exhausted, I dug the walking stick I'd picked up at Hawk Mountain Shelter into the muddy wet leaves as I trudged up the steep Georgia Trail. Slipping and sliding, I was determined to reach the shelter before nightfall. Retracing my steps in search of white blazes was too overwhelming to consider. Soaked to the bone, I anxiously peered over another crest. Like magic, white glistened on the bark of a stout oak tree. Relief shivered through me, at least from the possibility of being lost, but not from the bone chilling weather or from the questions that quaked within. Why was I plodding my way to Mt. Katahdin in this wet, cold, March rain? Two thousand miles remained before I would fulfill my childhood dream to thru-hike the Appalachian Trail. I shivered in the icy wind. Such an objective now seemed to be poor rationale for spending five months alone in the woods. The goal spiraled around interconnected paths, as crucial as white blazes would be to my northbound process. I would hike through gullies, around switchbacks, over summits, and in ravines before the purpose of the goal would be clear.

That night, as I lay on the hard Cold Springs Shelter floor, I listened to nature drum patterns of my story on the roof that protected me from the icy rain. "Stories are medicine with power. They require only that we listen," I remembered Clarissa Pinkola Estes writing in *Women Who Run with the Wolves*. "The remedies for repair or reclamation of any lost psychic drive are contained in stories. They are embedded with instruction which guide us about the complexities of life"(15-16). Stories set the inner life in motion as though we are inside the story, rather than the story remaining outside of us.

Around my Vermont home, the wind swaying in white pine trees and the water babbling over New England brooks provided an arena for me to play out my fantasies. As I walked over massive mountains, looked into spacious skies, and ran through voluptuous valley, I heard the first chapters of my story spinning in my soul. Swirling through my blood and bones like the salt and spices that season life with structure and strength, a symbol would spin my story.

The white blazes first appeared to me during a family vacation at the Dolly Copp Campground near Pinkham Notch in the White Mountain of New Hampshire. My family and I were walking on part of the Trail that leads to New England's highest peak, Mt. Washington at 6,299 feet, when the Trail markers called me. I was only ten years old. With brows as knotted as entangled tree branches, I gazed up at a four-by-six inch rectangular white mark on a large tree and asked, "Mummy, why is there white paint on that tree?"

"That's a white blaze. We are on part of the Appalachian Trail," she answered.

"Really! How long is the Trail? Where does it go?" I asked, reaching on my tiptoes to touch the white stencil mark.

"The Trail goes all the way to Georgia. It begins up in Maine."

"Wow! I could walk in the woods for a long time!" And, so the dream was born.

I had no idea where Georgia was. I remembered hearing it mentioned in the movie, *Gone with the Wind*, while watching it with my grandmother. The Georgian characters in the movie talked a lot different than people in New England. I knew it must be a long ways away. What I didn't know was that hiking the Appalachian Trail meant following a rugged continuous footpath for over 2,000 miles for nearly six months. On that summer day in the early 1960's, my mother had no way of knowing what I was thinking, nor the power of initiative that would evolve from the simple answer she gave her oldest child.

My mother took us to the White Mountains because her parents had taken her to the Wawbeek Resort on Lake Winnipesaukee just south of the White Mountains. She cherished memories of staying in cabins on the Ellis River and fishing with her father. I, too, later swam in the lake, rowed around the islands, and climbed the nearby slopes. These visits wrote the early chapters of my story.

We also visited great Aunt Polly at her cabin Red Fox, on Lake Winnipesaukee. My brother, sisters and I spent hours diving off Aunt Polly's boat dock counting the fish that hid among the boathouse piles. I'd sleep under the tall pines and watch for foxes as an excuse to sleep outside. It didn't matter that I never saw a single fox. Listening to rain pound on the tent roof, hearing the wind whistle through pine trees, and guessing what kind of animal howled across the valley satisfied a craving in my soul. Sleeping in confining claustrophobic houses separated me from the night sounds and fresh air.

The hand water pump in the kitchen also intrigued me. After priming, I'd put my ear to the side of the pump and listen to the water gushing up the pipe. Although the grownups repeatedly warned me not to waste the water, I was enthralled by the primitive pump and thought there was no better water in the world.

The outhouse also fascinated me. The grownups thought it was far too primitive and discussed replacing it with indoor plumping, but I loved the crude wooden structure with its pictures of nature tacked all over the walls. After gazing at the pictures, I enjoyed leaving without having to flush. I felt flushing was a terrible waste of water. Little did I know the day would come when I'd live among nature for five months, with few opportunities to flush a toilet. Years would pass before that chapter evolved.

When I was eleven my parents divorced; and my mother moved her children to Keene, New Hampshire. Leaving my Vermont farm and adjusting to the loss of my father during puberty had a profound impact me, but I had learned to find solace in the woods. Movies and television bored me. My values were askew from my classmates. Daddy had taught me to find joy in nature. Enough joy to wait thirty-five years before my dream to hike the entire Appalachian Trail would come to fruition.

At age sixteen I drove my 1952 English Ford to the northern end of Lake Winnipesaukee and took a job as a chambermaid at the Rob Roy Motor Lodge in Moultonboro. I received permission to camp in the town councilman's apple orchard. Although I had a six-person tent, cot, bedding, camp stove, picnic table, and a lantern, I lived quite primitivly compared to other young people who worked in the Lakes Region for the summer. Civilized living complicated and cramped me. I needed space and simplicity. During that summer I read Henry David Thoreau's masterpiece, *Walden.* His principles of oneness with nature, simplicity, and purpose complemented my own values. "The spartan simplicity of life and elevation of purpose" (68), spoke more sense to me than congregating on city sidewalks or crowding in front of television sets. The whole of outdoors was a living room. Although I suspect Thoreau would have been appalled at all the equipment I hauled to the orchard, the experience was preparation for the future. A crystal creek with a waterfall and a pool flowed through the middle of the orchard. Years later as I followed blue blazes in search of water, which needed to be purified before using, I realized how fortunate I'd been to have clean assessable water.

In the fall of 1968 I wrote to Washington D. C. for topographical maps of the fourteen states through which the Trail passes. But I could not yet commit to a thru-hike. I had two more years of high school and plans to attend college. In September of 1970 I headed to Northwestern Michigan College. When the semester ended the grant money I'd received ran out, and I returned home.

In the summer, I headed to the rocky coast of Maine where my mother and step dad moored their boat in the Kennebunkport Harbor. I received permission to camp in the yard of a house designated for young people to stay in while working in the area. I had kitchen and bathroom privileges, and ran an electric cord from the house to the tent. I doubted that Thoreau would have condoned the electricity, but I justified the luxury so I could read his books after dark. I became the first woman to get the job of ferrying people across a saltwater inlet. Folks paid fifty-cents for a ride across the river in order to avoid driving through the village and having to search for parking on the beach. Sunburned and sandy tourists waved at me to retrieve them from the other side of the inlet at the end of the day. In the evening I worked at a coffee shop in the fishing village. I balanced participating in society and living in nature. However, change is the only constant in life. Like spirited seagulls diving for lobster boats in harbor, it was time for my life to make a monumental swoop. Timing is of the essence when responding to one's story. Impulsive actions open or impede the process of one's journey. As the summer came to an end, I longed for someone to take me away to a new lifestyle. That spiritual longing was answered by moving my story far away from New England to a town only a few miles from the Southern most terminus of the Appalachian Trail. Although it was years before I accepted the rationale behind this chapter in my life, I responded to a primal ancient calling to go, seek, be free, and be in love.

Waving from a dock on the river on Labor Day of 1971 were four young men wearing boxer trunks. I curiously paddled my rowboat to the landing. Their thick southern accents were clues they were not natives. Southerners from Virginia, they were enjoying the coast enroute to Canada before returning south. When they learned I was a local, they asked me to lead them around the customs at the border. My summer job was over. I had no plans for the immediate future, no funds to hike the Trail, and no reason to go home. I agreed. Little did I know that after touring Montreal I'd go South with the man wearing purple shorts, my favorite color, and become his bride.

As Tom and I became acquainted, we joked about the differences between Southerners and Northerners. Such jokes would later fuel rivalries between my future in-laws and my heritage. I learned the War Between the States is still very much alive below the Mason / Dixon line. He also talked about his Seventh-day Adventist friends in Georgia. I had little experience with organized religions, so I accepted his invitation to go south and study the Bible. We were married on January 9th, 1971 and settled in Ellijay, Georgia, a Seventh-day Adventist community only a few miles from the southern terminus of the Appalachian Trail.

I developed the green thumb I'd inherited from my father and grew a vegetable garden. Soon children filled our home with responsibilities and joy. Katie was born in 1973. She was just six months old when her dad and I joined the Polar Bear Backpacking Club. I carried Kate and Tom carried the heavy pack with gear for three. We never missed a month all winter. In 1996 David Emerson was born. As soon as David could sit in a backpack, we began climbing Ramrock, Justice, and Blood Mountains and staying at Hawk or Gooch Gap shelters. I was content to put my dream on hold.

In 1985 we moved to a trailer on my in-laws' land in Lenior City, Tennessee. The children and I built a tree house from saplings we hauled from the back of the land. In it we played school, ate picnic lunches, and slept out. My creativity flourished while homeschooling the children. I taught them to multiply with pinecones, create poetry about nature, and read from Bible stories and National Geographic. When the children were old enough to be in scouts, I became a church-scout director. The hours I spent planning, organizing, and packing for Smoky Mountain backpacking trips or buying, carrying and repairing gear were another Appalachian Trail preparation chapter.

However, transitions often take place through movement. The children needed a wider world; so did I. A new chapter waited. Feeling like a dinosaur loosened from the depths of a cave, I let go of the familiar and stepped forward. Our home schooling days ended when I put Kate, at age nine, in the church school I'd helped to organize in the basement of our church. I volunteered in the school and continued to home school David until he entered the third grade. Adrienne Rich in *Of Women Born* (1986) said, "The process of 'letting go,'— though we are charged with blame if we do not—is an act of revolt against the grain of patriarchal culture. But it is not enough to let our children go; we need selves of our own to return to" (37). I would move with the process vulnerably, yet eagerly. I needed to develop my life beyond child needs and wife duties. The words of Gautama Buddha made sense, "This existence of ours is as transient as autumn clouds. To watch the birth and death of beings is like looking at the movement of a dance." My story and the children's had been one inseparable dance. Dance is the only art form, aside from singing, in which we are the stuff of which it is made. In the same way that dance moves through music to the soul, change closes one experience while opening another. As I moved into my thirties, the primal messages I heard in the wilderness of my childhood danced me into me into my chapter. Sacrificing one phase of life for another would balance my story. But, the disruption felt like death. The chapter closed as rapidly as rhythms in the wind.

When David joined his sister in the hands of the school system, I took steps to complete the education I'd begun thirteen years earlier. Hiking the Trail was a personal goal, not a financially enterprising endeavor. I would express creativity in a classroom. A goal since my own third grade teacher had allowed me to be creative with my learning. I would respond in order to remain creative. The rewarding comfortable rhythm of homeschooling the children and being a stay-at-home mother disappeared as quickly as waves collapse sand sculptures on a beach. Gone were the days of picking flowers, having picnics, and playing in the creeks. Difficult as it was, I believed I'd find power if I closed the chapter on what had once worked. I needed a new vision, a new way of looking at the world. Sonja in the film *Mindwalk* reminded, me, "What works is not always good for the system." In 1983, I was accepted into the teacher education program at the University of Tennessee.

Vulnerable and frightened, I believed the transition would propel me forward. Where, I did not know. I tuned my listening skills to hear more than wind and rain. The voice of professors became cords to empowerment. However, fears of inadequacy plagued me. After thirteen years out of the classroom, I was afraid my skills were too weak to succeed. For years all I'd read were children's, self-help, and Christian books. I also worried that my husband's inconsistent work would cease providing a roof over our heads and food on the table. Foremost, I feared his declining emotional support and flaring temper rages were red flags that indicated securing a stable home would eventually become my sole responsibility. I hoped financial aid and grants would continue until I graduated.

At the University of Tennessee I joined 28,000 students jumping academic hoops. College was an awakening, enriching culture shock. The constant pressure energized me. The late nights in the library were a calming modification of creativity. My experience echoed Chopra's words: "The world of energy is fluid, dynamic, resilient, changing, forever in motion. And yet it is also non-changing, still, quiet eternal, and silent. But the combination of movement and stillness enables you to unleash your creativity in all directions wherever the power of your attention takes you"(21). The hours I spent studying in our crowded trailer living room, after all wife and mother duties had been tended to, prepared me to have choices. I felt empowered. I had only known power as a dominating tool.

Over the years, anthropologists and historians have used the patriarchy as a tool to define the structure of pastoral and nomadic societies. In recent times, it has become a manipulative system of male dominance over women. I was no longer willing to live as a victim. I no longer wanted to be among the masses of women who live under the unequal roles of the patriarchal nuclear family. I feared I would be doomed to live under eternal submission if I didn't accept the knowledge that there is more to life than dishes, dust, diapers, and dissension. The chapter of contentment I'd found when small children romped under my feet, bread dough swished between my fingers, and early green peas popped from their shells had closed. In college, I searched for the power of a new voice.

The language of patriarchal power insists on a dichotomy that for one person to have power, another person must be powerless. My marriage was an example of this kind of relationship. The idea of power becomes the power of an idea. The idea of falling in love, expressed as sexual love, is later often redefined as power over. The idea that love begets marriage and the marriage union requires one person to have primary power is a configuration of doom. I'd fallen for this trap and had been living powerless. Submitting to my husband did not insure his support or care, only his control. Such treatment led me to depression, guilt, and low self-esteem. I took the blame and shaming treatment, but knew as long as I believed I deserved it, I would remain powerless and my psyche would die. My survivor instinct surfaced. I wanted options. I sought power from within not without. I needed an anchor. The dream to hike the Trail resurfaced. In 1985, twenty years after my first inquiry, I wrote to the Appalachian Trail Conference in Harper's Ferry, West Virginia. I received a sample data book page, Trail maps, order forms, and a list of post offices. I studied the material with determination. But, the time had not come.

After four long years, graduation day arrived. My mother came from New Hampshire for the celebration. I, alone, knew that the graduation party gathering at my in-law's home was more than an educational milestone, it was a step toward freedom. It represented the birth of a transition and the death of a marriage. Within the month, I filed for divorce and moved the children to Knoxville, Tennessee, twenty-two miles from the country. We rented a house for a year and then I bought our first home. The house had nearly an acre to landscape. I'd work the soil creating gardens and water features while waiting for the day I'd walk the earth on the Appalachian Trail.

I got a job teaching grades three, four, and five in a private school for one year. Then in 1988, I sat in front of a Knox County supervisor for a public school interview. When asked how I thought children learned best I said, "children need exposure to the natural world, a variety of resources, and varied experiences. Teaching is a creative art." I was hired. For the next ten years I taught inner city children, whom I adored. Committed to giving children a variety of experiences, the students and I raised the money for a four-day wilderness experience to Tremont Institute in the Smoky Mountains. We joined with students from area schools to participate in nature lessons, evening programs, and pillow fights. I was in my element and my students were in awe. During those glorious days in the Smokies, I fantasized about the day I would take to the Trail alone. Nurturing the dream kept it alive. Intuitively I clung to Este's words as tightly as I later clung to trees on the ledges. "The most important thing is to hold on, hold out, for your creative life, for your solitude, for your time to be and do, for your very life; hold on, for the promise from the wild nature is this: after winter, spring always comes." (191).

Struggling as a single parent to raise teenagers was not easy, but professionally I was on the rise. I received 21st century computer training and the Knoxville Junior League sponsored our Tremont trip. However, emotionally I was plunging. Climbing professionally left me no room to breathe. The larger my portfolio grew with teaching awards, writing projects, workshops taken and given, and grants received to escort students on fields trips to Washington D. C. and Tremont, the tighter my soul became. My efforts to make a difference felt stifled. The longer I stepped to the beat of the stale structured system, the stronger the need swelled. I longed to step to the beat of my soul. Thoreau's words spoke to my conscience more powerfully than my growing portfolio. I wanted to experience the words I'd underlined in *Walden* at age sixteen. "I went to the woods because I wished to live deliberately, to face only the essential facts of life, and see if I could not learn what it had to teach, and not, when I came to die, discover that I had not lived" (67). I didn't want to come to the end of my life not having accomplished the dream that had pulled at my heart since childhood.

First, I needed to be able to stand in the face of power, because ultimately some part of that power would become mine. I was experiencing a disrupted relationship with what Estes refers to as, "a wildish" force. I had energy in the classroom, but I felt confused, without soulfulness, chronically stuck, doubtful, blocked, inert, and uncreative. Examining my motives and core, I reached inside and found integrity, balance, honesty, and awareness. I needed to understand what Jung call, "the moral obligation." There had to be a way to be both productive and true to myself. I would strengthen my intentions, gather new ideas, redirect my focus and prepare not to allow predators to rule my life.

The stress of teaching inner city children was undermining my creativity. Increased credentials would expand my opportunities. Again I applied to the University to Tennessee, this time to the graduate program. The following year, after teaching all day, I took classes and wrote a thesis. In 1995 I graduated with a Master's Degree in education with a cultural studies emphasis. I looked forward to a less hectic school year. However, the Universe knew my story.

During the summer, budget cuts made it necessary to cut a teacher from the faculty. I became the only fourth grade teacher. I also managed the 21st century computer lab, without assistance. The students had low independent work habits, high attention deficiencies, low cooperative learning skills, and high enthusiasm. Maintaining discipline in two rooms was not teaching. My elevated position had given me more financial security but less inner peace, greater responsibilities but less chance to be creative, and a wider range of stress with less opportunity to release it. I followed a pattern indicative of women culture climbers. By increasing my education and professionally advancing, I'd sacrificed myself. I'd allowed the system to take advantage of me. Drained of the creativity that had once identified me as competent, authentic, and unique, I felt as stripped and stark as a dusty desert under a scorching summer sun. I had to take control of my thirst in a soul-strengthening manner. To do so would require a powerful act of a wild spirit and trust in the Universe. From my soul I sought power not to be a victim. I knew if I remained only a survivor, without moving or thriving, I'd limit my energy and power in the world. I wanted my story to say more than that I only survived. I respected my creative life more than cooperating with oppression. The timeliness of my decision closed a chapter and moved my story forward.

The following year our school and two other inner city schools voted to merge. One hundred and eighty five inner city students had been challenging enough. I was not looking forward to three times that many. Enough time, discontent, and pressure had been brought to bear. I would hurl myself into a new life for my behalf. My own children had left home. My spacious landscaped yard, flowing with a twenty-five foot creek I'd built between two ponds lined with wild flowers, had lost its attraction. I would quit my job.

In the spring of 1992 I had met Dr. Suellen Alfred, a professor at Tennessee Technological University in Cookeville, Tennessee. We had become close friends. She proposed an idea that would change my life. "They are looking for instructors to teach study skills classes in the Academic Development Program at the University. Teaching time management and organization skills would get your foot in the door at the college level," she encouraged. Me teach college? I had given adult workshops, but what did I know about teaching college? I knew how to manage time. But how would I teach it and what would it pay? Maybe money was not the primary reason for increasing my education. Tennessee Tech was located a hundred miles west of Knoxville. Changing jobs would mean starting all over. Suellen seemed to read my mind. "I can put you in touch with Elizabeth Boucher, the director. You could come for an interview during spring break next week. You're welcome to stay at my house."

"I'll give her a call," I was more excited than I let on. In March of 1996 I found myself driving around the campus looking for Foster Hall where I would interview for the job. I had not a clue how significant the meeting would be. One year later I stood on Springer Mountain ready to hike the Appalachian Trail.

Within minutes after meeting Elizabeth, I was hired. However, she wanted to be sure I understood one detail. "You have the credentials we need. With your background, you would be an asset to the program. However, I can hire you only for the fall. We have an overflow of freshman that need study skill classes, but only for the fall semester. I sincerely hope you will come aboard, but I want you to understand you won't have a job in the spring." She could not have been more eager to hire me, nor more clear about the lack of a spring position. I contemplated the risk. I was quitting a tenured, secure position for one semester of adjunct teaching. I would have to sell the home I loved and move. However, as long as I worked for a school system that operates from August until May I would never be able complete the Trail in one season. Changing careers would give me the opportunity to hike the entire Trail in the spring and summer of 1997. Responding to the call of the Trail would change my future and my life. I could hear the clock on the wall ticking seconds into minutes, into hours, into days. The sound seemed to go faster and faster like soggy snowballs spinning down steep New England slopes. Like snow that melts in the warm sun, I did not want to melt from the commitment I'd made to my soul. No matter what the future held professionally, I needed to listen to the needs of my heart. The room spun with the speed I had been traveling during these past years. In my imagination, I heard the wind on the ridge, the birds in the trees, and water in the wilderness creeks. A new chapter began with five words. "I will take the job." More than a job change called. I left the office feeling fearful and ecstatic. My journey would be filled with the same mix of emotion. It was time to prepare for a dream come true.

The end of school year was full of the usual end-of-the year activities, including taking my fourth grade class to Tremont for the last time. These trips were the highlight of my year. Many of my inner-city students never left the asphalt sidewalks of housing projects in the summer. Watching their eyes light up as they caught salamanders and frogs in the creeks, climbed trees, and listened to nature lessons by Kristen Austin, their teacher naturalist, was worth all the preparation. Leaving my job would mean I'd never again share moon light walks and campfire stories with poverty-stricken children. One Tremont experience stands out in my mind as particularly dear.

I can still see Derek stretching his nine-year-old arms around a large tree, hugging it tightly, and chanting: "I love you, tree. I won't never cut your bark again. I don't never want to hurt you. I love you, tree. I won't ever hurt you no more. I won't cut on nothing as long as I live." I had caught him jabbing a tree with his pencil in an attempt to carve his name in the bark. When I asked him if he would want someone to write on his house or make marks on his skin, he flippantly responded, "I don't care. I get marks on me all the time and our building has writing all over it." Just before the trip, Derek had been caught spray painting curse words on the back of school. He, like many of the other children, was saturated with street knowledge. They knew more about knives, guns, destroying property, and drugs than they did about math or English. I changed my explanation. "Trees hurt just like people when they are stabbed. If trees get hurt enough they will fall down and die. If all trees died you wouldn't have forests to play in and the animals wouldn't have homes. Do you want that to happen?"

His round face softened. He sprang up off the ground where he had slumped in defiance and lunged to hug the nearest tree. "I love you tree." he chanted. Hearing Derek's mantra, his classmates circled him. In so doing they hugged Derek against the tree in a circle of love as they chanted the lesson they had all learned about love and respect. The chanting voices Kristen and I heard on that warm spring day were not the same voices I'd heard in the classroom. Lessons taught in the wilderness had a far greater impact on the children than lessons taught in the classroom. Seeing students learn lessons in the classroom were rare. In the woods, learning evolved naturally. As we hiked along the children jumped up and hugged trees all along the path. In nature, opportunities to relate practical instruction to discipline and social skills present themselves in ways classroom lessons can't possibly offer. I can still see the huddle of eager learners hugging each other as they chanted with all of their hearts. Such experiences aren't suggested in teacher's manuals, at workshops, or taught in college method courses. Who would take the children if I left? I would miss the students. They would miss me. But, discipline challenges, and bureaucratic procedures had escalated into constant stress. It was time for someone else to work with the children. It was time for a career change, and time to literally take a hike.

I kept the news of my decision quiet so I wouldn't jeopardize my credentials and risk leaving in good standing. My colleagues would think I was out of my mind to quit my job for a financially insecure future. Over the years when students and parents had been particularly challenging, I'd jokingly threatened to get a substitute to finish a school year and "go do the Trail." This time I wouldn't be joking. As I waited for spring, I felt positive about power of transitions. It was time to make personal use of the phrases I used in the classroom such as: monitor and adjust, focus, and foster the positive. My job now was to find a way to balance creativity with purpose. I knew not to create solely under my own steam. I had spiritual, nurturing friends who listened. Many had experienced corporate lay-offs or job loss casualties. They helped me calculate my risks and speculate the rewards of following a dream. My friends' nurturing spirits moved me.

My own children's independence freed me from home responsibilities. They supported my decision. The merging of the three schools into one made my decision to accept the temporary college teaching job appealing. I had the support of my friends. The transition was no reason to vacate emotionally from the space we held in each other's hearts. The time had come to hike the Appalachian Trail. However, crisis arose. My plans were impacted by the tragedy of cancer.

# Chapter 2

## *"Line up fellows, the Cancer Lady is here!"*

### A Goal with A Purpose

Laura, a fifth grade teacher at Lincoln Park Elementary School where I taught, was diagnosed with breast cancer a few weeks before Christmas in 1995. The faculty and I were stunned. Laura and I had spent many hours discussing effective ways teach our students as we planned field trip, projects, and shared computer knowledge. Her emergency surgery and battle with the devastating disease became a lesson in faith and courage for the whole school. Determined to prepare her students for middle school, Laura taught as often as she could. Feeling helpless and powerless over the disease, the faculty pulled together like family. Her co-teacher, Greg Lassiter, and I helped with her students when she was absent. Laura returned the following year cancer free, but the cancer returned. She lost her fight in April of 1997.

Breast cancer was the first of many cancers my grandmother had battled until she died in 1987. She was diagnosed in 1970, the year I graduated from high school. I could not comprehend why her breast had to be removed. Someday I vowed to help change the prognosis. Over the years, I discussed the complications, cures, and consequences of breast cancer at women's conferences, in education circles, and with concerned friends. Because there is power when money is involved, I decided if organizations could do walks and runs for charity, I could walk from Georgia to Maine to raise money for breast cancer. My grandmother and Laura's experiences were the catalysts that turned my goal to hike the Trail into a breast cancer campaign I called, "Hike for Healing."

I approached the Knoxville American Cancer Society with a proposal to solicit $10,000 from family, friends, businesses, and corporations. They said that no one individual had ever proposed a campaign involving such a long physical commitment, but they agreed to write me a letter of support. I would begin the campaign as soon as I relocated in Cookeville. By the time school was out, I had the house ready to sell. I needed it to sell fast, so I decided to sell the house myself. An advertisement came out on a Wednesday and the house sold on Sunday. The rapid transaction sealed my decision to fulfill my dream. I moved to Cookeville as soon as school was out.

As I walked into class on the first day of school, I spotted a young man sitting on the front row wearing an Appalachian Trail tee shirt. "Have you hiked the Appalachian Trail?" I asked as the class got settled.

"Yes, my brother, a friend, and I finished it two years ago."

"Really! I'm leaving March first. Will you tell me what to expect?

"Sure, I'll make a list of what we took and places to stop for food." Every day after class Greg and I rode the elevator together. He told me what to take and how to prepare. This positive omen was one more example that I was where I needed to be, and was about to do what I needed to do. My friend Deb had finished the Trail ten years earlier and gave me advice from a woman's point of view.

In class I met goal setting and time management objectives by explaining how I was preparing to meet my goal. Based on the 150 days between the March first and the end of July, we discussed how much food to put in Ziploc bags and how many baggies to place in twenty-three maildrop boxes with toothpaste, rolls of film, moleskin, toilet paper, and maps.

I also taught sociology and a walking course at Volunteer State Community College. As my students walked in sneakers, I broke in hiking boots. In sociology we discussed the necessity of developing a positive attitude in order to adjust to cultural changes. By using my goal to reach Katahdin as an example, I explained the importance of proactive problem solving, the necessity of acquiring skills, the development of action plans, and the importance of realistic time frames. Weeks later, while struggling up mountains in the rain, I reflected on the long-term planning lessons I'd given and knew they'd been as much for me as they had been for the students.

I was out of work when the semester ended. However a power greater than myself hovered over my life. The director of the Cumberland Career Equity Center, Dr. Maggie Phelps, asked me to give goal setting, time management, decision making, and problem solving presentations in the public schools during January and February. As I worked up the program and presented the topics, I gave myself pep talks about the decision I was about to put into action. "Goals need to be measurable, realistic, and consistent with your values," I said to the students. "Make use of schedules, think in terms of time, and be willing to monitor and adjust your plans. Something magic happens when you pick up a pencil or a pen and apply your thoughts to a piece of paper, so write down your goals and they become real. Change takes time and effort. Goals aren't reached quickly or easily. My goal to do the Trail has been a thirty-five year process." I later applied my lectures.

In October, I took my plans to Cookeville's most widely read newspaper, the *Herald-Citizen*. The living section editor, Debi Rami, interviewed me for an article about "Hike for Healing." With the color photograph and article, Knoxville American Cancer Society support letter, and my flier I began soliciting funds. For Breast Cancer Awareness month in October, I spoke at the Noon Rotary Club, the Lions Club, for Mr. Nash at the V. F. W. and the Ladies Auxiliary Club. I explained the importance of early detection, risk factors, and the need for research. The members of the Rotary Club enjoyed my presentation but resisted financially supporting Hike for Healing. After the meeting an American Cancer Society board member, Al Profant, grasped my hand and graciously applauded my plans. But he too had no more intention to donate then the other members. I needed to know why. "Mr. Profant, why are folks reluctant to give?"

"Your Knoxville support leads people to believe the funds will go to the Knoxville Chapter. I would be happy to connect you with Angie Beaty, the coordinator for this region. I am sure with a letter of support from our Cookeville branch, the community will support you." I had no idea moving would deter me from gaining support for a national cause. The next week I met with Angie and Al over coffee at Poet's On the Square to discuss my plans. Angie was excited to be part of my journey and promised me a Cookeville letter of support by the end of the week. I redid the flier to read: "The fund raiser operates in conjunction with the American Cancer Society in Cookeville, TN." With a reworked flier, a new support letter, and the newspaper article, I began campaigning again November first. I hoped to raise $10,000 before Saturday, March first.

Tennessee Tech's television station, WCTE, heard of my project and asked me to do a twenty-minute program. I was filmed putting Trail food in boxes, packing my backpack, and displaying my equipment as I explained my goal to raise $10,000 for breast cancer research. WKZX Channel 28 interviewed me for a segment and the *Nashville Banner* published a column. With publicity and a local support letter, the funds began to come in and many positive experiences began to happen. One such experience took place at the Putnam County Transportation garage. In the supervisor's office I held out the newspaper article and began, "Good afternoon, I'm Ellen Wolfe. Remember this article that appeared in the Herald-Citizen? Well I'm the one walking to Maine to raise money for breast cancer research. I'm sure you would like to be part of this campaign. One out of every eight women will get breast cancer. With community support research can find ways to treat the disease."

As the supervisor reached in his pocket he asked, "Do you want to ask all the fellows for a donation? It is quittin' time and they're out in the garage waiting to go home at 3:30." I peered behind me at fifty men milling around the large garage.

"Sure," I said. I followed the man into the middle of the open space where he hollered, "Come on fellows, the cancer lady's here! She's got something to tell ya."

Some of the men ambled forward. Others headed for the door. A few of the men sitting on folded chairs got up. Others appeared to be glued to their seats until they could head for their parked cars. The men leaning against walls looked as if they thought the building might cave in if they budged an inch. I glanced at my watch. I had only five minutes if I hoped to raise any money. I would have to work fast and choose my words carefully. I suddenly remembered how I used to get the attention of my students when they had only the impending dismissal bell and waiting school buses on their minds. I stepped boldly to the middle of the room, while keeping my eyes on the men nearest the door and said, "Come on guys, make a circle right here. I am sure you have all heard of breast cancer. Everyone knows a woman who has had it."

At the mention of the word "breast," I felt a dozen pair of eyes shift to the front of my blouse. Feet shuffled toward me. For a second I wanted to run. Grounding myself to the reason I'd called the men to surround me, I focused on my purpose and turned to the man nearest me. "Thank you for being the first one up here. May I borrow your cap? Let's make a circle starting right here," I reached for the cap. Talking fast, I kept up my instructions to join the circle until all the men had peeled themselves off the walls, out of chairs, and away from the door. "Breast cancer is not just a woman's disease. It strikes one out of every eight women. I'm sure you fellows know eight women. She could be your wife, your daughter, your niece, your sister, your aunt, or even your own mother. Only by contributing to research can we hope to stop this disease. I'm going to hike the entire 2,160 miles of the Appalachian Trail from Georgia to Maine as a personal commitment to find a cure. I know you will contribute."

I walked around the circle holding the cap in front of each man. They dug into pockets and donated to what was now our cause. Sensing their discomfort, I suspected they wondered if I was a survivor. After sharing with them that my grandmother and a school colleague were my impetus to walk for a cure, I felt them relax. Raising $100.00 in five minutes at that garage was just one of many miracles that happened during my campaign.

As I moved in and out of businesses, lumberyards, beauty shops, service stations, and factories, I listened to stories of lives affected by the disease. As bosses, managers, and owners supported my 2,160-mile commitment, I knew I was where I needed to be, doing what I needed to do. Some folks talked about hiking. Dr. Philip Bertram told me he'd hiked parts of the Trail. J.R. Nash, who graciously donated my maildrop boxes and gave a donation, knew the importance of taking his children to the mountains.

Concern for Trail safety came from men rather than the women. Many women wished that they could leave behind the stress of managing kids, work, and a household for time in the woods. It was the men who were horrified I planned to hike alone. They suggested I learn karate and carry everything from guns, to knives, to clubs. When I informed pharmacist, Mr. Bassett, that I only planned to carry the smallest Swiss army knife, he insisted I take his two-inch pocketknife. Honored by his concern, I took the knife. When I returned the knife in August, I was happy to report I did not once have to open it.

After hearing the purpose of, "Hike for Healing," Mr. Coe asked, "You are going to carry some pepper spray or mace aren't you?" I told him I had it on my list. When I returned a few days later to pick up his donation, he asked as he handed me the check, "Have you bought pepper spray?" I confessed I had not. Pulling the check out of my reach he said seriously, "You can have this, but promise me you'll buy pepper spray and attach it to the front of your pack." I promised and drove immediately to see David at Cumberland Outdoors Sports.

"You may need to use this to scare off wild animals. A friend of mine told me he was having a picnic in the middle of the Trail in the Smokies when a big bear came lumbering toward him. He didn't have time to get the food picked up so he sprayed a circle around the area where he sat. The bear came as close as the circle, sniffed all the way around it, and left. Wild predators might be a bigger threat than human ones."

Compression sacks were new since my scouting days. David explained how they save space. "Pull on straps evenly and sit on the sack as you pull." I purchased pepper spray, socks, compression sacks, and large bottles of Skin-So-Soft to keep the gnats and no-see-ums away. Mr. Ballenger, the owner of the store, stressed the importance of taking care of my feet and keeping down the weight. "Your feet are your primary concern. If they break down, you won't go anywhere. Cut the strings off tea bags, put all your food in baggies, and don't take anything you don't plan to use every day. Carrying a light pack is essential. Put a new pair of socks and sock liners in your maildrops every five hundred miles. Your socks may not have holes, but after a hundreds of miles the support is gone. Your feet and your morale will get a boost to have new socks." When I opened boxes in Virginia, Vermont, Pennsylvania, and New Jersey, my feet as well as my attitude appreciated new socks. Graciously he sold me a Lowe internal frame pack at wholesale. It proved to be very comfortable and withstood the whole trip without repair. I attached the pepper spray to a front strap where it still hangs unused.

The campaign led to conversations about things other than backpacking and breast cancer. One woman who runs a radiator shop with her husband asked me what I planned to eat. I told her I had been a vegetarian for twenty-seven years and planned to take dried beans, trail mix, pastas, rice, nuts, dried fruit, peanut butter, hot cereals, and soups. She said she needed to lower her cholesterol. I promised to bring her some recipes. When I returned, she smiled. "I haven't had any meat since you were here last. I've been walking and feel so much better." The experiences showed me I was not only committed to raising money, but to helping people in a community I now called home.

Returning to New England on foot was about taking literal steps through the mountains that had distanced me from my dream. It was about connecting with my homeland. It was about a calling to fulfill a spiritual and emotional need to walk to the soil of my childhood. The words I'd underlined in *Walden*, when I was sixteen applied to women as well as to men. "If I do not keep pace with my companions, perhaps it is because I hear a different drummer. Let me step to the music I hear, however measured and far away."(78). After stepping away from my companions, I would watch nature come to fruition despite freezing nights, flooding storms, or even trampling hikers. I would cross creeks flow ing from the rugged peaks. By reaching inward to the place I'd known long ago but had forgotten, I would search for a self obscured from the world. Toors referred to such a journey as, "a gathering from within to that which is often denied and repressed." (2) I'd be on such a journey among both the flesh and spirit. Among the leaves and rocks I'd discover a deeper self. By touching what had been wounded and is incomplete, I would tap a vision quest to heal the feminine and claim wholeness.

This pilgrimage would be different from trips I'd made to New England. Zooming up and down the interstate for vacations was not the same as hiking a single footpath. Trips to New England had been planned around the holidays and seasons or traveled to meet a crisis, most painfully my father's funeral in 1986. This time I was in control of the circumstances. It was time to step away from schedules, careers, and responsibilities. I would respond to my own voice. The ancient primal calling to return to the womb moved me to breathe with the earth. Soft moss to rest on, deep caves to retreat in, tall trees to shelter under, fruit bushes to nibble on, and clear water to drink from beckoned me. I'd listened to an inner voice that dared to unravel the ties that had bound me to the models, molds, patterns, and paths that had rattled the wild nature of my soul while trying to be submissive, compliant, and docile. No more would I walk false, foreign, and fruitless steps. I would hike the Appalachian Trail.

The Trail is never far from logging roads, dirt roads, two-lane highways, interstates, and even the Palisades Parkway only twenty-three miles from New York City; yet it offers a wilderness experience. The inhabitants of the Eastern United States' megalopolis seldom notice its entries and exits. It is the longest continuous walking Trail designated only for foot travel in the world. Winding through grassy fields, over cliffs, in deep water, above swamps, and through pine forests, the narrow path called me to follow its unpretentious route, not merely as a geographical south to north bearing, but inward. Too often unheeded messages of desires, aspirations, and yearnings grind themselves into the fibers of our bones begging for release. I would respond to that gnawing. My soul cracked and groaned with a need to find balance between my transient lifestyle and a permanent dwelling. By walking my truth, I would free myself from feeling uprooted and unsettled among the perplexities and bureaucracies of society. Walking over Appalachian roots I would connect the years I had spent struggling to establish myself as a Northerner on Southern soil. My years of searching for Southern permanence would come full circle as I make this circuit. As I placed the arched contour of my boots along the arched contour of the 2,160 miles of Appalachian Mountains, I would gain control.

In 1971, my hasty relocation in the South had been attached to the nebulous premise of pursuing roots in family values. Back in the north Georgia Mountains where my adult years began, my journey would connect my years in the South with my northern childhood. I did not want to come to the end of my life without making intimate contact with the wilderness of the fourteen states surrounding the linear pathway between these two segments of my life. I would connect yesterday and tomorrow as I physically, mentally, emotionally, and spiritually walked over the Appalachian Mountains. I would remain faithful to finding a solution to my grandmother's and Laura's diagnosis. The question I'd had asked my mother still tugged at my heart, "Is there nothing we can do so they don't have to take Grammy's breast off?

Choices are the key to movement and change. "Unto they own self be true." My mother had instilled Shakespeare's words into me. Serving others began with a firm sense of self-esteem and self-respect. The idea had stuck as firmly as the children had stuck boards together to build our tree house. Hiking the Trail was a piece of my personal journey. During my turbulent marriage, I had often been tempted to move back to New England. But the time had not been right. I hoped to know why I had remained south of the Mason / Dixon line since that fateful day in 1971 when I wound my way down the Blue Ridge Parkway on a 350 Honda behind my future husband. Determination to see through the process had kept me rooted deep in Southern soil and service. I hoped to understand why I had gravitated to Tennessee on that long ago crisp autumn day when I left my roots and all that was familiar with only my clothes and a daypack on my back. One quarter of a century later, I was making the journey again, in the opposite direction this time. A sense of purpose and personal control was in charge. My escapade from the coast of Maine to the mountains of Georgia with the southern bachelor had carried me to Washington D. C. on the motorcycle. We continued south in a station wagon. A quarter of a century later I would retrace my steps north on the very route we had careened south. Only this time I'd walk alone on a footpath with a full pack rather then ride on an asphalt highway with a daypack.

The timing of the universe called me to embark on an experience that would merge many faucets my life. Estes calls this sensing, "a psychic ability."(396). I would process through things I had learned, heard, longed for, and felt. I would process ideas and energies to implement soulful tasks and find new creative endeavors.

The list of equipment had grown long and I was a long ways from my goal, so I asked for donations for my forty-fourth birthday in October and for Christmas. At a bon-voyage gathering, friends came with donations and written words of good wishes. With melancholy sadness, my friends encircled me as I read the words I later taped in my data book. I was never without their love. The first message was from Suellen who would send the maildrop boxes and would gather me from the base of Katahdin. "Please take with you love, safety, endurance, growth and faith." Suellen. "I hope for you that a sense of wonder will be your companion along the way," wrote Jane. "May your path be firm, your feet steady, and your heart at peace as you journey," said Cindy. "I hope that on your journey your presence and appreciation of the universe is supported and heightened" wrote Jo. "May your eyes and your heart stay open, may you feel yourself weaving the blessings of creation," wrote Kim. "May you soar like the wind. May you meet yourself and God. And may you know both better mile by mile. I wish for you dry socks, cool clean water, a warm shower now and then, strong shoulders, and friends old and new," wrote Judy. Many others wrote wonderful messages like, "Enjoy the wind in your hair." "Serenity, safety, and insight." "May your journey inspire you with scenic vistas and natural wondrous travels." "I'll send you energy every morning of your hike." "May the darkness cradle you in her safe bosom."

Suellen laminated the following poem and message on a Susan B. Anthony coin, "Like you, Susan B. Anthony was a courageous woman who followed a dream and suffered for it. Keep this coin as a reminder of courage, perseverance and hope. As long as you have it with you, you'll never be broke."
*For Ellen on the AT:*

> One step after another,
> Plodding moving toward the North,
> The place that spawned you into the light,
> Walking home, toward the old haunts,
> Toward blessings, completion, and new beginnings,
> Moving though the leaves, through chipmunk haunts,
> Through bird song and deer paths,
> Through mountain views and valley narrows,
> Through fatigue and hunger, and rain and sun and hope,
> Through solitude and the magic time,
> When you and 'Nuppie*' alone know the way,
> An outward journey from Springer Mountain to Maine;
> An inward journey though labyrinths of the heart and soul,
> Walking your way to yourself."

*Nuppie is the name I have given my spirit guide. It is a nickname my daddy used for me when I was little.*

From a piece of birch bark that grew near the pond at Daddy's house, my step-mother Gloria inscribed, "Ellen, this is your good luck charm from the birch tree by the pond on Priest land in Putney." A miniature harmonica from Susan and laminated photographs of Suellen, my dog Lars, and Cornbread the cat were tucked in my backpack and traveled with me all the way to Katahdin. Between October and March I received over $5,000.00 from friends and relatives. $5,000 more came from the Cookeville community. When I left I was $55.00 from the goal. Within a month, two more donations arrived. I had reached my goal! My friends, family, and the community supported "Hike for Healing," with part of the money used in support of the trip, and the rest donated to breast cancer research. Together we believe someday surgery will not be the primary solution to breast cancer.

# Chapter 3

## *"Guess what Mom, I have three weeks off!"*

### Springer Mountain, Georgia to Fontana Dam, North Carolina

The 1996 *Backpacker Magazine* rated One Sport as the only brand of boots in which hikers had been able to complete an entire thru-hike with only one pair. Bob, the owner of Gatlinburg's Happy Hiker camping store, helped me fit my 8 1/2 double wide foot into a men's size 10. Bob kindly gave me a discount because I was a thru-hiker and was hiking for breast cancer.

From Campmor Catalog I bought a Thinsulate lite loft Firelit sleeping bag rated to 15 below zero to use with my full-length therma-rest mat. I would add the contents of my Ziploc bags to boiling water on a new International Whisperlite stove. I started out with a PUR Scout water filter, but had nothing but trouble with it. Nineteen days into the trip, at the Happy Hiker, I bought an MSR Water-works. After caring for a family for fifteen years, I looked forward to providing for only one. However, such was not to be the case at the beginning. It was a cold January morning. Sorting through the mail at the mailbox, I was delighted to get a letter from my daughter.

"Dear Mom,

Thank you for the Christmas gifts. I love the wheelbarrow and the new cat cage. The cats will love the cage when we travel. It was great having you at my house for Christmas. I wish we didn't live so far apart. Come visit again real soon.

Love, your daughter, Katie.

PS. Oh, I almost forgot to tell you. I have three weeks off from work and can go with you on the Appalachian Trail. Johnny will pick me up in Gatlinburg. Isn't that great? I'm so excited! Call me and tell me what I need to take."

I'm always glad to hear from my children. Having Katie and her boyfriend Johnny host the Christmas gathering at their house in Calhoun, Georgia had been a special change. At twenty-three she had grown into quite a mature young woman. At twenty my son David was head and shoulders taller than I and doing fine working as finisher in Atlanta. I had told the children of my plans over Christmas dinner. I remember the occasion like it happened yesterday. "My university teaching job is only for the fall and I'm not going to look for another job. I'm going to hike the Appalachian Trail."

I thought they would tell me to find a hiking partner. Instead they were concerned about how it would be for me to leave my community. "But, Mom won't you miss your friends? You'll be gone a long time."

"Yes I'll miss everyone but I need to do this. It's finally time."

As Kate finished off her pie, she offered support. "Walking home, that's real neat. I'm proud of you Mom."

My introspective son had been quiet. Grinning he asked, "You think you can still do it, Mom?"

"I think so." I grinned back. Neither of them mentioned going with me.

I had never looked for a hiking partner. This was my goal alone. Over the years friends had considered going, but not seriously. I wanted to be self-sufficient, free, and alone. Now, there was Kate's letter. I stopped in the middle of the yard and stared at the words. She had three weeks off and was going with me. Where had the idea come from? I was in shock. A close friend chuckled when I shared Kate's letter, "Sounds like time for mother-daughter bonding." Her comment reminded me of lines from, *Women who Run with the Wolves.* "When a woman goes home according to her own cycles, others around her are given their own individuation work, growth, and development, too." (281). Perhaps there was a lesson in this for Kate as well. I let her decision rest.

On the phone that night Kate and I chatted briefly before turning the conversation to the Trail. "Kate, I got your letter. Are sure you want to go? I mean it will be a lot of walking each day. It will be cold and you'll need equipment and…."

"I know Mom," Kate cut into to my laundry list of concerns. "I can do it. We used to backpack all the time. Tell me what I need and I'll put it on the credit card. It won't be too cold in March. I think it will be fun. Don't you think?"

"Well, yes. I hope you will come look at the maps and equipment catalogs. There's a lot more planning involved in this trip than there was in ones we used to go on."

"I know, Mom, but I can't come to your house. Johnny and I have plans for all the weekends that I don't have to work between now and March first. I have a Campmor catalog and a pencil. Just tell me what I need."

An hour later Kate had ordered five hundred dollars worth of equipment. She would get her own trail mix. I would supply the breakfasts and suppers. She promised not to complain about hot cereal breakfasts and vegetarian suppers. I hung up the phone with mixed emotions. Kate was so excited. It would be good to have her support.

On February 27, Suellen and I loaded the backpack, food, and a box of supplies in her van and drove to Kate's house, a half an hour from Springer Mountain. On Friday Kate and I loaded, unloaded, and reloaded the backpacks. All of Kate's equipment had arrived. She borrowed a backpack from her dad and a therma-rest from me. We tested the stove, put trail mix in baggies, cut the cardboard out of toilet paper rolls, and looked at maps. We ended up packing extra straps, bungi cords, rope, buckles, pins, short sleeved shirts, and enough food for an army. Our packs weighed nearly sixty-five pounds apiece.

At Amicalola Falls Kate and Johnny got a motel room. Suellen's sister

Judy and our friend Jane, from Knoxville, joined Suellen and me in a cabin. The children's father and David joined us for breakfast at the lodge before driving to the Trailhead at U.S.F.S 42 near Big Stamp Gap. I was ecstatic. The dream was about to become reality.

David, Tom, and Judy joined Kate and me for the nine-tenths of a mile climb up Springer Mountain. At the southern-most terminus of the Appalachian Trail, Kate and I signed our first register. As we turned to leave, the first of many miracles happened. "If you don't mind," Tom began. I was surprised to see him choked with tears, "I would like to have prayer for you two before you begin this hike. Ellen, I know how important this is. I'm real proud you."

"That would be fine," I said reaching for my son's hand.

Tom prayed a sincere prayer for our safety and health. He finished by saying, "I know if any woman can hike this entire Trail, my ex-wife can." I was touched. I hadn't had much contact with him in the ten years we'd been divorced. Most of our fifteen years together had not been particularly amicable. The children had told me he'd returned to church and his character had mellowed. I hoped this was true for the sake of his good wife Diana, the children, and his own well being. Now, back in the same place where he and I had hiked with our children nearly twenty years before, Tom supported me. I was moved by his gesture. So were the children. Our lives had come full circle. It was fitting and right that four individuals who at one time enjoyed the southern Appalachians as a family, should gather at Springer Mountain to recognize that all is not lost when the term family no longer applies. With our divorce, our children had witnessed the sacredness and value of people being true to themselves, rather than continuing in an arrangement unsuited to individual needs. Also on the summit, Kate and I met our first thru-hiker. Dan McGraw from Florida, known as Chief, became part of my Trail family.

At the edge of the Trail, Kate and I planted native flower seeds in honor of women who had been stricken with breast cancer. Suellen read a prayer she had written for the occasion. "On this paper are the names of women who were stricken by breast cancer. Katharine S. Ordway, Laura LeCoultre Lawson, Fran Bell, Elizabeth Dooley Biggs, Denise, Latrina, Nichols, Katherine Davis Porter. May they live and rest in peace and may the wild flowers planted here symbolize the beauty of their lives and the hope that we who survive will never be so stricken. May the contributions generated by 'Hike for Healing' lead to a quick and certain cure so that our daughters and their daughters can live free from the fear of breast cancer. Amen."

At last it was time to shoulder packs and head to Hawk Mountain shelter, 7.6 miles up the Trail. Cameras flashed, tears were shed, and promises to write and be careful were made. As I hugged Suellen good-bye I could only utter, "I would not be out here if it weren't for you." The weeks ahead would prove how much I meant those words. Kate and I waved until our friends and family disappeared from sight. Suellen called after me, "Wisely and slow, they stumble that run fast."(297). Quoting the Priest in Shakespeare's play *Romeo and Juliet* was fitting. It had been my father, Emerson "Pete" Priest, who taught me the value of walking softly over dried leaves while on long walks through Vermont woods. My native homeland was nearly two thousand miles away, but Suellen's parting words reassured me that my father's Priestly ghost would travel with me.

The walk up the hill was tough for Kate. She was nauseous by the time we reached the shelter. I hoped food would make her feel better. We had tried out our new stove, but the instructions escaped us. "Here, let me help you. We have a stove like that. They're kind of hard to get going at first." A man with an accent I immediately recognized reached for the stove.

"You're from New England aren't you?" I asked

"Yes, New Hampshire. I'm Ron Derby and this is my wife Pat." He motioned for a woman about my age to join us as he lit the stove. Ron had just retired. They were using the hike as time to contemplate their next step in life. They hoped to finish the Trail by September in time for their first grandchild to enter the world in West Virginia. We Southerners dubbed them the Kentucky Derby's. Hikers identify themselves by Trail names. I dropped the E from my last name and called myself, "Wolf Woman." There are so few women thru-hikers, that I wanted my name to connect to my gender. Because Kate's clothes were blue, she called herself the, "Blue Snail."

The basic necessities of food, shelter, water, and companionship connected Gumby, Woolly, Peppi, the Admiral, Boone, Snake Eyes, Stork, Tippy Canoe, Ron and Pat Derby, Grasshopper and her dog Bailey, Chief, Kate and me. We became part of the twenty-two thru-hikers who left for Katahdin on March first. The 1997 Trail community christened new sleeping bags in new tents or on the hard floor of our first weathered three-sided shelter built to accommodate eight to twelve. Pat and I stayed connected by way of the Trail journals until we lost touch in upstate Virginia.

Kate was sick throughout the evening and slept fitfully, but in the morning she was willing to keep going. Getting everything back into the backpack proved to be quite an ordeal. I knew I didn't need all the stuff we'd brought. Kate and I were last to leave for Gooch Shelter, 8.5 miles away. It was nearly dark and raining when we reached the blue blaze Trail leading to the shelter. With impending doom we called, "Anyone up there? Room for two more?" With renewed energy, Kate's young eyes lit up when she spotted the shelter.

"Hey, Wolf Woman and Blue Snail, you guys made it! There's always room for thru-hikers heading for Maine." Boone's New Hampshire accent revitalized our spirits as we followed the sound of her voice. Boone, Tippy Canoe, Stork, Snake Eyes, and Chief moved their gear over for our second night on the Trail. "You know, you guys," Boone began, "Less than ten percent of the folks that leave for Katahdin make it. I want to, but I'm going to have a good time just

23

in case I don't."

"I read that too," I said between bites of granola bars, bread, and peanut butter. "This won't be easy; today sure wasn't, but I'm going to Maine." As I drifted off to sleep, I wondered if Boone would finish. She was such good company and her herb pipe helped to keep the mice away. As I hung our food in the rafters so the mice wouldn't get a free meal, I wondered what effect doubts and fears would have on finishing. Katahdin was so far away. After only two days all I could think about was getting to Hiawassee and lightening the pack. I wouldn't make it carrying sixty-five pounds. Little did I know how necessary a positive attitude would be. I got out my journal and flashlight. *March 2: Boone and the guys made room for us. The AT community feels good. Kate is better and likes the young folks. I'm ecstatic. The day was perfect. The packs are way too heavy but we will make it to Hiawassee. Being here feels like a dream, a dream come true.*

Our hike to Georgia's highest peak, Blood Mountain at 4,400 feet, was our first twelve-mile day. Because there is no water on the summit Kate and I cooked supper at the stream below. Boone, Stork, Tippy Canoe, and Snake Eyes had already staked out spots in the damp stone structure by the time we arrived. Built in the 1930's, the shelter had a door and gaping widows. Kate greeted Ron and Pat at their tent with a silly poem she'd made up before settling in. Just as the *Thru-Hiker Handbook* predicts, we had a visitor. "Oh! Shit. A skunk!" trembled Boone.

"Be still. He won't spray if we're quiet. Light up your pipe." I suggested in a steady voice. The small, speckled skunk wandered back and forth between our heads and the back of the shelter. Boone lit her pipe and the skunk waddled out the door.

"Wow, we're above the clouds. Hey, you guys come out here and look at the moon. I can't see a city light anywhere." Stork had hopped out barefoot in the night air with his sleeping bag zipped around his shoulders. "It's cold but absolutely gorgeous." Pulling on our fleece or wrapping up in sleeping bags, we joined Stork under millions of stars. A huge yellow moon spilled streaks of silver light across the treetops. Thick white puffy clouds cradled the valleys between the mountains. We were truly above the world.

"We are on an island surrounded by a floating lake," Kate murmured.

"Only three days out and what awesome beauty," I mused. We stood in sacred silence until the stirring night breezes seeped through the cracks of our wraps with subtle suggestions we return to the stone shelter and got some sleep before sunrise.

Kate and I reached Walasi-Yi Center at Neels Gap on the fourth day. On the wide stone porch we let our packs fall and dug out a pack towel and clothes. "I wonder if anyone will take our gear while we're gone." I mused.

"Don't worry about that," said a middle-aged man with a wide brace on one leg and one arm dangling at his side. "Usually when you leave your pack where hikers hang out, you'll come back to find things added to it rather than anything missing. Hikers want to get rid of weight. You thru-hikers? I'm One Armed Bandit, OAB for short."

"I'm Wolf Woman, headed for Maine. This is my daughter Kate, the Blue Snail. She'll get off in Gatlinburg. Right now we're headed to the shower. I'd love to get rid of some weight. Want some trail mix?" I handed OAB a bag on my way to the shower.

The next shelter was too far to reach before dark, so Kate and I camped near Baggs Creek Gap. We created a tent by wrapping tarps and ponchos around branches before cooking polenta to eat with vegetarian pate and fruit bars. The night sky blazed with a thousand diamonds. As the moon rose, Kate talked of her job, plans she and Johnny had, and her struggles to find direction in her life. My friends had been right. This piece of the journey included a chapter on bonding with Kate.

*March 4: Life is so simple and peaceful. Kate and I are doing fine. She is sore but pleasant. We made a great shelter. My body is doing well. All I can think of is all the stuff I need to get rid of. Not only stuff, but attitude. I need to feel less compelled to rush. I need to lighten my mind, as well as my load. One day at a time, I will make it. The trip makes life so trivial, incidental, and quality times with people, especially Kate, so important. By leaving civilization, I'm learning to appreciate the value of people.*

The fifth day out began bright and sunny, but by afternoon, the sky was as heavy and swollen as a woman expecting a child. Black as night, the air hung heavy with a pending storm. Low Gap Shelter was built in a bank above a bubbling stream. Broken Road and Pilgrim, brothers from Massachusetts and their friend Tacet from Pennsylvania were there. Tippy Canoe and Boone hurried down the path a few minutes ahead of OAB and Two Winds, who joined us just as the rain hit. Crack! Boom! Thunder and lightening ripped through the gap like stampeding horses on a narrow track. Feeling like primates hovering in a wilderness cave, we sat with our back against the wall, our knees pulled up to our chests, and our sleeping bags tucked around our shoulders. We could hardly hear each other talk above the crashing storm. As we snuggled close together, OAB shared with us his struggles as a hiker with handicaps. "I want all of you to know I'm an epileptic. I hope that doesn't scare anyone. I haven't had an attack since last year but if I do, just roll me on my side so I won't swallow my tongue. The seizures don't last long. The doctors thought I was going to die when I had a brain tumor. I don't have use of my left arm and wear that brace on my leg. It is hard out here, but no harder than it would be anywhere. I've hiked many sections of the Trail several times, but have never done a complete thru-hike. I hope to this year. I hear you're going to write a book, Wolf Woman. I'd like to write one about hikers with handicaps. Do you think it would sell?"

"Sure it would. I respect you for being out here. My brother is a mycrocephlic and a diabetic. He's in his forties and he can't read, but he's very capable in other ways. I used to teach kids with learning disabilities. It's no crazier for you to be out here than it is for the rest of us. We probably all have folks back home who think we are nuts. Actually, I am not so sure we are too bright to be sitting in the middle of a thunderstorm; but we didn't invite this fury any more than people ask to be physically or mentally challenged. Sure I think you can write a book and people would read it."

OAB was a wealth of information about the places to stop and Trail conditions. We shared many shelters together until he headed to Damascus for Trail Days in May. The Trail rumors reached me that he'd hitch hiked to Katahdin and would be hiking south. Thru-hikers who know they will run out of time before Baxter State Park closes in October can flip-flop by catching a ride to Katahdin, climb, and then hike to where they got off the Trail to complete the trip. I didn't see OAB again after leaving Virginia.

"I'm freezing! Is anyone else cold? The temperature has really dropped." Boone huddled into her sleeping bag. The rain had stopped, but wind whipped though the forest.

"My thermometer says it is 10 degrees," OAB confirmed Boone's predication. I didn't have long to wonder how Kate would do with the wind and cold.

"Mom, is it going to be cold like this all day? Can't we lie here until it warms up?" Kate was trying to be pleasant.

"No honey, we need go on. I'll heat water for cocoa and oatmeal."

"I can't believe it got so cold so fast. Yesterday was nice and warm. I was planning to take a bath in the stream. Forget that idea!" Tippy Canoe sipped steaming coffee. We huddled together trying to escape the roaring wind. The longer we sat, the colder we felt. We needed to move if we didn't want to freeze to death.

"We'll warm up once we get moving. Be careful, stay safe, and stay warm," I added to the standard parting lingo as Kate and I hoisted on our packs. Kate was feeling better, but her hiking zeal was diminishing. This was not going to be a day to push for extra mileage. The wind made our eyes tear up and visibility nearly impossible. If we rested we got chilled, and if we kept going we were exhausted. If bone-chilling weather wasn't enough, coming around Chattahoochee Gap a speck of dust blew in Kate's eye. I examined it but I didn't see anything in her bloodshot watery eye. I suggested she let it run and not rub it, but Kate was in a state of panic. "Mom, this is too much. Let's get off the Trail in Helen, Georgia. Can't we get out of the wind for just one night? Maybe if I have a good night's sleep I'd feel better."

"We'll make that decision three miles up the Trail at Blue Mountain Shelter." At the shelter Boone tried to flush Kate's eye out with purified water and calm her. But Kate wailed. "Mom, I can't stand it."

I fashioned a bandage over her injured eye so she could see through the good eye without having to force the injured one shut. I wouldn't have considered taking a day off, had I been alone. However, I had a hiking partner, who happened to be my daughter. Chilled to the bone, we hiked until the Trail crossed the highway. I hurried across the road to a parking lot and asked a hiker the direction to Helen. I got back to Kate just as a car passed and stuck out my thumb. The driver brought the car to a screeching halt. In Helen we checked into a motel. While Kate showered, I went to a Wendy's for food. When I returned, Kate's eye was still swollen and red and she was sick to her stomach. With tears flowing down her cheeks she asked, "Mom do you think I should just go home? This could happen again. I've been sick the whole time. I've tried not to complain. I wanted to hike with you, but this is a lot harder than I thought it would be. I didn't want to disappoint you or let myself down. All day I've been thinking what will my friends say if I quit after only six days."

The questions were critical. If I encouraged her to get back on the Trail she would do it; but she was right. Her eye probably would keep bothering her, and if not her eye than perhaps something else. If I suggested she go home she might feel I didn't want her with me. She might interpret such a suggestion as a lack of my confidence in her. I knew she could make it to Gatlinburg. However, the weather would probably stay cold. This section was one the toughest on the entire Trail. We still had a hundred and fifty miles to go. "Kate, I want you to do what you feel is best. What do you want to do? I will respect whatever you decide. Why did you want to go with me in the first place?"

"Oh Mom, I just wanted to spend some time with you. I'm so proud of you and I wanted to be part of the experience. I thought this would be fun. But, I want to go home." Sobbing, Kate picked up the phone and called Johnny. He was home and promised to come right away. As I sat on the motel bed running my hands through her long natural curly brown hair, I realized how quickly decisions change our lives and what a monumental impact seemingly small incidences can have on our plans. "After I get home we'll plan some time together. It is more important that you wanted to be with me than making it to Gatlinburg. I love you. I'm not mad at you."

"Oh Mom, I don't want you to be upset. Doing the Trail is real hard, cold, and miserable. I know you can do it. I mean, you have always wanted to and it's important to you. You're not like most people, Mom. Not everyone is strong and driven like you," Kate sat up and hugged me. Strong and driven. Is that how my daughter saw me? Is that what it was going to take to get to Katahdin? Within an hour her gear was in the truck and she was on her way back to Calhoun. Alone in the Helendorf River Inn parking lot, I gazed through the German decorated village and waved good bye to our Appalachian bonding experience. I'd been unsure about wanting Kate to join me, now I unclenched my back teeth and let the tears flow. I already missed her. Perhaps the array of emotions I'd felt during our fifty miles together was best described by Adriene Rich, ". . . there is no thing in human nature more resonant with charges than the flow of energy between two biologically alike bodies, one of which has lain in amniotic bliss inside the other, one of which has labored to give it birth. The materials are here for the deepest mutuality and the most painful estrangement" (226). Kate had reached out because she needed me. In order to touch our own strength as women we need our mothers. The dream was mine, but I needed to know I was where I needed to be through Kate's eyes. The physical and emotional steps that Kate and I took together affirmed the cry of that female child in us that need not be shameful or regressive but is the germ of our desire to create a world of strong mothers and daughters.

After Kate left I turned to practical matters. I would lose a day in Helen. Suellen planned to meet me in Hiawassee, but not for two days. I picked up the telephone. "Suellen, Kate just went home and I'm in Helen, Georgia. Can you come tonight?" It only took Suellen a second to respond. "Good, I'm at the Heledorf River Inn. See you soon." After showering, I sorted out supplies for Suellen to take home and journaled.

*March 7: I made it through the first week. I'm glad for the chance to get rid of unnecessary weight although I now take on the weight of the tent and everything Kate carried. I feel stronger. Climbing is much harder than I thought it would be. I'm learning about endurance and perseverance and, yes, about making use of being strong and driven. I'll miss Kate.*

Suellen was on spring break from teaching and was able to slack pack me for three days. She would drive the pack between connecting roads so I could hike with only a daypack. After a big restaurant breakfast, Suellen dropped me off where Kate and I had gotten off the Trail and then drove to Tray Mountain Road USFS 79 to set up our six-person tent. The following night we camped at Dick's Creek Gap and then at Deep Gap USFS 71. Turtle, a retired fellow who was walking the Trail as a healing process after losing his wife to cancer and his only daughter to a car accident, joined us at Dick's Creek Gap. I felt melancholy at the loss of Kate and Suellen was exhausted from working on a book. We boosted each other's spirits with stories. Turtle told tales of his travels abroad. I recalled my first days on the Trail. Suellen, a gifted story teller, kept us in stitches with stories she'd collected for the story telling book that she and her colleagues Sandy Smith and Dr. Betty Roe were compiling, entitled *Teaching through Stories: Yours, Mine, and Theirs* (1998).

For the next two days I carried only lunch, rain gear, toilet paper, camera, and my journal as I flew through the forests, unfettered by the heavy pack. As a child I'd been attracted to the elusive, mobile, migratory lives that I believed birds and Indians lived. I was ten years old when my father told me I couldn't grow up to be a bird or an Indian. However, I remembered his saying, his blue eyes sparkling as clear as a New England sky, "You can always pretend." For three days I thought I was one, the other, or both as I flew down the slopes and stalked slowly up them. Each night Suellen and I cooked polenta or soup around a campfire and slept in a tent, almost as big as a tee pee.

On the tenth day I looked up to see the small wooden sign that signified I'd accomplished my first seventy-five miles. The initials GA-NC were fastened to a tree. I snapped a picture. Mt. Katahdin was over two thousand miles away, but every landmark was a milestone and daily victories were important. On the morning of March 11th, I took up the pack. I missed the easy companionship of Suellen and the deep connection I had found with Kate. Truly alone for the first time, I set my own pace into the deep forests. I hiked twelve-mile days for the next two days and camped each night beside beautiful streams. Carrying a tent freed me from the fear of not being able to make it to a shelter before dark or possibility of finding them full. I enjoyed the quiet time, yet I missed company. My life long battle between wanting people in my life and pushing them out plagued me. I was surprised these complicated concerns had followed me into the wilderness.

The AT community would be a necessary part of my experience. Hikers communicate by signing and dating the journals or registers in the shelters. Camping alone at Betty Creek Gap and later at Winding Stair Creek Gap, I missed the nightly chatter of my Trail community, but I had quiet time to write.

*March 12: I made it to a camping spot after a rough nearly 13-mile day. The climb up Mt. Albert was a hand over hand experience. The pack is still too heavy. I can think of little else except what else I can get rid of. I get anxious about making it to shelters at night. I can't do this for five months unless I send more gear home. I am not discouraged, but carrying everything at such a slow pace is overwhelming. Having my tent takes the pressure off making it to shelters, but I am not sure carrying the four extra pounds is worth it. I know I am supposed to be here, but why, I don't know. What is the point of carrying 50 pounds a day? The answer will come if I keep writing, thinking, and walking. I will make it to Wesser, North Carolina, and mail things home.*

The following day brought a drastic change in the weather. I tucked the pack cover over the backpack as whipping cold rain lashed my face. Struggling up Wayah Bald and into Burningtown Gap, North Carolina, on my thirteen-mile hike to Cold Springs Shelter, I questioned the sanity of subjecting myself to biting wind and chilling rain. What was the point of this journey? The teacher in me rose as high as the water in my boots as I pondered the lessons I needed to learn. What was the point in making it to each shelter, only to spend another night in the cold? Reaching a dirt road that intersected by another equally deserted road, I hoped I was at Burningtown Gap. I walked across the fog filled clearing before starting up the steep log steps. It was painfully difficult to lift my drenched body and the pack up the steep embankment. I crumbled on the steps. Balancing the pack on the upper step, I stared at the road in a trance. It would be easy to walk down the road until I found civilization and hitch a ride home or at least to a dry place for the night. Loneliness suddenly soaked into my misery as thoroughly as the rain had managed to seep through my Gortex rain jacket. I remembered David at Cumberland Mountain Outdoor Sport saying, "Only plastic or rubber are completely water proof. Gortex is only guaranteed for a certain number of hours in soaking rain, then expect to get wet." The fore-warning had filled me with fear that the rain would continue before the inevi-table happened. The combination of loneliness and soaked misery was as dan-gerous as mixing vodka with orange juice.

While working with recovering alcoholics in Knox County, I recognized the necessity of not dwelling on drinking in order to maintain sobriety and to work a recovery program. Harboring such thoughts puts alcoholics at risk of relapse. It occurred to me that just as the alcoholic cannot entertain the thought of a drink, the thru-hiker cannot entertain the thought of going home. Thru-hikers, like alcoholics, who wallow in self-doubt, self-pity, and despair, are in danger of not meeting their goals. Both the alcoholic in recovery and the Katahdin-bound thru-hiker must focus one step at a time on a pity free positive attitude. Having witnessed people build one sober day on top of another through the determination to stay clean and sober gave me strength to get moving. I had to believe if I kept moving my conditions and my attitude would change. Rec-ognizing the detriment of negative thinking, I focused on the fact that each step moved me closer to Katahdin. I paraphrased the familiar Prayer of Alcoholics Anonymous. I needed to learn to accept the things I could not change, such as the weather, and have the courage to change the things I can, such as my atti-tude.

"Anyone there? I could barely see the shelter through the rain and fog. Turning the corner, I was thrilled to see Broken Road, Pilgrim, and Tacet huddled in sleeping bags cooking supper. "Boy am I glad to see familiar faces. This rain has really got me down." Broken Road jumped up to take my pack.

"Wow, your pack is heavy. What have you got in there? I don't know how you carried it up here." He shook his head in disbelief as he hung it on the shelter wall. "It's good to see you, too. We've been wondering how you were getting along."

"I'm going to ship a bunch of stuff home when I get to Wesser." Shivering, I dragged out my sleeping bag and dry clothes. Holding my sleeping bag in front of me, I grasped it with my teeth to make a curtain before easing out of my wet clothes. I tried not to drip on my dry clothes while trying not to expose my nakedness. The fellows respected my situation and continued with their sup-pers. Even with dry clothes on I chattered uncontrollably. Tacet handed me a steaming cup and said, "Sip on this. It will warm your insides. In this kind of weather you have to guard against hypothermia." I knew I was losing body heat faster then I was replacing it and was in danger. I was aware of the warning signs: walking with uncoordinated steps, speaking slowly, losing appetite, feeling unusually tired, or acting peculiar. I didn't feel hungry and wanted to sleep. The hot liquid connected to my chilly core like a powerful medicine. I was grateful for their kindness. "Thanks, this hits the spot. What is this? I'm so glad you guys are here. I've been camping the last several nights and haven't seen thru-hikers for several days."

"You're drinking hot jello," Pilgrim answered, as I handed Tacet back the cup.

"It's good to see you. We camped out last night, too. I have some hot water if you want it. No reason going out in the rain when we have plenty. Where is Kate? I heard she got dust in her eye and had to get off the Trail."

"Thanks for the water and for asking. Her eye is okay. We never found anything in it, but it was real red and swollen. She was having a hard time with the cold and mountains. She got off the Trail in Helen," I added Lipton soup mix to Pilgrim's hot water. After supper, I reapplied moleskin to my heels, a thru-hiker nightly ritual. Blisters were an inevitable part of thru-hiking. As I snuggled in my sleeping bag I looked up to see a drenched woman backpacker round the corner. She stood in amazement.

"Oh, dear, I didn't think anyone would be in here. There are two more people coming. Can you can make room?" We shuffled our belongings closer together. Soon two more women and a small dog arrived. "Thanks so much, we really appreciate it," said the first women. "We are up from Florida for a week. This storm came up fast."

I noticed how much easier it was to change with someone holding the makeshift curtain. The little dog shivered. One of the women dried him and invited him into her sleeping bag. We followed his example and wiggled into our bags on the shelter floor.

"Everyone warm enough?" Broken Road asked.
"I'm fine. Thanks a lot you guys." I said.

"Yeah, thanks to all of you for making room," the women answered. With renewed spirits and gratitude for the thoughtfulness shown by the Trail community, I jotted down a few notes in my journal by flashlight before drifting to sleep. *March 13: I hiked nearly 15 miles in the rain today. I got very frustrated with my poncho. I couldn't put it over the pack by myself in the wind. I bought a long mens. It drags the ground and is useless. I enjoyed the fog. The Goddess was with me. I thought about my grandmother, Grammy Kay. She loved the wind. The company and warmth of six people is comforting. I constantly vacillate in my need for people to be around and my need for privacy. Tomorrow at Wesser I will send supplies home. I still wonder why am I out here.*

*My mother said I come by this traveling vagabond lifestyle naturally. John*

*Ordway, from Hebron New Hampshire, was one of a few well-educated men recruited to go west in 1805 on the Lewis and Clark expedition. My mother's maiden name was Ordway. John was the first cousin of Bradshaw Ordway who was the great great grandfather of my grandfather, Richmond Ordway. John's journals provided valuable information about the history of Lewis and Clark's Cores of Discovery. The success of their journey west was contingent upon the kindness of strangers, comradeship, and their ability to maneuver over the land. I will succeed on my trek north because of Trail Magic, support, and my ability to persevere.*

*Although I depend on maildrops and stores, this experience taps into the core oneness with Mother Earth as a primary provider. With her power, I'll move through the unknowns. Earlier today I thought I was going to die. Now I'm full of peace.*

Knowing I was about to lighten the pack made it feel lighter during the eleven and one half-mile hike to Nantahala Outdoor Center in Wesser, North Carolina. I knew more about the necessity of having a positive attitude than about how much weight to carry. Spring beauties and May apples poked through the ground as I listened for traffic. Rounding a bend, the wide river came into view. I knew I was close. My head whirled as I reached US 19. The cars sped by, and people moved too quickly. I got a bunk in a cabin with Preacher and Crazy, showered, then joined Broken Road, Pilgrim, and Tacet at the River's End Restaurant. We watched Kayakers on a slalom course as we ate. "We've been hiking two weeks. I can't believe it," I said between bites of vegiburger and salad."

Broken Road swallowed, "Yup, next stop is Fontana Dam." Thru-hikers pace their journey by anticipated stops. Reaching the "Great Mountain" is every hiker's goal, but 2,160 miles is too overwhelming a distance to calculate the days by. Maildrops and restaurants kept me going; not the water falls, mountain summits, rivers, or vistas, despite the beauty. I needed to connect to the culture I'd left in order to live in a culture I constantly moved through. Unlike home where life is constant, safe, and predicable, Trail life is elusive, unpredictable, and full of unknowns. Thru-hikers must trust that the distances between shelters are what the data book indicates and that water sources won't be dried up or full of debris. The elevation maps added to the fantasy, as do weather conditions and companions. There was little room for fear, only a healthy respect for strangers, animals, weather, and dangerous terrain.

At the center I bought a two and a half-pound bivy tent and a two-ounce closed cell mat. I mailed home the L. L. Bean tent, therma-rest, extra paper, pens, socks, lighters, a pan, the wooden spoon, candles, a compass, and a few Band-Aids, which lightened my pack by five pounds. I put extra moleskin, paper, ibuprofen, soap, sun screen, bug spray, shorts, batteries, and food in a box and sent it priority mail to two maildrops ahead. If I needed anything, I'd pick the box up and take out what I needed, or ship the box on to the next maildrop without added charge. I ended up shipping the box from maildrop to maildrop all the way to Monson, Maine.

At Rivers End, I met Stick-In-Face, Magot, Daddy, Vagabond, Crazy, and Preacher for the first time, but earlier they had become part of my Trail community by way of the journals. Admiral was struggling with his decision to go home. His wife supported his desire to do the Trail, but had never really understood. Believing his marriage was more important than thru-hiking, he decided to catch the next bus home. "When I called her and told her I was coming home, she said it was the smartest thing I'd said since I retired!" he said happily. I had to admit that hot showers on a regular basis sounded appealing. My heart tugged at the mention of home, but I'd vowed not to entertain thoughts of home.

After breakfast and doing laundry, I took another shower, taped moleskin on my heels, and shrugged into a considerably lighter pack. The day was perfect for hiking. Several hours into the day I encountered Trail Magic. Descending into Stecoah Gap, I spotted a woman with a daypack at the edge of the Trail. "Hi, my name is Swan of '95. I'm known for my Oreo cookies, help yourself. Are you thru-hiking?"

"Yes, I left Springer Mountain March first and hope to finish by early August."

"What other Trail Magic have you encountered?"

"Making it to the shelters before dark, finding water, and now you standing here with food." I said, referring more to the presence of a woman than the cookie.

"I don't see many women. I'm surveying women's Trail experiences for a book. Would you mind filling one out and sending it to the address on the back?" I pulled a copy of the survey out of my pack.

"I'd be happy to. Don't be in a rush about writing the book. People will be finishing until October, or until it snows in Baxter State Park. South-bounders will be finishing until Christmas. It will take a while for the impact of the trip to settle with you."

"I didn't realize people finished so late. I've only met four women but have left surveys in the shelters. I'd like to do a book of women's stories too." We talked about my plans until Crazy joined us. "Thanks for the cookies and for taking the survey. I have miles to go before I sleep."
"Look for a fellow with fruit, soda, and beer at the gap."

"Beer, all right!" sang Crazy.

"Fruit! I hope he has apples. Thanks again," I added, following Crazy.

Hiking with Crazy made me realize how alone I felt walking by myself. Just a few minutes of conversation lifted my spirits. Interaction, conversation, and stimulation, givens in society, are missing on the Trail. Being alone is a way of life. Most thru-hikers, including myself, are introverts. I hadn't expected difficulty being alone. Some folks I'd talked to while campaigning had admitted loneliness would prevent them from thru-hiking. Missing people is one-reason hikers return home. I was not lonely for society, but I just missed contact. Finding Vagabond, Magot, Lynx, and Stick-In-Face with Swan's friend nearly made me cry. Kindness is the corner stone of Trail Magic.

"Hey everybody, good to see you guys. You do have apples and oranges." I said slipping out of my backpack to enjoy the fruit and fellowship.

After eating and taking pictures, I stuck another apple in my pack and bid my Trail family good-bye, "See you on up the Trail. Stay safe."

These words were passed back and forth among thru-hikers as commonly as, "Drive safely," is at home. I left ahead of the others, but knew they would pass me. I was slower than the younger hikers and always the last one to drag into the shelters. The lighter pack did not increase my speed.

The evening at Cable Gap Shelter was like old home coming. Broken Road, Lynx, Pilgrim, Tacet, and everyone from Stecoah Gap talked about Fontana Dam. A fire warmed our spirits and bodies. I played my harmonica. Crazy helped me pitch my bivy tent. I emptied my pockets into the food sack before hanging it out of reach of mice.

*March 16: Meeting Swan and eating fruit were today's highlights. I'm struck by the importance of connecting to landmarks. No one talks about the beautiful scenery. Hikers grumble about the hard steep climbs without recognizing the incredible views. I want to acknowledge the beauty, as well as the energy it takes to move through it. The bivy tent feels claustrophobic. I can't put my feet in the air to stop the cramping. I will send the tent home with Judy at Fontana. The Smoky Mountains are next.*

# Chapter 4

# "Get off the ridge if it snows!"

### Fontana Dam, North Carolina to Hot Springs, North Carolina

Spread like a deep blue oasis, Fountain Lake sparkled through the leafless trees. Steep and massive in the sunlight behind the dam, the Great Smokies Mountains' mighty peaks beckoned me to risk balancing ecstasy with fear. I hurried down the hill eager to shower at the Visitor's Center before Judy arrived. I was waterproofing the bivy tent on the pavement when she drove up. We hugged as if years had passed.

"I have salad and muffins from the Fresh Market. I can't believe you've hiked a hundred and sixty-three miles already. Everyone sends their love. How are you?"

"Just fine. Look out there," I motioned. "The Great Smoky Mountains are next. I hope to do them in six days, including a day off at the chalet in Gatlinburg. Hiking these mountains is like coming home."

"They sure look rugged to me," Judy mused.

"They are, but I want to do more than just knock off seventy miles of the trip. I want to understand why I'm out here. It is not enough to just say I'm fulfilling a childhood dream, walking for breast cancer, or I have the time to do the Trail. I want to understand the significance of having the time."

"You will," Judy promised. "Keep searching, you will."

In Fontana Village Chief, Magot, Broken Road, Pilgrim, Lynx, Crazy, and I entertained Judy with stories of our first seventeen days while we washed clothes at the laundromat. My Trail family was envious that Judy had driven seventy miles to see me. I was grateful. It would be miles before I'd understand the purpose of people.

Early the next morning Pilgrim gazed at the sky from the Fontana Hilton porch. "Anyone want a weather forecast?"

"Sure, what is it?" responded a sleepy voice from the large wood shelter, so named because it holds twenty-five hikers on four platforms.

"Looks like a clear sky, no rain in sight."

"Maybe that storm the locals were predicting went north," I sighed.

Rain in lower elevations could mean snow in the Smokies' 6,000-foot elevations. In recent years hikers had to evacuate the Trail until the snow melted enough to hike. Weather is the greatest friend or the most dreaded enemy. I knew rough terrain would slow my pace, but I didn't have time for a delay.

I needed to look at textbooks before I looked at anthropology students in

August. Just before I had left home in March, Dr. Donna Darden, the chair of the sociology department at Tennessee Tech University, had hired me to teach three anthropology classes. I wanted time to visit my mother on her boat in Maine before returning south. First I needed to hike from Fontana Dam to Davenport Gap. It was comforting to know I had a place to stay if I needed one, but lounging around Gatlinburg was not an option if I hoped to climb Katahdin in five months. I dressed while still zipped in the bag, a feat I'd mastered during the low teen mornings in the Nantahala Mountains. Shivering over breakfast with twenty other hikers, I tried to be positive.

Boone was not among us. Trail rumors speculated that she had not been prepared for the frigid temperatures and had gone home. I hoped she'd enjoyed her time on the Trail. I watched ominous black clouds looming over the last slice of rosy sky, barely visible on the horizon, as I ate hot cereal, dried fruit, and nuts. I wondered what the warning, "pink sky in the morning, sailors take warning," meant for hikers. Threatening weather for a thru-hiker is a signal to be aware. Everything I needed hung from my back. Like a massive restless giant, reaching up to grab the swollen sky, the straight barren trees of the Smokies loomed straight ahead. I'd made it through the rugged Natahalas. I was ready for these mountains, just not a crippling snowstorm.

By 7:30 a.m. only a few hikers were left pulling on boots and packing up gear. Morning after cold morning I marveled at the young men's speed and efficiency as they packed gear, prepared meals, and got on the Trail. Broken Road, Tacet, and Pilgrim were notorious for munching on pop tarts as they headed up the Trail before it was even light. Remembering how difficult it had been to get teenagers out of bed, I couldn't imagine these same fellows displaying this same energy and exuberance when faced with getting ready for work or school. But then, neither did I. Preparing for the day was part of the experience, a 2,000 mile experience that could last as long as six months. Most goals have greater degrees of flexibility. Vacations are shorter and are much less intense, goal orientated, or anxiety-filled. No experience has the same degree of unfamiliarity and vulnerability, or splendor and individualism as does hiking the Trail end to end. The only requirement is to keep walking. What could be simpler and yet more difficult?

The route is narrow and linear. Hikers who get off the Trail and hitch hike, or get rides between sections and miss part of the Trail, are called "yellow blazers." Sometimes town stops last longer than hikers intend, causing them to resort to yellow blazing in order to make up lost time. Skipping difficult sections, escaping bad weather, or catching up with friends are reasons hikers use to "yellow blaze." True thru-hikers don't yellow blaze. Often I'd read journal entries from folks I hadn't seen for weeks and were suddenly days ahead of me. Yellow blazing was not honest. Just as there are numerous ways to move up the Trail, there are also numerous reasons for leaving the Trail. Injury and sickness occasionally send hikers home. But managing time poorly, losing focus, and getting side tracked are the main reasons hikers quit. I didn't have time or money to spend time in the towns. Skipping sections would defeat the purpose of enjoying the scenery while focusing on the moment. Working an honest program is the philosophy of the Alcoholics Anonymous program. I vowed to apply the one-day at a time principle, and I took one-step at a time, putting one foot in front of the other.

"See you up the Trail; stay safe, and dry," I called out to hikers still packing up. "Be careful and watch the sky," I added out of motherly instinct.

Before crossing the bridge, I stopped at the Visitor's Center to make one last phone call to Suellen, who had insisted that I keep in touch with her. "I'll call you from Gatlinburg. No, it is not raining yet. It may clear," I added with more hope than I felt. I said goodbye to Suellen and headed over the dam.

A park ranger pulled up beside me. "You a thru-hiker?

"Yes Sir."

"You hiking alone?"

"Yes Sir, but I know hikers headed for the next shelter."

"The weather calls for heavy thunderstorms, possibly turning to snow in the high elevations. Keep your eyes to the west. You can see the storm coming. You don't want to be caught on the ridge if it storms. Use the Trail Ridge to get off the mountain if you need to. Be sure you get to a shelter by nightfall, and get off the ridge if it snows!"

"Yes, Sir," I said, fearing further comments would give him the chance to tell me I shouldn't be hiking alone or should wait and see what the weather was going to do.

"Oh, and be careful." he added. I'd taught my fourth graders that careful meant to be observant, vigilant, and mindful. Adjusting and adapting would be particularly necessary today. The first four miles climbed and climbed. Birch Springs Gap Shelter was five miles away if I needed to stop before reaching Russell Field Shelter, twelve miles away. Covered with dead leaves, the stark land and barren terrain looked drab and colorless. Winter hung in the air. Heavy and holding, the sky resembled two hundred-pound football players inching their way down the field. My pack burdened me with a heaviness I thought I'd gotten used to. Suddenly I stopped. At this slow pace I noticed tufts of moss struggling to grow around the bases of barren trees. Barely visible, May apples poked through the hard ground. Spring was making a noble effort to push its way through the cold earth. Year after year, after long harsh winters, nature brings forth spring. Encouraged, I hummed the Rogers & Hammerstein song, "You'll Never Walk Alone," in the rhythmic soothing motion of a comfortable rocking chair scooting slowly across hard wood floor. I too, scooted slowly along a wood filled living room.

The morning came without a sunrise. A swollen, pregnant sky asked for relief. The twelve of us at Russell Field Shelter donned rain gear, pulled on pack covers, and zipped up gaiters before walking into the bleakness. Relieved of pressure from the held back flow, cold hard rain fell. I fearfully obsessed that the rain would never end. My feet became soaked. Thinking gaiters would keep my feet dry in deluge was a false expectation. After realizing I couldn't get any wetter, I stopped avoiding the puddles and splashed through them like a child. I practiced staying in the moment. With the distance I'd traveled behind, and the miles ahead in the future, I enjoyed soggy scenery. The fourteen-mile hike became an exciting exhausting adventure of mud sliding and puddle sloshing. I gasped as I rounded Silas Bald Shelter. I will never forget the scene before my eyes. "I wish I had a movie camera! Is there room for one more?" I asked.

"Let's see." Leaning over the top row of bunks, Pilgrim counted, "There are nine down there and eight up here; Wolf Woman, you are up here." He and Broken Road, Tacet, and Lynx were the only thru-hikers. The rest of the hikers were referred to as spring-breakers, because they were students backpacking during a school break. I stood in awe. Seventeen men had crammed into a shelter built for twelve. Seventeen pairs of filthy, soaked boots lined the shelter. Seventeen hikers sat cross-legged or lay on their sleeping bags in front of their stoves, strategically holding pots of simmering suppers. Seventeen pairs of eyes looked at me. Sagging ropes with the weight of soggy clothes crisscrossed the rafters. As I pulled off my boots to join the community, I was aware of an unpretentious respect each hiker had for his neighbor's right to the limited but adequate space. I couldn't recall ever seeing guys with such boundaries. I was accustomed to guys being loud, obnoxious, and overbearing while demanding space in lines, parking lots, and crowds. Here in the wilderness a unique reverence prevailed. The scene made me wonder how much space people really need. The Silas Bald community did well with very little. Perhaps the order resulted from an ancient voice for basic needs.

Pop tarts, candy bars, trail mix, and hot water along with lighters, water filters, and flashlights were carefully passed among the weary hikers. Gratitude was the topic of discussion, not how miserable the day had been. Talking of success developed resiliency. Foul weather is an integral part of thru-hiking. A positive attitude was a necessity. As a thru-hiker I accepted crummy weather, crowded conditions, and the company of all males. Compared to the truly catastrophic experiences of our forebears, the early explorers, and the first Trail blazers, having field-tested equipment, shelters, and a well-marked Trail, we were not truly roughing it. The experience felt like home. I was content in the woods on this rainy cold March 19th, with seventeen guys.

After using a poncho to change under, I added my wet clothes to the sagging line. A fellow from Middle Tennessee State University in Murfreesboro held out a hand and hoisted me and my sleeping bag, supper, flashlight, data book, toilet paper, pen and journal to my space. I was part of the scene that so fascinated me. We chatted about our experiences in the mud and rain, ignoring the ever-present fear of snow.

I spent many more nights with only guys, but never again with seventeen. Their company renewed my faith in men to be sane, sensible, rational, and reasonable. That is, until someone farted. A symphony of smells and sounds, which had begun as an innocent explosion, sparked a nightlong contest between the guys on the top and the guys on the bottom. The man-made air attacks were muffled and reasonably spaced at first. However, as soon as someone let one loud enough to have blown the poor fellow out of his sleeping bag, the shyness ended, signaling a siege of self-propelled firearms. I always wondered if the guys on the top lost because they had one less participant. I had remained silent. With my sleeping bag over my head to block out the odors, I chalked the night's escapade up to sheer insanity among fellows who had been doing so well in such close quarters. Spending the night with seventeen fellows, who probably couldn't remember their last shower, had not been exactly odorless from the start. But who was I to talk? I'd chosen to be among them and my weekly showers didn't come any more often than theirs. After all, I was still trying to figure out what was so sane about walking to Maine.

The next morning frost sparkled on the frozen crusty ground. The temperatures had dropped into the low 20's, but the rain had stopped. Sun peeked into the valley as I began the 12.9 hike to Gatlinburg. My shadow swayed rhymthically as I hiked nonstop to the ramp below the 6,643 summit of Clingmans Dome, the highest point on the whole Appalachian Trail. I dropped my pack, pulled on a windbreaker, and continued up the spiral walkway. Thick Clouds engulfed the valley and then quickly parted, returning the magnificent scenery. Knowing I'd walked further than I could see overwhelmed me. Chilly gusts motivated me to snap pictures and head to the warm chalet.

The cold hard Trail of iced over puddles and water turned into a pine needle pathway. Vacillating between rocky terrain and soft ground, the Trail to Newfound Gap changed as often as the weather. I became lost in the glory of hiking as rainbows on the white crispy ground resonated with the promise of renewal. I was reminded that movement guarantees change. The tourists in the Newfound Gap parking lot reminded me I had not had a bath in four days, but within minutes I sat in the front of a Cadillac on my way to the Post Office with a local businessman who said he was honored help thru-hikers. I picked up my maildrop and caught another ride to the Happy Hiker.

In the presence of supportive friends, I spent the day soaking in a hot tub, waterproofing my rain gear, and enjoying Linda's home cooked food. By eleven the next day, Dennie, Linda, and Susan accompanied me to Ice Water Springs Shelter. I laughed about how long it took them to decide how much water, lunch, and gear they needed for the three-mile hike. It put my planning in perspective. Everything I needed was always with me. Cold wind nipped at our faces as we hiked. Lunch was melancholy. It would be months before I would see my friends again. With tears, I bid them good-bye and headed for Peck's Corner Shelter, seven miles further. They returned to warm homes.

Back at 5,000 feet, the weather had turned very cold by the time I arrived at the shelter. Nestled between two ridges, it had a homey atmosphere. A couple struggled to light a fire with damp wood. I encouraged their efforts while preparing macaroni and cheese. A round yellow moon casting radiant light across my sleeping bag woke me in the night. Bright and luminous, it arched high in the sky like a pregnant woman filling the space in an empty room. I snapped pictures from my sleeping bag and journaled by moonlight: *March 22: A cold windy day. Linda, Susan and Dennie walked with me to Ice Water Springs Shelter. I cried when they left. Am I finally realizing how important friends are? What keeps me going? I'm lonely yet content. It's easy to make a gratitude list. I'm amazed at the energy nature gives me. This shelter feels sacred. Even in its cold barren state, the Trail is alive with energy. My goal is as alive as the moon's round face.*

Freezing, in the early morning, I dressed while still in my sleeping bag. As I started up the short, blue blaze Trail to the main Trail, the fellow who'd built the fire peered out from his sleeping bag. "Have a good hike," he mumbled.

"You too! Thanks for the fire. I commend you for getting out here in this bitter cold. I hope it warms up. Be safe," I said, as I disappeared down the Trail thinking about all the activities young people could do rather than coming out in the freezing cold and carrying heavy packs up steep mountains. But these young people were not unique. Something primal calls the young and old alike into the mountains under all conditions. Looking into the cloudless sky, I wondered how it could possibly snow through the piercing blue. A majestic sight waited.

During the night snow had fallen. Thick, luscious, and white, it lay like icing across the treetops. Like comforting breasts, the gentle ridges of the mountain had protected the shelter. Here at higher elevations, the thick evergreens were heavily laden with several inches of snow. The thick branches filled with powder shielded the Trail from vanishing. Under my feet, hoarfrost crunched and sparkled in the sun. Like miniature rainbows glistening in the early morning light, the multicolored snowflakes resembled the flaked crayons I'd ground in my blender for art projects. As I hiked over the crystal translucent snow patterns, the rainbow-frosted shavings appeared to have been hand brushed in intricate color and designs. Symmetrically sculptured and creatively carved, the trees were a magical fairy world. Bent over, I felt like a troll burrowing through the white tunnels in a maze of authentic wilderness. At a clearing, I stood in sacred silence. "For me?" I mused "No one but me will see this. Is this really, just for me?" Snow flurries dusted my face from a clear blue sky. Touching the soft wetness anchored me in the reality that what I saw was truly a spiritual reassurance of a power and energy greater than myself. The silent message told me I could have both snow and the Smokies. Soon the sun would melt the beauty. Stopping to ponder, I accepted the raw, primitive, basic joy of being alone in the mountains. Experiences such as this don't happen in classrooms or homes. I had to come to the wilderness. Just one year ago I was presiding over a classroom as a teacher. Now I was the student in need of being present. This journey wasn't only about a calling to my roots, but a calling into the wild.

As I walked along the narrow ridge of Mt. Chapman, Mt. Sequoyah, and the approach trail to Mt. Guyot, frosty, white snowflakes drifted from a regal sky. Hiking through the snow filled me with a deep sense of promise. I'd only been on the Trail three weeks and was not even halfway through the Smokies, yet I felt secure. I felt freed from the perils of a crippling blizzard. My attitude had changed. What was there left to fear? I had hiked through wintry cold rain to the warmth of lower elevations. The snowy mountain reassured me that my journey would find balance.

In olden times people feared the mountains. Their rugged heights brought terror to those attempting to climb. Only by walking into them did people learn to trust the mystery of their depth. I too, often felt overwhelmed. However, standing on equal heights with the views, I become one with their splendor. I'd balanced my energy with my goal from a profoundly spiritual place. Accepting the connection between body, soul, and mind kept me from shutting down in fear and losing sight. Because fear comes from a lack of connection, I accepted my impermanent, transient, and unstable position. I was free from assuming disaster is based in unknowns. As I pulled the cold mountain air deep into my lungs and exhaled it back in the cycle of energy, I accepted my responsibility to move through the journey. Life was right around the corner, not fear of what if, but a life of what is. Synder defines this vagabond feeling: "the condition of true 'homelessness' is the maturity of relying on nothing and responding to whatever turns up on the doorstep" (105). The snow was a message of faith, not fear. The magical beauty taught me to believe I would move through the Smoky Mountains and on to Katahdin.

Coming from the cold of winter to the warmth of spring during the eighteen-mile hike to Cosby Knob, the Trail now was carpeted with pink and white spring beauties. Tucked around rocks and tree roots, plush green moss banked the moist ground. The energy of movement, the rhythm of the Trail, and Mother Nature's changing forces had guided my seventy-mile trek through the Smokies. However, walking through a forest fire was not how I had imagined my week in the Smokies to end. Black smoke grew thicker the farther I hiked. At a stream two hikers were filling water bottles. "Where do you think the fire is headed?" I asked the fellow leaning over the creek.

"I was about ask you the same thing."

"There's nothing to do but keep going," I said stuffing my fear. "Stay safe," he called after me, as I walked away into the smoke filled Trail. When the

Trail came to the Interstate 40 intersection, I cross the bridge and left the black smoke. On Snowbird Mountain I stopped and looked back. Smoke had engulfed the mountain I'd just come from. No flames were visible, but neither were fire trucks. Trail Magic had kept me safe.

Climbing Snowbird Mountain took me longer than I had anticipated. Hiking in the snow had also slowed me down. I wouldn't make it to Roaring Fork Shelter. The data book indicated water and camping at Brown Gap. I arrived just before dark but found neither. A cold supper would have to suffice. A black sky predicted rain. I covered the pack with the rain cover and pitched my tent. I hoped it wouldn't rain and that no local would spot my tent as I crawled in feet first, vowing to make it to shelters from then on. It was just as easy to assume it wouldn't rain and that I'd be safe than to fear otherwise.

A sharp pain in my right leg woke me. Tossing and turning in my limited space, I tried to get comfortable. The ibuprofen was out in my backpack under the pack cover. Fitfully, I drifted in and out of sleep until dawn's gray light seeped in my tent. I examined my leg while washing down ibuprofen and Trail mix with the last of the water. Nothing looked wrong. Hot Springs, North Carolina was twenty-two miles away. Judy was coming to see me and in two days Suellen would bring my third food box. The pack was light because I was low on food. I'd hiked two, twenty-mile days. My right shin was very tender and painful, but I walked on.

Stryder and OAB passed me. We agreed to meet on top of Max Patch. As I limped over the grassy windy summit I hollered, "I'm starving." Stryder sat licking peanut butter off a spoon. Our paths had crossed frequently since meeting in Georgia. His long pony tail, tall gangly body, and sweet nature reminded me of my son.

"Help yourself," he said, handing me the jar and some crackers.

"I'm so hungry. I could eat this whole jar," I snatched up the jar taking Stryder up on his offer. True to my word, I polished off the peanut butter.

"So your appetite finally kicked in!" chuckled OAB. "It usually takes about two weeks, sometimes longer for women. Good thing you'll be in Hot Springs tonight. Staying at Elmer's? He has great vegetarian food."

"No, Suellen made reservations at the Duckett House Inn for Thursday. They serve vegetarian too. It sure took a while for my appetite to kick in. I didn't eat much for supper last night because I camped at Brown Gap and I couldn't find any water so I couldn't cook. Where did you guys stay?"

"We camped on the bottom of Max Patch. Did you see the moon last night?

"Yes, it was incredible!" I answered between bites. I remembered the pain in my leg waking me up and seeing the moon. "I have a pain in my leg. It's a dull ache clear to the bone. You know what it might be?"

"Sounds like shin splints," said OAB. "You'll have to stay off your feet and let your leg rest. Shin splints can get so bad you won't be able to walk. I've had them."

That was all I needed to hear. "How am I supposed to stay off my feet and hike?" I didn't mean to sound smart, but I didn't have time for injuries. "Suellen isn't coming until Thursday. I'm two days ahead of schedule." I dreaded being away from my Trail community and off the Trail for four days. "Judy is a nurse and will know what to do."

As I pulled on my pack, I looked down at Stryder who had leaned back on his pack to catch afternoon rays through the chilly wind. "I owe you a jar of peanut butter, brother! I won't forget. Thanks a lot. See you on the Trail. Be safe."

"Ah, don't worry about it Wolf Woman. See you in Hot Springs," he drawled.

"More likely in a few minutes when you guys come flying pass me."

"Getting to Maine is all that matters," Stryder mumbled, half asleep.

Stryder was right, it didn't mater how slow I was as long as I kept hiking. For a nineteen-year old Stryder was a very responsible. He and the other fellows treated me as a comrade. Stryder occasionally called me Mom when the guys weren't around. I remember the time I'd left the shelter ahead of our Trail family and I was picking my way around a narrow section in Georgia. Slippery wet leaves filled the Trail and streams intermittently crossed the path. Several miles down the Trail Stryder came loaping by; his long legs barely touched the ground. I thought of suggesting that he slow down before he fell, but I knew that would sound too much like motherly advice. I only had time to say "Hi," as he careened by. Rounding a bend I found Stryder sprawled in the middle of the Trail rummaging in his pack for his first aid kit.

"Stryder, are you all right?" Dropping my pack beside him, I moved into my nurturing role.

"Just skun it up a bit," he mumbled.

"Yup, looks that way," I said, sizing up the bloody scraped knee as not a major wound but one in need of good washing. "Good thing you had shorts on or you would have torn up your pants." Scraped knees healed, clothes had to last. "Good thing there is a stream here too."

"I fell just after I passed you, but the data book said water was ahead."

I held Stryder's boot up in the air so water wouldn't run down his leg and soak his socks as he washed, dried, and applied antibacterial cream to the cuts. Cold wet feet could be a worse problem than a scraped up knee. Bandaged up, Stryder filtered water.

"Thanks," he grinned handing me my water bottle. It was on the tip of my tongue to suggest he slow down, but figured such talk would be as useless as suggesting streams run up the slopes instead of down. Casting me a backward glance Stryder mumbled, "Thanks, Mom, see you down the Trail. Be careful," he grinned playfully as he took off at an equally fast clip.

But this afternoon, I was the one who was hurt. The pain in my leg was bad. My shin was swelling, but my adrenaline was racing. I was determined to make it to Hot Springs before dark. The last five miles were nearly straight downhill. As dusk fell, the lights of Hot Springs appeared through the bare trees. I walked up the steps of the Jesuit Hostel. "I'm sorry, we are not open until after Easter. Try the Elmer's," the man replied when I asked for a room. I was hoping to stay one night. Hobbling through town, I made my way to Elmer's and limped up the driveway. Magot, Daddy, Lynx, Preacher, Broken Road, Pilgrim, Tacet, Crazy, Stick-In-Face, and Vagabond sat clean and showered on the porch. Delicious smells coming from the kitchen made my mouth water. "Wolf Woman, your pack is crooked," someone said.

I ignored the comment. I was too glad to see everyone to let criticism get in the way of connecting. "It's just my pack cover that's crooked." I haven't seen you guys for days. Is there room?

"I think the last place was just taken. Go in and ask," Preacher suggested.

I dropped my pack and opened the door. Standing in the middle of the warm kitchen full of wonderful things to eat, I was aware of how bad I smelled and how desperately I needed comfort. "Do you have room?" I asked.

"I'm sorry we're full. You can probably get in at the Duckett House Inn."

I was crushed. I wanted to be with my community more than I wanted a place to sleep. I walked out on the porch, picked up my pack, and walked past my Trail family without a word. Grinding my back teeth to keep from crying, I headed for the road. I felt disoriented. The walk through town was emotionally and physically painful. I didn't mind being alone in the woods, but being in town was different.

Peeking through the screen door of the Duckett House Inn, I could see someone on the telephone. Setting my pack on the porch, I gathered all the assertiveness I could muster and walked in. "I'm a thru-hiker and am exhausted. I have reservations in two days. Elmer's is full and I desperately need a bath, food, and rest. Please let me stay."

The tall man with a long brown ponytail and gentle eyes covered the receiver and said, "I am Brian. Sure you can stay. I'm going out to visit friends, you'll have the whole place to yourself." Impulsively I reached up and gave him a hug. In so doing, I tangled us both up in the long telephone cord he was attempting to hang up. Brian hugged me back, "We don't usually feed thru-hikers supper but since you are alone you are welcome to the week-end leftovers." He led me into a spacious kitchen. "Have some gingerbread and salad. Hikers don't get enough vegetables. We have bread, peanut butter, and vegetarian casserole," As Brian pulled dishes and containers out of the refrigerator, I thought I'd never seen so much food. I ate three pieces of gingerbread in five minutes.

Brian handed me a bag of ice cubes and told me to stay off my leg. He led me to a room furnished with antique furniture and a bathroom with clean towels. "Make yourself at home. You can use the phone in the hall," he said as he walked out the door. I took my time soaking, scrubbing, and savoring in the tub before eating all I could hold. After calling Suellen, I climbed into bed with the bag of ice on my leg and pondered why I was so distraught at not being able to stay with my Trail family. Every night I read in the journals how many days ahead they were. Magot, the only woman in the group, could keep up. I could not. I often saw them in towns, but that was not the same as being with the crowd. There was something about staying connected with the people I had started the Trail with that touched a needy place in my soul. Maybe it didn't matter. Life is transient, changing, and full of upheavals. Life had taught me to survive, shift, and make substitutions. Even Brian had taken me in and left. All I'd said I needed was food, shower, and a bed. Why was I sad? The whole scenario was typical of ignoring emotional needs in order to care for the physical. If gingerbread, soap, a bag of ice, and a comforter are all I need, why even in the woods, was the gnawing need to be accepted rearing its ugly head? Like mice scrambling in search of morsels, thoughts raced for ways to stay connected.

*March 25: This journey is complicated with my need to be with people and to be alone. I thought I'd be glad to be away from people. During the first weeks, the shelters were too full. Now I miss the community those weeks provided. This bed is comfortable, my body is clean, and my stomach is full. If comfort, cleanliness, and cuisine sum contentment, then why do I choose to stay in an experience that separates me from creature comforts? Even my childhood idol, Thoreau, had Walden Pond, a cabin, and food growing in a garden. Perhaps it's the vulnerability and rawness of the experience that pulls me like a magnet to the primitive. Like a swirling whirlpool beneath a powerful waterfall that constantly pulls water forward, I feel like a crushed maple leaf bubbling to the top of the rapids, only to be sucked back down. Is there no relief in the struggle to belong, even on the Trail? Are not the contents of my backpack enough?*

# Chapter 5

# *"She needs to stay off her feet for at least two weeks!"*

## Hot Springs, North Carolina to Damascus, Virginia

"Oh Sweetie, I'll rub muscle relaxer cream into your swollen leg as soon as I get lunch ready." Judy spread pimento cheese, fresh bread, fruit, juice, and vegetable salad on the picnic table in the yard of Duckett House Inn. As we ate, Judy told me the news while rubbing my leg. While my leg soaked in the cream, my body consumed nutrition; and I absorbed the attention. It seemed like years since I'd been home. I told Judy about my spiritual snowy hike, eating Stryder's peanut butter, and my rainy night with seventeen guys. When my skin began to burn, Judy stopped rubbing and we examined my shin. Ice hadn't worked and neither had this. But I had laundry to do.

At the laundromat Judy and I met Ron and Pat. They were staying at a motel and hadn't seen much of our community. Pat was having trouble with her Achilles' tendons and I showed her my leg. She and Ron planned to stay in town a day or two before going on. I couldn't consider such a thing and hope to get to Maine in five months. We joked about being older and not having the stamina of the younger crowd. I wasn't so sure it was a joke. Being healthy and strong was as important as being motivated and determined if I planned to climb Katahdin. Judy listened to us cast doubts about our middle-aged bodies as long as she could before jumping into the conversation. "At least you two are out here going at it! Look how far you have come already, nearly one hundred and seventy-five miles! That's more miles on the Appalachian Trail than people will ever boast of. People a lot older than either of you have done the Trail. It doesn't matter how slow you are as long as you get there! Your bodies have carried you this far, they'll carry you the rest of the way!" Pat and I needed her words.

"I'm slow, but I'll make it to Maine!" Pat declared, hugging me as a seal of commitment. Pat was only slightly older than I and shared my fears as well as my determination. We often wrote encouraging words for each other in the shelter journals.

"I'm going to Maine, too. It's getting finished before school starts that's worries me but one step at a time, one day at a time I'll keep going. I hobbled up to visit Wingfoot at the Appalachian Trail Center this morning and am impressed with all the programs he has on the computer."

"Your book will keep you going too." Pat said, as she stuffed laundry in a sack.

"I've been sending home two rolls of film and lots of journal notes at each maildrop." I hugged Pat before following Judy to the car. "See you up the Trail and take care of that leg," Support would keep me focused. After Judy left I stretched out for a nap in the warm sunshine. Suellen's positive spirit would soon offer special support.

"Anybody in there?" Suellen's voice filtered into the shower.

"Suellen! I'll be right out. How good to hear your voice."

When thru-hikers have access to water, one shower is never enough. It was late and Suellen's trip from a conference had been taxing, but she wanted to hear Trail stories. Talking about the trip solidified the significance of each detail. Suellen had stories too, but hers came from a world that seemed remote. I missed the people, but the culture and routines I'd left felt alien. I couldn't remember life in Tennessee.

The next morning, joined by Gumby, whom I hadn't seen since the first days of the hike, and his parents, Suellen and I enjoyed Brian's vegetarian omelet and homemade scones for breakfast. Also at the table was past thru-hiker Lum, who was back to hike from Hot Springs to Nolichucky. He shared stories of the terrible weather in '95, "You're fortunate to only be experiencing cold weather, not crippling snow."

Redness had spread around my leg. From my ankle to my knee, the skin was very painful and tight. At Suellen's insistence, we scoured nearby Asheville, North Carolina, for a doctor, ending up in an emergency room. After a long wait and signing tons of papers, we were ushered into a small cubicle where a gentle nurse with smiling eyes looked at my leg. When I told her about my journey, she asked, "Is this injury giving you a message?" Suellen gave me a knowing look. I knew she thought I should slow down. Apparently the nurse did too. When I told the doctor I had done nothing except to walk from Georgia to Hot Springs in twenty-six days, the last three being twenty mile days, he looked down at me with a statement of doom. "You have a bad case of shin splints. You need to stay off the leg for at least two weeks. Aleve pain pills will help with the pain and swelling, but nothing will cure it except rest." I said nothing. There was no reason for a discussion. I was getting back on the Trail on Sunday and that was final. We bought Aleve pills and ate lunch at the Laughing Seed Restaurant before going back to the Duckett House Inn.

"Just come home for one week. I'll bring you back next weekend. I'm afraid if you don't let your leg heal you'll damage it so badly you won't be able to finish," Suellen insisted.

I would hear none of it. "Those are the chances I have to take. I can't lose time and hope to finish in five months. I have to keep going. I'm not going home!"

Lum offered his advice. "I had shin splints. Just stop and put cold water, mud, or leaves down your socks every chance you get. Sleep with a water bag and take the Aleve. That worked for me. You probably wouldn't be still if you go home anyway. Shin splints are the result of going too fast down hills, so take it easy with the descents. You're on a roll, keep going." Lum's veteran advice sounded good.

Suellen had no choice but to let the issue go. After breakfast I loaded the pack with food and we drove to where the Trail crossed the river. A gentle spring breeze blew and the sun was warm. It was Easter Sunday. Together we followed the Trail along the river and up the steep incline. Stopping at a bend in the Trail, Suellen said softly. "This is as far as I'll go. I'll see you in Damascus. Take care of that leg. Call me if you need me." She paused, "I know you'll make it. I believe in you."

"Thank you for saying that. It means a lot. Thank you for coming and for taking me to town. Say hi to everyone. I'll be fine, don't worry." I swallowed hard as she encircled me and my forty-pound pack with a hug. I watched Suellen head back to the van before continuing up the hill. This would not be the first time friends and relatives would leave me in the wilderness and return to safe cars and homes. As I climbed I thought about the connection between Gary Snyder's words in the *Practice of the Wild,* and my journey. "There is nothing like stepping away from the road and heading into a new part of the watershed. Not for the sake of newness, but for the sense of coming home to our whole terrain" (154). I was indeed walking home. But there was more to the journey than a pilgrimage to my roots and a fulfillment of a childhood dream.

Questions flooded my mind. What was the significance of leaving Hot Springs on Easter Sunday enroute for Damascus? While the Christian world sits comfortably in church pews in clean clothes, I hike along the Appalachian Trail. My Easter clothes are comfortable and they were clean when I left, although I could already feel sweat gathering on the back of my neck. My Easter clothes were the same ones I'd worn for Saint Patrick's Day, and would wear for Arbor Day, Memorial Day, Mother's Day, Flag Day, Father's Day, the Fourth of July, and all the Sundays I'd spend on the Trail. Being sweaty and dirty is a way of life. My attire fit the culture I was living in the same way the attire folks wear to church fits theirs. Sweaty hiking clothes did not deter me from being receptive to spiritual lessons. My church was in the woods, the choir wore feathers in the leafy tree lofts, and the preacher was Mother Nature's messenger.

Nature offered sacred opportunities in larger dimensions than the four walls of a church. Gary Snyder says that being in nature was sacred because it took me out of myself and into the mountains. I had taken up the primitive practice to go, be, and do a wilderness pilgrim's step-by-step, breath-by-breath walk up a trail into fields carrying all on the back. This ancient set of gestures brought a profound sense of joy (*Practice* 94). I found joy in movement. People attend church seeking a message. I, too, was on a search. Only I wasn't sitting still to receive it.

This simple act of mobility provided opportunities for conscious mindfulness. Hiking is an active primal response to attentiveness. The act of putting one foot in front of the other is the only requirement. It felt spiritual to propel my body through space and reach destinations by muscular force. I trusted my ability, energy, and will to use the simplest and most basic of movements. But the goal of traveling on foot for five months required a more concrete purpose than just putting one foot in front of the other. Walking two thousand miles is a rather obsessive compulsive goal, even if walking is an ultimate exercise. So why had I pit myself against the risks and taken up this vulnerable challenge? The answer lay in my choice to commit to the process. Katahdin bound, I would wait for an answer.

Because "brisk" is not always the pace and "observant" is often the manner, sauntering might be a more appropriate way to speak of how thru-hikers move through the forest. The word "sauntering" was first derived to mean "idle people who roved about the country in the Middle Ages as they asked for charity under the pretense of going *al a Sainte-Terre,* or to the Holy Land until the children said, 'There goes a Sainte-Terre,' The word also comes from the term *'sans tere'* which means without home,…equally everywhere" (Thoreau, *Timeless*, 3). A thru-hiker saunters as an expression of being at home in nature. For the thru-hiker, the line from the Wizard of Oz, "there's no place like home," refers to rough open shelters. Staying in different shelters in different locations with different people expresses the juxtaposition of a vagabond life full of enticing adventure and raw exposure. It provides awareness of the vices of vulnerability and the value of variety. I accepted this wandering lifestyle with its lack of permanence.

The Buddhists refer to being homeless as leaving the householder's life, temptations, obligations of the secular world, and imperfections of human behavior behind (Snyder 104). Zhiangyan, the fifth-century poet, enlarges the scale of the homeless by saying the proper hermit should "take the purple heavens to be his hut, the encircling sea to be his pond, and roaring with laughter in his nakedness, walking along singing with his hair hanging down" (Watson, 82). So homelessness means being at home in the universe and finding an innate comfort level in the wilderness. It has always been a part of basic human experience to live in a culture of wilderness. To the inhabitants of the Trail community, who are constantly in motion and annually replaced, nature is not a place to visit, it is home. Therefore, the temporary community depends on the crude wilderness shelters for a sense of grounding. Fears and insecurities come from unexpected invasions of objects, humans, or experiences that threaten safety and familiarity. People fear that which they do not understand. They return to the familiar homes because home provides security and familiarity provides stability. The best security on the Trail is the contents of the backpack. Unknowns are around every corner.

On this Easter afternoon I understand why I breath a sigh of relief every time I round a bend in the Trail or top a ridge and see my night's lodging. More than having arrived at a place to lay my head or finished another section of the Trail, I sigh because I'm home among family. I am part of a community that values chance and change above the constraints of the communities we left behind. Home is direction and destination, not the customary nor the common.

Another Easter lesson is to develop trust in the blazes marking the Trail. The four-by-six inch stenciled white Trail markings are a powerful testimony to the magical meaning of symbols. Leading me to shelters nestled in clearings, along streams, or on mountains, the symbol leads me day after day. Hearing voices as I approach assures me I'll spend the night with people who share my culture. Each morning as I hoist life's basic necessaries on my back and resume my trust in the white blazes, I look forward to another night in a crude but cozy home with a Trail family.

So my Easter morning's message is to recognize the spiritual significance of walking and the soul stabilizing need to connect with like-minded companions while accepting and trusting the unknown and unfamiliar. Living in and moving through Mother Nature provides a primal connection with the womb of wilderness. Every section has natural wonders seen only by those who stay on the Trail after the sun and the temperature drop below the hills or the skies become cloudy. I walk regardless of the weather. Permanence and constancy come with faith in the process that I'll arrive at a shelter of familiar faces. Knowing I, not machines or vehicles are responsible for the day's progress motivates me north. The changing scenery and seasons became part and parcel of my culture. As my feet move up and down the narrow winding path that connects the southern Appalachians with the northern, my soul listens to a more personalized message than I could have heard within the walls of a church. Walking teaches me that all mountains have summits, that animals fear me more than I do them, and that I will dry after a storm. The vulnerabilities of hiking have more to do with addressing internal fears than being alone in the forest. Like there was for St. Paul, profound messages wait on my one hundred and eighty-mile road to Damascus. I will stay in the moment and move, one step at a time toward Mt. Katahdin, my ultimate goal.

A gentle rain was falling as I arrived at Spring Mountain Shelter. Lum was eating supper with his dog, Sally. I dropped my pack and headed to the stream for water. Tippy Canoe, OAB, Stryder, and two Dartmouth students arrived. Getting back on the Trail after a break in town is hard. We spent the evening reminiscing about pizza, fruit, and hot coffee, and dreaming of soft beds, hot showers, and warmer weather.

Talking about the weather prompted Mother Nature to visit us. As we huddled in our sleeping bags, the temperature dropped. My cold fingers could only journal a few lines.

*Easter Sunday March 30: It was hard to leave Hot Springs. My leg is better. I hiked slowly down the hills. I shortened my step with my right leg to take the pressure off the shin. Stuffing wet leaves down my socks helped. This shelter is small, but with the weather so cold we'll stay warmer. Tomorrow will be one month on the Trail. It doesn't seem possible one fifth of my trip is over and I'm still adjusting to carrying the pack.*

By morning two inches of powdered snow covered the ground. The temperature hovered in the teens, but the trees were beautiful. "How are we going to find any jelly beans under all this snow?" OAB asked, kicking under the powdery white cover.

"Maybe the Easter rabbit decided to bring white jelly beans this year and got overzealous with scattering. I joked, "If the snow tastes sweet we'll know it's sugar, not snow and it will melt when the sun comes out."

"That's a bit far-fetched," Stryder mumbled from deep in his bag. "No wonder our kids are messed up. Did you teach your students that rabbits bring snow?"

"No, but that would have made a good line for a writing assignment. Speaking of lines, I wish we had some real Vermont maple syrup for sugar on snow like I used to get at Harlow's SugarHouse in Vermont. The Harlows would pour thin lines of hot syrup on clean snow packed in a horse drawn wagon. After the syrup hardened, we'd pick it up and eat it in long thin ribbons. They'd serve sour pickles so we'd be able to eat more. This is sugaring time right now. The nights have to be freezing and the days warm for the sap to run. The season only lasts for about three weeks between late March to early April. If we had some we could drizzle it along the Trail and eat our way to the next shelter."

"Sounds good to me, but who's going to carry the extra weight?" asked OAB.

"The Easter rabbit could hop along the Trail and drizzle as he goes." I suggested.

"An early April Fool's to you too. I'll settle for today's sugar coming from State Line Grocery store three miles down the Trail. Is anybody stopping?" Tippy Canoe asked.

I hadn't gotten off the Trail during the day before, but snow in April deserved a change in the routine. After hours trudging through the beautiful snow filled forest, we gathered around a pot belly stove in the Allen Gap country store located on the North Carolina and Tennessee border. I loaded up on cheese, crackers, granola bars, and chugged down a quart of grapefruit juice with Aleve pills while the guys munched candy bars, chips, and soft drinks. By taking pills every three hours and stuffing snowballs down my socks and up my pant leg, I had kept down the pain and swelling.

In the warm store my pants dripped all over the creaky wood floor. If snow in April was a bit out of place, the ambiance of the country store definitely put me back in time. The warmth and comfort of the sparse decor and woodsy aroma reminded me of New England general stores. But those days were as long gone as the next shelter was a long way up the Trail. With snowy, wet packs back on we headed into the woods. Snow sparkled and flurried in the air. The ground was warm enough to keep the Trail visible. Splotches of wet snow mingled with the white blazes marking the Trail. The fellows were soon ahead. Accustomed to hiking alone, I relived New England winters.

As the Handbook mentions, Jerry Cabin Shelter had an inside fireplace, light switch, and telephone. Only the fireplace worked. A sign on the wireless equipment asked hikers to keep their phone calls brief and to turn out the lights when they left. The humor made for delightful conversation. A fire blazed and hikers cooked supper. So many incredible changes occurred in the scenery, weather, and environment each day it seemed like years since I had left Hot Springs or stopped at the store. With numb fingers, through gloves, I journaled. *March 31: Hiked 14.6 miles today. The ground was too wet to sit down and the air too cold to be still. Slow, steady pacing was the rhythm for the day. The trees and ground were beautiful. I love snow. The cold air felt refreshing circling through my lungs. A wonderful warm fire blazes. The temperature is in the low teens. We are sleeping with our water bottles in our sleeping bags and our boots upside down. I am learning to be grateful for simple things.*

It was bitter, cold, and windy; but the view from Big Bald was breathtaking. I fought the wind until I reached Low Gap where Lum had set up camp. As we ate, he marked my Handbook with places to eat and hostels to stay in. I noticed he wasn't using a filter. "You don't filter your water?"

"No, I use iodine crystals called Polar Pure. I put two caps full in a quart of water and wait twenty minutes. Fill the bottle with water and the crystals will be ready to use again in twenty minutes. If the water is real cold, use an extra capful. Polar Pure is much cheaper then a filter and doesn't have to be replenished like iodine tablets. Just be careful not to break the glass bottle. I keep it in a Ziploc on the top of my pack. Pick some up the next time you plan a break. Hiking alone can get to be a very lonely proposition."

I nodded. I had already taken off six days in only the first two hundred and sixty eight miles. The next stop was Damascus. After I got over Mt. Rogers, I'd lighten up my pack by sending home winter gear. I could solve problems and make decisions, but I couldn't control the weather.

I peeked out the tent door at daybreak just in time to see Lum hoist up his backpack. I lay back and watched my breath escape into the air. The cold, sunny sky filled me with contentment and harmony. I was not unafraid to be alone in the middle of the forest. I felt way out in the woods even though Spivey Gap at U.S.19 was only two and a half miles up the Trail. Thinking of roads triggered homesickness, so I concentrated on watching the tall trees stretch their branches like angels interlocking protection over my camp. I was grateful to be living in such a sacred sanctuary. As I moved heel-to-toe over the pine needle strewn, leaf-filled, mud-gulled, rock-piled, grass-swishing paths, I saw how Mother

Nature consistently covered the earth. I needn't have worried about my lodging. However, I often did.

A minuscule uneasiness vacillated within. It stemmed not from fear of the unknown, but from detachment. Although my lifestyle was temporary, I felt like a bird or a Native American. Daddy would have told me I could be both. Maybe I was a sophisticated vagabond. But, birds and vagabonds don't go home at the end of five months. They are home. Soon home would have four sides instead of three. I missed nothing tangible, only people. No colleagues, team workers, or family members were around to make proposals, suggestions, plans, or create havoc. I was competent to be my own administrator, but it was difficult being my own best friend.

At the thought of friends, I remembered Linda who lived forty miles off the Trail in Kingsport, Tennessee. At the gathering in October she had offered to come get me for a night's rest and home cooked food. While in Hot Springs I'd left a message on her answering machine, telling her I'd be in Nolichucky at 2:00 o'clock on April third. I knew the chances of my arrival in Nolichucky coinciding with her work schedule were slim. I had no way of knowing whether she'd gotten my message or had plans for Tuesday. There was a chance I would hike into the village with no place to stay and not enough time to make it to the next shelter before dark. I also needed to pick up a maildrop in Erwin before the Post Office closed. In civilization communication is taken for granted. On the Trail I always wondered whether people would show up. I never knew where I was in relationship to highways or towns on the outside world. The world I'd known for forty-four years was now, the "outside" world. I could hear the river as I slowly wound my way down the steep decline. I'd wrapped my leg in an ace bandage OAB had given me so I could hike faster.

Lum looked like a hiker in a costume as he rested on the porch at Nolichucky with clean clothes on. I called Linda, but only reached her answering machine. Lum had arranged for a ride to town, but would wait until 4:00 to leave. I showered and called Suellen. Just as I was growing fainthearted, Linda's car turned the corner. When she jumped out of the car, her long legs moved toward me. "I'm so proud of you! Don't worry about your maildrop. Post Office gave it to me."

Running to the car, I shouted like a child on Christmas morning. "Linda, I knew you would come! Thank you for getting the maildrop. What Trail Magic."

"Here are crackers and a banana to hold you over until we get home," she said as I hoisted the pack into her trunk.

"Thanks, let me share some with Lum." Lum had watched the reunion from the porch. Linda and Lum shook hands. I was stirred with melancholy sadness as I hugged Lum goodbye. "Thank you for your advice and company."

"I'll call you when I visit my daughter in Tennessee. I can't say, 'see you down the Trail,' but enjoy the trip." Lum's daughter would take him to an airport so he could fly back to Minnesota in time for tax season. I, too, would be leaving the Trail, but only temporarily. Suddenly I wasn't so sure I wanted to be removed from the simple routine. I allowed the miracle of Linda's arrival to entice me into the car door as she held it open. The door closed on my decision to leave the Trail.

My Trail life was showing me what wonderful friends I have and how much I needed them. One step and experience at a time, my faith in humanity that had disappeared over the years were being renewed. Not wanting to deal with fluctuating emotions, I asked Linda to tell me the news as we headed to a sporting goods store for Coleman fuel and Polar Pure crystals. On the highway the cars flew by. I felt as though we were traveling a hundred miles an hour as trees zoomed by like black birds.

The Trail had changed my perspective about comforts that I'd taken for granted. I felt privileged in Linda's comfortable home. I would be more grateful after the hike. However, I did miss hearing the wind. Being warm and dry kept me from analyzing.

My pack was still too heavy. Linda agreed to take a box to Brown's grocery in Hampton, Tennessee in Dennis Cove at USFS 50. I would carry food for less than a week and either send food ahead or get off the Trail more often. Thru-hikers who use maildrops only for traveler's checks and news get off the Trail every couple of days even though it takes time to hitchhike into town, find a store, and get back to the Trail. I usually didn't have trouble getting a ride, but losing time made me anxious about getting to shelters before dark.

After a hardy breakfast, I pulled on long underwear, supplex shirt and pants, and my fleece jacket. The weather was still bitterly cold and windy. By eleven o'clock I was back at Nolichucky. I had been off the Trail less than twenty-four hours. "See you in August. It's been very important to be part of your journey," Linda smiled.

"Thank you for everything and say hi to everyone." Although I vacillated between the sadness of leaving a familiar culture and the joy of getting back to the Trail, I wasn't as close to tears as I'd been the last time a friend had left me in the woods. The mention of August rattled the reality of what I was doing. August was far away. Today was only April 4th. Linda helped me find the white blazes and walked with me to a bridge over a gentle creek. She took pictures and waved as I walked away. I was alone again, but something inside had snapped. I knew I'd make it. The miracle of connecting with Linda allowed me to let go of resistance and fear.

Clyde Smith Shelter was fifteen miles away. The climb out of the Gap and over Beauty Spot was steep and foggy. Thoughts of Grammy Kay moved through my mind as consistently as fog over the valley. Her strong positive spirit had given her many good years after her breast cancer surgery. I could see her brown hair whisping around her strong face and her deep brown eyes watching me play giant steps across her lawn. I didn't mind the bitter wind or lack of scenery. Memories of her spirit swirled about me.

With each switchback over Unaka Mountain the incredible terrain changed from deciduous trees to evergreens, from scrubby bushes to rocky patches, and on the summit to a pine scented grove towering over carpets of green moss. Massive pines and hemlocks canopy grew so close, I expected an elf or troll to appear. The sun cast low shadows in the gathering dusk. I could have stayed for hours, but three miles remained to the shelter. I promised I'd return, as I hurried down the mountain. The teacher in me wanted to scoop up pinecones, but I was content to capture the beauty in photographs.

The comforting sound of barking dogs guided my steps in the dark to the shelter. Stryder, Monarch, her companion with their two dogs, and two puppies welcomed me. "Hey Stryder, It's good to see you. And Monarch, how are your dogs?" She and her friend were taking photographs of the Trail for a college class out west. They'd gotten off the Trail at Nolichucky to find a veterinarian for a sick dog. Monarch and I had visited while I waited for Linda and she waited for her friend.

"He's fine. The vet says he's exhausted. It's a long ways down the bank for water. We have plenty." The woman with matted sandy blond hair handed me a full water bag.

The chore of going for water after a long day of hiking was never appealing, and even less so in the dark. "Thanks so much. How kind of you! Do you need food? I just stocked up. Are you sure you don't need the water? This is the first time I've gotten into camp after dark. I didn't leave Nolichucky until 11:00. What perfect Trail Magic."

"Trail Magic will happen for us. Use what you need. We can get more in the morning. We have plenty of food to get us to Elk Park, our next stop. You want a dog? These two puppies are strays. I wish we could take them. They will starve in the woods."

"No, I have a dog. How about you, Stryder?" I asked, as I put dried beans and rice into the water. I was still in disbelief at her kindness. Thru-hikers were such thoughtful people. No matter who made up the community, we operated like family. The Libra in me struggled to do things fairly. But, she was right. Trail Magic would come to them, too. Now, what was the right thing to do about these dogs?

Stryder had been playing with the puppies. "Actually, I've always wanted a dog. This is rather a strange time to get one though. What do puppies eat?

"Anything until you can get off the Trail and get packs for them to carry their own dog food. I gave them some of our dog food when we got here. They'll be a lot of company. Looks like they've taken to you. Try peanut butter." Monarch suggested.

Stryder stuck a finger into his peanut butter jar and held it out to the two-month- old fluffy pups. The puppies lapped his finger clean in seconds.

"That answers your question. Looks like they'll do fine on peanut butter. I think you should take them." Monarch and I encouraged the nineteen-year-old as he struggled with the decision to have not one, but two puppies of his own. The four of us slept safe with four dogs stretched among us. The puppies snuggled closest to Stryder. *April 4: Unaka Mountain was covered with moss and pinecones. I would have gathered handfuls but thru-hiking is teaching me I have what I need. Enjoying the moment does not mean walking off with the beauty. This shelter feels like home with four dogs.*

I would have given anything to have a movie camera the next morning as Stryder coaxed the puppies down the Trail with peanut butter and bread. The scene reminded me of the story of *Hansel and Gretel*, renamed *Stryder and the Puppies*. All day I followed three sets of prints to Roan High Knob Shelter. I was accustomed to seeing hiking boots, but not eight paw prints. I smiled as I analyzed the patterns. The puppies seemed to have kept up with Stryder's long legs. In fact, they appeared to have stayed right under his feet. The puppies obediently trusted their new owner with the peanut butter fingers. Following their docile patterns was sobering. Would I ever trust the process of my journey completely? And I had a data book and ever-present blazes. The scenario reminded me of walks with my children. They would tag behind, be right under foot, or run ahead. I was grateful that they were happily living on their own. Growth and change provide the balance and space people need in order to be whole. I was glad Stryder had taken the puppies. I was equally as glad they were under his feet, not mine.

I'd been averaging high teen mileage and thought I was used to climbing, until I started up Roan Mountain. I'd reached the summit on every mountain so far but now I had my doubts. I'd heard the fourteen-mile climb to Roan Mountain shelter was rough.

The last section was hand-over-hand rock climbing in a narrow boulder-filled gully. A storm threatened. Bitter winds whipped about me. Not making it to the shelter before dark was a real possibility. Expecting to see Stryder and the puppies kept me going. It was difficult to reach my legs over the ledges. Stryder probably had to carry the puppies. The wind and gathering dusk rattled my emotions. Just as the rain began to fall, I spotted the shelter nestled up the blue-blaze Trail in a stand of evergreens. I pushed open the door. The stone structure was empty. Dropping my pack, I picked up the journal. Stryder had stopped but had decided to continue on to Carvers Gap for puppy food. At least he and the puppies made it over the rocks. I tossed the journal down and dropped the flaps on the windows to keep in the warmth. Doing so plunged me in darkness. I fumbled for my mag-lite flashlight, fleece jacket, sleeping bag, and water bag. I had to act quickly if I was going to find water before dark. Using Polar Pure made me extremely thirsty. I'd been out of water for hours.

At the end of a narrow path, I found a tiny stream barely trickling into a shallow pool full of pine needles and debris. By capfuls I dipped water into my bottle while taking sips to quench my thirst. After a frustrating hour, I returned to the shelter with half a quart of water. Freezing and fighting depression, I huddled in a corner and tried to count my blessings as torrents fell from the sky. By flashlight I lit my stove. I discovered I'd drunk more water than I should have, without enough left over to thoroughly cook macaroni and cheese. Disgusted, I ate half-cooked pasta. During the night I made frequent trips to the woods, hunkered under my rain jacket. I hoped my queasy stomach was the result of raw pasta and pine needles, not giardia. Burrowing deep in my bag on the hard concrete floor, I wondered why I was lying in the dark, cold, stone structure with no water, no bathroom, no light, or no company. How slight of faith and memory I was. Companionship made all the difference.

Closed up in the cell-like building, I didn't wake up until nine. Having nowhere to go, except to Katahdin, I decided to wait until it quit raining and trust I'd make up the hiking time. Peacefully I munched on Trail mix, dozed, and journaled. *April 5: Sleeping with wet puppies wouldn't have been as enjoyable as the dry ones. Each day I feel more strongly that I'm where I'm supposed to be. The backpack feels like a part of my body. I couldn't tell whether the "black things" in last night's supper were dirt or pine needles. The wind continues to howl. Fourteen miles a day seems to be my pace. Moving through changes is what is this trip about. Today I walked ridges and roads and saw my third "Welcome to North Carolina" sign. I climbed a 6,200 feet rock gully. The thruhikers have thinned out to other rhythms. I have found mine walking one section at a time and trusting the process, at least most of the time. I hope I can get used to the thirst from the iodine. I panic when my mouth feels as dry as cotton and I'm out of water. Tomorrow monitor and adjust and take tiny sips to make it last longer.*

About noon, sunlight peeped under the window flap. I packed and headed for Overmountain Shelter, six miles away. A huge, red, renovated barn, reminding me of New England, offered excellent views of Hump Mountain and the valley. The picnic table was inside and out of the wind. Sleeping platforms had been built under a porch-like roof. Water ran out of a pipe in front of the barn. Such a fantastic night's home deserved polenta, crackers, and hot tea, especially after last night's specialty of raw pine needles.

From the loft's wide-open windows I could see a U shaped valley receding below an arch of pine trees that gradually angled toward the sky. The open fields topped with peaked mountains looked like delectable creations served in a Ben and Jerry's ice cream parlor. As I finished my last bite of supper, I sensed something was moving. Like puffs of stream rising from a boiling teakettle, delicate white fog rose up out of the valley. The puffs danced up and down in the air currents before disappearing in the clear sky above the mountains. In seconds the scene was completely swallowed up in a rolling blanket of fog. My visibility was gone. The rows of pine trees and the long valley were completely socked away. The thick grayness brought dampness into my cozy loft as the magical vapor completely concealed my world.

In one mysterious motion, a heavy veil covered the land, totally engulfing me in fog. Just as magically, a pink lining crept back into the horizon. The rosy hue drifted across the arena and nature reappeared unchanged and unharmed. Snuggled in my sleeping bag, I was mesmerized by the evaporation process. Up and down the pyramid of mountains, the gray fog ebbed and flowed like mighty ocean waves on a rhythmic sea. Like loving arms clasped across a woman's breast, the mountains' massive forms folded across the backdrop of natures' floating movie screen.

The swirling patterns never altered the power of the mountains. I stared into the darkness as the sun slipped behind their solid forms, dropping the temperature and ending the cycle of fog and clearing. The spirit of the Appalachian Mountains was with me. The experience moved more than moisture. It moved trust into the barn. Just as the beautiful experience ended with a change of atmospheric conditions, so too would adverse conditions. By walking I would watch changes moving through the mountains. The power would be mine for being attentive. I'd walked through snow, rain, fog, sun, and wind. The land had changed from dips and ditches in the deep woods, to switchbacks around the mountains, to vertical climbs up summits, and to swishing Trails through grassy fields. I'd spent nights in crowded shelters and in solitude. I'd climbed- soaked, sweating and miserable- under the strain of a heavy load and breezed down gentle slopes, barely aware of the pack. The magical gift of movement created the change. I wanted the spiritual barn experience to last forever. But Katahdin was my goal. There would be more magic.

As darkness settled over the valley, I prepared for bed. Millions of stars filled the sky. I pulled my sleeping bag to the loft window. In the darkness a particularly bright light caught my attention. Two lights low to the ground moved toward the barn. The darting lights looked like flashlights. As the lights moved below the loft, I flashed my own light toward the Trail.

"Is anyone up there? Wolf Woman, is that you? Thank God! Do you have a stove?" A woman's voice sounded desperate.

"Yes, Monarch, what's wrong?" The dogs sniffed about the barn.

"You won't believe what happened. One of the dog's packs came unbuckled and got lost in the woods. The dog food was all gone and we had put our Whisperlite stove in pack. Now the stove is gone too. We spent three hours today tramping through the woods looking for it. Could we borrow your Whisperlite to cook supper? We have food and gas. It has been a long day and we're starved. What a beautiful night and a fantastic barn."

"Of course you can. It's all set up on the table. I have plenty of fuel if you want to use mine. Come on up. I can't believe this place either. I'm the only one here. Stryder's journal entry at Roan Mountain said he was getting off the Trail for dog food. I loved following puppy prints yesterday, did you?"

"Yes. They were so cute. This place is amazing. Thanks for letting us use the stove." Monarch flashed her light around the spacious barn.

"I'm glad I was here to return the Trail Magic." It was hard to believe only five days had passed and Damascus was five days away. I drifted off to sleep with misty memories of the mysterious movement of moisture.

Leaving my barn mates and the dogs sleeping, I headed for Humpback Mountain. Walking into howling winds at a 5,000 feet elevation was difficult. I was thankful the skies were blue instead of black. The Trail came to the road leading to Elk Park and then on to the Walnut Mountain, Campbell Hollow, and Buck Mountain Roads.

Just before turning into the woods two dogs lunged at my heels barking ferociously. I beat them off with the walking stick I'd carried since Springer and escaped into the forest unharmed. I later learned that when Ron and Pat passed through, one of the dogs bit Ron in the back of the leg, fortunately only bruising the skin and not tearing his wind stop pants. The local people were not pleased when the section was rerouted though their community. They had painted misleading blazes on the trees and placed barbed wire and fishhooks along the Trail. I sensed the hostility. The Trail was a series of steep short ups and downs that seemed to go nowhere. No sooner had I climbed up a steep bank and crossed a narrow creek than the pattern began again. I was usually not afraid to sleep alone in the woods, but these woods felt eerie and I was not going to make it to the shelter. I set up the tent on the Trail, cooked supper, and prepared for the worst. After covering the pack and purifying plenty of water, I got out my knife and mace.

After a cold night, I woke to thick frost crackling on the tent. The crushing crackling leaves sounded like frosted flake cereal. I couldn't believe it was April 7th. I dragged my clothes out of the bottom of my sleeping bag with my toes and dressed. With freezing hands, I boiled water for the last of my hot cereal before pulling apart the tent poles and loading up my frosted backpack. At least eleven miles before reaching Hampton. Exhausted, I grabbed at trees and clambered up and down the steep banks. An old injury in my left knee ached with each step. A journal entry at Mooreland Gap Shelter referred to the area as "serious knee crunching." I agreed. A poster about a hostel in Dennis Cove hung in the shelter. I copied down the information. All I could think of was getting to Brown's Store for food and to Laurel Fork Shelter before dark.

As often was the case at roads, I didn't know which way to turn. Across the street was a sign like the poster offering breakfast and lodging for a three-dollar donation. Another sign advertised a closer hostel with a hot tub, but for a steeper price. I headed left for a half-mile walk to Kincora Hostel. Two people stood in the driveway as I approached. "Welcome, you look tired. Do you need a room? I'm Bob Peoples and this is my wife Pat." Bob extended a hand.

"I'm Wolf Woman, a thru-hiker. Glad to meet you." I said, grasping his large strong hand and noticing his thick New England accent.

"Do you know how far it is to town? I'm out of food and need to pick up a box."

"Over the hill. I'm headed that way." Bob opened the door. "Toss your pack in."

"Thank you so much. Today's hike was tough. Are you from New England?"

"Yes, Boston, originally from Vermont. I was the director of a school for disadvantaged teenagers. We retired and moved to Tennessee a couple of years ago to start a hostel. Do you know Magot and Stick-in-face?" he asked, changing subject. "They were our first hikers for the season. Daddy, their companion, came a day later. He fell on Roan Mountain and broke his thumb. We took him to the bus station to go home." Bob's friendly nature and wonderful Boston accent was comforting.

My food box looked like a gift beneath the counter. I was overcome with a desire to buy everything in the store. Constraining myself, I only picked up a few granola bars, apples, and cheese. Back at the hostel, Bob showed me the washing machine, dryer, shower, and bunkhouse complete with a potbelly stove. It felt good to be inside after last night's experience in the frosty nerve-racking woods. "We don't usually feed hikers, but we have some leftover apple pie and I'll make you a cheese sandwich." Bob offered. "Pat is out for the evening and I'd enjoy hearing about your adventures."

"Sounds like Trail Magic. I'll be in as soon as I shower and put clothes in the machine. I'd like to hear about Vermont. This break was meant to be."

Bob told teaching stories while I ate three cheese, tomato, and lettuce sandwiches and two pieces of pie. It was refreshing to talk about something other than the distance to water and shelters. Bob had taught children from the same socio-economic background as the students I'd left in Knoxville. His stories confirmed my decision to leave public school. "I lived in Westminster and Saxtons River. This hike has something to do with hiking home, to Vermont." I wasn't sure what I meant. Being in the presence of a kindred spirit was no accident. When a cool breeze reminded us the hour was late, Bob offered to build me a fire. I rolled out my sleeping bag on the couch while Bob lit the wood stove.

Tonight's Trail Magic was warm because I'd listened to my gut and kept moving. Bob and his wife had come from Vermont to make Tennessee their home. Maybe I had, too.

I snapped a picture of the hostel as I walked down the driveway the next morning. Full and buoyant, Laurel Falls was beautiful. Spring beauties, trilliums, and bluets lined the switchbacks to Pond Flats. As I rounded a curve on the Flats level top, I heard what sounded like squirrels scurrying in the leaves. The noise was too loud to be a squirrel; instead, it was a huge black bear shuffling under a tree. I pulled out my camera and focused. The bear was intent on pawing. Moving closer, I snapped again. I wanted a picture of his whole body. "Well ole bear, are you going to keep your head in the leaves or look up here for a picture?" I asked politely. The words were barely out of my mouth when he raised his head, took one fleeting glance, and bolted into the forest. Now the only sound I heard were trees crashing as he propelled his huge body out of sight. I put the camera away. Talking to the forest not the bear, I continued, "Getting your picture taken would have been less painful than banging your head through the forest, ole bear."

April 9th was the coldest night yet. Cruze Control, Two Gulps, Cowpenski, and a friend joined me for the freezing night at Vandeventer Shelter. Facing into the wind, we ate quickly before burrowing into our sleeping bags. The next morning I packed up quickly and headed for Abingdon Shelter, ten miles from Damascus.

Hikers often get discouraged and go home in Virginia because one quarter of the entire Trail passes through this state. I hoped to do twenty-mile days through Virginia's three sections. Finally, I would stop seeing signs for Knoxville and Interstate 40. Watauga Lake was my last view of Tennessee. Deer darting across the Trail made me want to run the last twenty-three miles into the town that hosts Trail Days. Like the Apostle Paul on his road to Damascus, these last two weeks had stirred revelations. I had balanced the power of movement with awareness and learned to accept the things I could not change. I had learned to trust my instinct and control my attitude.

# Chapter 6

## "Call me, I will come get you."

### (Southwest Virginia) Damascus to Pearisburg

"Welcome to Damascus," the sign read as I walked under the archway. Around the corner I spotted Ron and Pat coming out of the Dollar Store. "Pat, wait up!" I hurried up the sidewalk.

"We loaded up on snacks," Ron was as excited as a little boy on Halloween as he showed me his candy bars, crackers and cheese, and granola bars. Pat gave me a big hug.

"Looks like a deal. Can you believe we're almost a quarter of the way to Katahdin?" I eased out of my backpack and leaned it up against a store window.

"Feels good, doesn't it!" Pat smiled.
"The weather is supposed to hold, so we're hiking the nine miles to Sanders Shelter today." Ron explained.

"How long are you staying? It's good to see you." Pat hugged me again.

"Judy is coming tomorrow and Suellen will bring my food. Monday I'll hike the fifteen miles to Lost Mountain Shelter. Right now I want to get some walking sticks."

"Looks like you stopped at the right place." Ron said, opening the door to the Outfitter Sporting Goods Store. By getting a pair of Keki, I supported the Expedition Inspirations Fund for Breast Cancer Research. Back outside, I shouldered the pack and we walked to The Place. I hugged Ron and Pat goodbye and found a room. After a shower and then a pizza at Quincys, I left a message on Gloria's machine in memory of Daddy's sixty-seventh birthday. I called Suellen, Judy, my children, and Linda before stretching out on a mattress and falling into an exhausted sleep.

Pouring rain woke me. I wondered what happened to Ron's predication about the weather holding. When Judy arrived we hugged as if we hadn't seen each other for years. I had forgotten how nice human contact felt. The last time I'd seen her she'd nursed my shin splints. Now thirteen days later, thanks to Aleve pills, wet leaves down my socks, and TLC, my leg had healed; and I was in Virginia. If only the weather would warm up!

We caught up on news in the laundromat before driving to Linda's house. She was out of town, but had opened her home for me to get a good night's rest. Judy stayed until Suellen arrived. "See you in August. You'll make it."

Judy was positive, but we all knew I'd face many challenges before we'd see each other again. I was moving fast, the driving distance was getting long, and finding road crossings to coordinate with friends' days off was getting too difficult to predict. Suellen's visit was a mixture of ecstatic exuberance and melancholy sadness. Bickley and Pam, friends from Johnson City, joined us for dinner. As rain poured and wind howled, I was grateful for warm quilts, hot water, and support from a very special friend.

I slept late and then repacked the backpack. Part way through the process I burst into tears. Suellen held me while I cried. I missed everyone. I didn't want to go home, but I just wasn't sure I could make it to Katahdin alone. I was already exhausted. Having made it through the Nantahalas, I knew I could do it physically, but hiking to Katahdin depended on my attitude. I released my fears in the safety of Suellen's friendship and talked my way clear through from thinking that attempting a thru-hike was the dumbest idea I ever had, to knowing there was no way I could possibly turn back.

"You aren't doing this alone. Lots of people support you," she assured me. Cold wind still howled, but the rain stopped by the time we returned the Hostel. Cruise Control, Two Gulps, and Cowpenski were taking a day off. Stryder was just leaving. He'd gotten the puppies to an animal clinic, but it was closed so he'd left them in the yard. OAB was staying in town with friends. Magot, Pilgrim, Stick-in-face, Broken Road, and Preacher were up the Trail. Tomorrow I too, would face Virginia's challenges.

At dawn I pulled my fleece over long underwear and hoisted up the pack. After a hot breakfast in town, I hiked the long road walk back to the Trailhead. Crossing the Creeper Bike Trail brought up memories of a bike trip with Judy and Susan a year ago. The event felt like yesterday. I recalled Judy's words floating back to me in the wind as we passed a backpacker. "That will be you next year." My trip at that time was in the planning stage and felt like a dream. Today Judy and Susan were back in Tennessee and I was moving through the Virginia forests with a full backpack.

Built in 1994, Lost Mountain Shelter still looked brand new. I boiled water for tea and enjoyed leftover, cold, Damascus pizza as though it were delicacy. Anything leftover postponed the already growing monotony of Trail food. Alone in the shelter my fingers ached with cold through fleece gloves. *April 14: I was real sad leaving Damascus, but the sun warmed my body and kicked me into the rhythm of hiking. Now it seems as though I'd never gotten off the Trail. Everyday I go through so many moods and feelings. I'll miss the support, but there is a sense of freedom now that I won't be trying to predict my hiking pace with friends' work schedules. I need to walk and let support come where it will. Many hikers have dropped off the Trail. I stay in between the groups. I'm excited about picking up my first maildrop in Bland. I wish spring would come.*

Rosy color eased into the shelter and across my sleeping bag early the next morning. Sitting up, I gasped at the beauty. As I exhaled, my breath looked pink. I held my face to the sun and blew at various angles. I created floating pink designs until Mother Nature called me to stop playing Color my Breath with the sun. Last night's cold pizza was long gone. I pulled off long underwear and pulled on my supplex pants and shirt and a fleece pullover. The same sock liners and socks I had worn up from Damascus would do until I reached Troutville. I laced up cold stiff boots, stuck a fleece hat over my ears, and found my toilet paper.

After my jaunt across the clearing, I lit the stove and set water on to boil for Wheatena cereal and tea. While I waited for the water to boil, I stuffed my sleeping bag into the stuff sack. After taking out a cup of hot water for tea, I stirred in cereal, chopped dried fruit, and nuts. I returned to packing power bars and trail mix in my waist pack. Stirring the cereal with a spoon, my only utensil, made me decide that breakfast had special meaning for hikers. I didn't know just how special until I held a spoonful of the steaming, sweet mush to the sun. By holding the spoon at just the right angle and blowing on the porridge with precise pressure, I transformed the steam into all the colors of the rainbow. My cold breath, the rising steam, and the splendor of morning light created radiant dancing visuals. The colors rose a foot before disappearing.

I exhaled. Breakfasts in shielded synthetic kitchens, with only specks of sunrises over neighborhood rooftops can't offer the magic of eating in sunny shelters. Being one with the experience of eating, breathing, and internalizing, not only nutrition but also, the color, warmth, and glory of the sun, was exquisitely exceptional. The higher the sun the more difficult it became to duplicate the phenomenon. As I ate my cereal, I realized the rainbow creations were a lesson for me to stay in the moment. The spectacle had given me a keener sense of *Carpe Diem.*

The highest mountain in Virginia, Mt. Rogers, was named for the state's first geologist William Rogers. The 5,729 elevation climbed past tall fir trees and thick moss. Wild edible ramps poked bright green leaves out of wet marshy creeks. I stopped to use the elaborate composting privy near the Thomas Knob Shelter. Magot and Grasshopper's journal entry said they'd spent their coldest night here. The weather was very cold for April. Lightening the pack by sending home winter gear would have to wait.

As I followed blazes over the rolling hills, outcroppings of white rocks glistened with mica chips in the sun. Fields of yellow grasses fluttered with meadow flowers. Tall pine trees soared over clusters of scrubby bushes. Dry air rustled through the grass. I felt like I was walking through an orchestra of natural reed instruments playing delicate tunes in perfect harmony. This was not mountain climbing. It was literally a stroll in the park. In the distance, mottled colored wild ponies nibbled grass.

Fifty yards off the Trail, one shaggy animal curiously lifted his head and came toward me. He picked up his pace and stepped into the Trail. More ponies joined the rendezvous. "Well, fellow, what can I do for you? I wish I had an apple. Fruit is a rare commodity for me too." I scratched the pony between the ears. The other ponies waited their turn. Their natural browns and tans complemented the landscape's soft earthen hues. "You sure are sweet. Your scraggly tails and manes need combing as much as my hair does," I said as I attempted to separate knots. The ponies followed me to the top of the hill before returning to familiar grounds. I hated to leave, but four miles remained before I'd reach my night's home.

Across the ridge, I could see the Wise Shelter tucked in the clearing. I was disappointed to find it empty. I hadn't seen a soul in two days. After dropping my backpack, I headed to the spring with my water bag and then cooked pasta with beans on the picnic table. The wind had stopped blowing and the weather was almost spring-like. After washing out my pan, I got out a granola bar and fruit roll-up before hanging the food. I purified water and changed into long underwear before journaling. *April 15: I saw precious wild ponies that would have eaten out of my hand. The day was perfect for hiking. I feel less stressful about making it to the shelters and feel better about staying in the moment. I hope to get some long mileage in the next few weeks. With a positive attitude I will not let the long weeks in Virginia get me down.*

Was I dreaming or did I hear something? I thought I was out of bear country. The noise was barely audible, but an animal snorted close to the shelter. I pointed my flashlight into the darkness. "Ah, how beautiful!" I gasped. A brown deer nibbled grass just a foot from the table. Relieved it wasn't a bear; I turned out the light. After my eyes adjusted to the darkness, I was able to see her feeding in the moonlight. Her strong body moved gracefully among the pine trees. For the second time that day, animals had been my companions. As I drifted in and out of sleep, I sensed the deer close by. I could hear her softly nibbling. The ease with which wild animals found food was a lesson for me to trust the process. If they weren't anxious about surviving, I had no reason to be either. Hearing the deer munch let me know support would come when I needed it. Creatures of the wild would fill the place friends and the hiker community had filled. A full moon offered her slant of comfort. Streaming through the forest, across the picnic table, and on my sleeping bag, a single sliver of light connected me to the powers of the night sky.

The deer still grazed near the shelter as I moved onto the Trail the next morning. She was a medium sized and light brown with a white tip on the end of her tail. As I raised my camera to take a picture, she slipped behind some bushes and disappeared. Perhaps she felt photographing our encounter would desecrate the sacredness of the experience. I tucked the camera away. Memories were all I needed to remember this Trail Magic. My needs would be met just as hers and the ponies are met in this scrubby barren land. Herds of deer ran in the woods during the rest of my hike. None were as comforting as the Wise Shelter deer. I never again saw wild ponies.

Even though it was April 15, the hard, cold ground crackled with frost. Iced over shallow puddles glistened in the sunlight. As the ice crackled and crunched under the weight of my boots, I thought of the hours I'd spent with my brother and sisters cracking ice as we skidded over frozen brooks in Vermont. Like I had as a child, I skipped from puddle to puddle opening up watering holes for the animals. By noon the sun had turned the icy patches to mush and melted the frost.

The terrain changed from open grassy fields to a thick deciduous forest as the Trail wound around the side of a mountain. Finally, it dropped into a ravine. I had almost decided the section would never end, when an empty Trimpi Shelter came into view. Bunks filled the space on each side of a stone fireplace. A clear spring flowed in front of the shelter. I decided to take my first sponge bath since the first week of the trip. Keeping an eye on the approach Trail, I stripped down, bathed, and wash out my clothes. Clean and refreshed, I prepared soup with humus and purified water. The absence of people seemed strange after spending nights in crowded shelters. By reading the journal I learned Broken Road had stayed here a day to wait out a storm. Where and for how long hikers take days off is part of what makes each journey unique. Weather conditions and hikers' attitudes are often the impetus for breaks. It doesn't matter how miserable a day's hike is or uncomfortable a night's rest, with each new dawn comes a new opportunity to hike. No soft munching woke me in the night. However, birds announced the dawn.

After crossing Highway 86 on the other side of Locus and Bushy Mountains, I headed back into thick woods. Rhododendron bushes growing along the banks of a fast-moving brook brought to mind the woods of my childhood in New England and of my adulthood in the North Georgia Mountains. Similarities and differences among the terrain, weather, and landscape made the sections unique as well as giving them a sense of continuity.

When the Trail began following a brook, I began guessing where I thought the Chatfield Shelter should be. I always disappointed myself. Learning to trust was an ongoing lesson. After letting go of my obsession to locate the shelters, they appeared. The creek that had wandered away now bubbled along as if it had never left. I even had to cross it to reach the shelter. After dropping my pack, I headed back to the creek with my water bag. The water soothed me as I ate dried beans and pasta topped with pesto sauce. I hoped that the strong wind that had picked up would subside when the sun went down. However the darker it got, the windier it became and the lower the temperature dropped. It had been a very cold trip thus far, and I was tired of it. Through the forest, I saw a light. Company would break the cycle of being alone for a third night. I hadn't yet seen anyone going south. I recognized fewer and fewer journal entries. Many hikers had abandoned their thru-hike plans.

As the light drew near, the familiar twinge of apprehension that I felt whenever I approached a shelter or was joined by newcomers returned. The hiker's legs looked cold in shorts as he picked his way across the creek. I wanted to establish ground first. "I'm Wolf Woman. Have we met?"

"I'm Luvtuhike. Don't think we have. I don't use shelters much. They are too crowded. I got soaked in the rain last night and my tent never dried today. Looks like no one will be joining us. If you don't mind, I'm going to set it up in the shelter. It will give some protection from the wind."

"Go right ahead."

"I'm from Florida, and I hate this cold weather. In Damascus they were predicting snow. It's going to get very cold."

"Snow again? I'm ready for spring. In New England snow is common in April, but this far south is ridiculous. Aren't you freezing? "

Luvtuhike had set up the tent and now huddled over his stove, sipping soup. "Yes, but I thought I'd get something hot inside me before I changed. I don't have any food left that doesn't have to be cooked. I've missed my first three maildrops because I'm covering ground so fast. When we get to Atkins, I'm calling home and tell my friend to send my boxes sooner and pick up some snacks. I'm a vegetarian and miss my pemmican bars. You planning to stop and eat at the restaurant?"

"I'm a vegetarian too and I eat pemmican bars every day. Here," I handed Luvtuhike a carob bar. "I have plenty. I hadn't thought about stopping, but celebrating one quarter of the way to Katahdin with real food sounds good."

"There's a motel near the restaurant. If we get this storm, I'm staying put for a night. The snow shouldn't last long. You're welcome to split the cost of a room with me. I hate springing for a room, but I hate walking in the freezing cold and snow. Rain, I enjoy, but cold is not only miserable, it's dangerous."

"Sounds like a possible plan. I'm on a budget and wasn't planning to do motels except in an emergency." I also didn't want to think about sleeping with a stranger in a motel. I changed the subject. "I'm going to call my daughter and mother. Kate's birthday is the 25th and my mother's is the 22nd. No telling where I'll be next week, and I can't forget them." I paused. "You have children?"

"Yes, a son and a daughter, they're both in their twenties. My son's in Florida. My daughter just got married and lives in Europe. She wants me to check in with her but the phone calls overseas are expensive."

"I know what you mean. I've called my kids more from the Trail than I do from home. My phone bill is going to be outrageous." Luvtuhike and I visited until we realized we were talking louder and louder to be heard above the wind. The temperature had definitely dropped. Luvtuhike put his stove away and crawled into his tent. As I pulled the drawstring around the top of my bag, I tried to make sense of the new turn of events. I was still alone, but not really. On the other side of the shelter was a stranger, who in all innocence had suggested I spend the night with him in a motel. A suggestion that otherwise might be regarded with suspicion. It felt good knowing no hooks or strings were attached.

The journey was not only teaching me to be comfortable in my own skin. While trusting that white blazes would continue, shelters would appear, and creeks would have water, I was also learning to trust people.

I slowly lifted my head. An icy blast and a winter wonderland greeted me. "You were right. It snowed," I announced to Luvtuhike who was still in his nylon cocoon.

"Is it deep? Can you see the Trail?" Came a trembling faint voice.

"Yes, but barely. We got a couple of inches. And it is freezing!"

"Then I'm not eating here. Let's pack up and head to the restaurant."

"Sounds like a plan. According to the data book, it's five miles to Atkins. We should be there by mid-morning if we don't have trouble." I said cheerfully. No matter how adverse the conditions, I was a morning person. This morning I was cheerful to have someone to hike with. Except for the first six days with Kate, I had hiked alone everyday so far. I deserved a change.

Luvtuhike climbed out of his tent dressed in all his clothes. It was too cold to talk as we packed. I glanced back at the shelter after stepping over the creek. I needed a picture. How quickly things had changed. Less than twelve hours ago, I had crossed the creek alone. Now I had a hiking partner. However, spending all day with a nearly total stranger sent a different kind of chill down my back than the kind the wind was sending. Maybe I couldn't keep up. What if I wanted to stop and he didn't? I suddenly realized I had been living a very self-centered life. Lonely as it had been, I hadn't had to deal with another person's disposition, personality, and idiosyncrasies. I remembered someone in Alcoholics Anonymous once saying that experiences like these are opportunities for growth. The snowstorm and appearance of Luvtuhike were circumstances out of my control. I decided to accept the things I could not change. It seemed like months since I'd worried about the possibility of snow forcing me off the Trail. I didn't know the worst storm of the trip was yet to come, and I would be alone.

Luvtuhike was no more accustomed to having a hiking partner than I. Our attempts at conversation were awkward at first. But talking helped pass the time and took our minds off our growling stomachs as we slipped and sloshed along the snowy Trail. Snippets of conversation evolved into accounts of our respective forty years. With each anecdote we became aware of the similarities in our lives. We had both been married and divorced for nearly the same length of time and had a son and a daughter about the same ages. We were both vegetarians and loners. I discovered I could comfortably trot right along behind Luvtuhike's long stride or lead a pace with which he was comfortable.

Snow clung to the trees, filled the air, and covered the ground all the way to the highway. Starving and cold, with clumps of snow clinging to our clothes and hair, we walked into Cumbow's Country Restaurant. Minutes later, we were served steaming plates of eggs, pancakes, English muffins, fruit, toast, and hot coffee. Thomas, his dad from Alaska, and Crash joined us. Seeing the father and son made me miss Kate. Proudly I shared stories of our six days together. I'd covered five hundred and twenty-seven miles since then and the adventures seemed long ago.

The fellows invited us to take showers in their motel room before getting back on the Trail. A hot breakfast and shower in the same day were unbelievable Trail Magic! After eating, Luvtuhike and I took turns showering and stocking up on snacks at the store. By 1:00 o'clock, with wet hair tucked under our fleece hats, we were back on the Trail. We needed to make good time to reach the shelter fourteen miles away. Fear crept into my world. If I hadn't stopped to eat and shower, I wouldn't be anxious about making it before dark. With the taste of cheese omelet still lingering on my tongue, I tried not to worry.

The snow disappeared under a warm sun. It was hard to believe that the day before we'd feared being snow bound. It was easy to hike three miles an hour across the lovely farmland. I maintained a faster pace when following someone. To my surprise, Luvtuhike took more breaks than I was accustomed to. I usually nibbled Trail mix or energy bars when I got hungry and stopped only when I had to. I was always exhausted at the end of the day. "Your body needs the rest and your mind needs the mental break. To stop only when you have to means you are pushing your body to the limit. I don't take a lot of days off, but I stop for ten minutes every two hours and don't hike compulsively."

"Compulsive uh? This is not the first time I've been told I do things compulsively. OAB used to break every hour, and so did Tippy Canoe. I sure hope we get to the shelter before dark, though."

"Most hikers stop regularly. We have my tent. There are plenty of creeks in this section. I usually eat when I come to water, fill water bottles, and keep going until dark."

He was right about the breaks, but I doubted I could sleep in a tent with a guy I barely knew. I preferred worrying about making it to shelters than to be burdened by the extra weight. Shelters had appeared with or without companions. I tried to stop dwelling on the, "perhaps inevitable," and concentrated on looking for beauty. "It must be up over the next hill. It can't be far." I said for the hundredth time.

"We'll make it before dark." Luvtuhike was being patient. Thirty minutes later, we rounded a corner and there it sat. We had made it in excellent time even with breaks every hour, but I was exhausted. "There's a creek half a mile up the Trail and still daylight. Are you staying here or going with me?"

"What? Go on? You're going to keep walking?" I was dumbfounded. My feet hurt and I wasn't walking another step. This option had not occurred to me. I knew he didn't like shelters, but if I didn't go on he would stay ahead and I would never see him again. The experience brought up abandonment issues.

"Pat and Ron are here," Luvtuhike was saying. "I've enjoyed the company. I'm sure I'll see you along the Trail. You don't need me. You're an excellent hiker." He gave me a fleeting hug.

"Will you sign a journal once in a while so I'll know how you are doing?" I called after him, grabbing at the chance to keep contact.

"Maybe. You have my address. Email me when you finish. Katahdin is our goal, not the shelters. See you." And he was gone.

"Bye, be safe, and thanks; thanks a lot. It's been fun." Fun, what was the point in fun when it ended so abruptly? I felt abandoned. What was the point in enjoying company for just one day?

"Did you meet someone?" Pat asked excitedly, sitting up in her sleeping bag. She hoped I would find a hiking partner.

"Yes, I mean no. For yesterday and today I did, but he doesn't like shelters and is going to camp by some creek." I didn't want to talk about it. "It sure is good to see you." It was nearly dark. I spread out my sleeping bag. I took out a couple of granola bars before hanging the food sack.

*April 18: Today was full of circles. The weather started out cold, turned warm, and ended up cold. It started with company, I ate a meal with a gang, and now I'm alone. Why were these events plopped in the middle of my solitary journey? People come and go on the Trail just as they do at home. I'm not sure momentary involvements are worth the energy. They bring a full array of emotions, most of which I don't want to deal with. I've felt everything from fear to joy to sadness, and now loneliness. A therapist told me all emotions fit in these four categories. No wonder I am so exhausted. I have dealt with them all, over and over.*

The wind died down by morning and the air wasn't as cold. As I moved through my routine, my emotions vacillated between deep sadness and mild relief at being alone. I was moving toward a place of accepting the process, but not always the outcome. I pondered the difference as I headed down the Trail. Watching Pat with Ron exacerbated my loneliness. It wasn't that I wanted a husband. A woman-hiking partner would be more to my liking. I remembered how adamant I'd been about not wanting anyone to join me, not even my own daughter.

The blessed energy of movement through beautiful Southwest Virginia propelled me forward. Ridge hiking offered spectacular views of rolling farmland and meandering rivers. Big red barns, narrow black roads, and sparkling blue ponds, interspersed with stores, subdivisions, and shopping centers stretched like a patchwork quilt. Farther along a section of the Trail had been controlled burned. The ground was scorched for several yards back from the Trail; a sooty smoky odor drifted up from the black ash. Thick blackberry bushes and tangled undergrowth grew in wild profusion just beyond the fire line. I pretended I was Dorothy in the *Wizard of Oz* following a yellowish green grass road with black sides instead of a black road with yellow lines. Snow had been flurrying since I'd gained elevation. A black, pregnant sky had replaced fluffy white clouds. Large white flakes nested in the black charred ground looked like white polka dots on coal black cloth. As elegant as white hair around the temples of a dark-headed woman, the snow added charm to an otherwise desolate dingy section. Unlike the evidence of aging, the flakes melted as quickly as they landed.

Chestnut Knob Shelter was perched on the crest of a grassy knoll. Stone and enclosed, it reminded me of Blood and Roan Mountain Shelters. Hearing voices as I got near, I was delighted to find Ron, Pat, and two Trail maintenance women enjoying lunch at the large picnic table tucked in the spacious shelter. The women had snack cakes, cheese, crackers, and fruit to share. I was beside myself with joy. "Food and company, what a surprise on a snowy day. Aren't the views gorgeous?"

"Yes, join us. Virginia is as beautiful and easy as everyone said it would be," Ron reached for a snack cake Pat handed him.

"You having a good hike?" Pat asked.

I signed the journal and set it back on the table. "Yes, I'm having a great day. It feels good to be hiking at my own pace too. This whole trip is about learning to walk my own walk, and I can't do that if I'm scurrying along behind someone. By the way, how do you two decide who's sets the pace?"

"I like to find a stick to use with the one we brought from home for climbing hills. Ron patiently waits while I scrounge in the woods looking for one. I set the pace up hills. We have fallen into a routine of walking slow in the morning. After lunch we pick up speed. Ron is real good about letting me set the rhythm." Pat smiled at her husband.

"That's a healthy practice," one of the women commented. "So many men take off and leave their female hiking partners to get along the best they can. Of course it's much safer for women to hike with someone."

I didn't want a lecture about hiking alone, or a reminder of my short experience with a partner, so I stuffed the remains of my lunch in my food sack. "We need to be on the Trail, too," said Ron, as he cleared the table. The women offered to carry out our trash and take our pictures, promising to send them to our homes. After the pictures were taken I headed out before Ron and Pat. My next stop was Bland. They were headed for Pearisburg and would pass me when I got off. The journals would keep us in touch.

The desolate, lifeless terrain leading to the Jenkins Shelter exacerbated the depression I'd been feeling since Damascus. I hoped a bath and clean clothes in Bland would lift my spirits, even though I had no idea where I would stay, and no one would be there to meet me. The handbook indicated only one expensive motel and one laundromat. As darkness settled over the forest and I prepared for my fourth night alone, out of the six I'd spent in Virginia. I didn't know that Bland would be just that, bland.

I ascended the last hill before the intersection that led to Bastian in one direction and Bland in the other wondering how I'd know which way to turn. Like a faithful friend, Trail Magic answered me. "Hi! Nice day isn't it!" I said, not wanting to startle a man and woman picnicking on a fallen tree across the Trail.

"Sure is," answered the man. "You hiking far?"

"All the way to Maine. I left Springer Mountain, Georgia, March first." I slipped off my backpack and hoisted it up over the downed tree.

" Maine! You a thru-hiker? You alone?" The woman asked.

"Yes, most of the time I'm alone, but I know lots of hikers." I changed the subject, "When I come to the road, which way is Bland?"

"To the left a few miles. The town is small. Need a ride?" asked the man.

"Yes, I need to pick up a maildrop tomorrow."

"We're staying at the Walker Motel, the only motel in town. If you'll wait by our blue sedan at the bottom of the hill, we'd be happy take you."

"Thanks so much. I'll be waiting." I pulled on my backpack.

The couple was right. The town was very small. "Thank you for the ride." I said at the Walker Motel. Thirty-six dollars was steep for my budget, but I had no choice. After showering I caught a ride to town in search of a restaurant and the laundromat. Finding nothing but a gas station with a deli, I ordered a sandwich and asked directions to the laundromat.

"The laundromat closed last year." the clerk explained. I was using last year's handbook. "No use crying over spilled milk," my grandmother would have said. I had dirty clothes and a couple hours of drying time left if I hurried back and scrubbed. Back in my room, I filled the sink with hot water. Soon clean clothes hung outside around the back of the motel. During one of my trips out to circulate them, someone call my name.

"Wolf Woman!" Crash, Thomas, and his dad waved at me from a motel room.

"Hey, give me a hug. How ya'll doing?" I got hugs from all the fellows. "We're okay but we're thinking about going home. Crash here, he's solid about going to Maine, but my son has been a doubting Thomas for a while and I miss my wife and daughter something terrible. We're just plain homesick. You don't look so happy yourself. I saw you on the telephone. Calling home helps, but you know what they say- 'There's no place like home.' I thought you were hiking with Luvtuhike."

"We hiked together for one day. He camped by a creek the night I stopped at Knots Maul. I haven't seen him since. I couldn't have kept up with him for long. I have been sort of depressed." "Sort of," was an understatement. "I'm going to Maine though."

"You're a good hiker. I can't believe you kept up with Luvtuhike. He's fast. Listen, Log Cabin Restaurant will be open for breakfast. Why don't you join us in the morning? Right now we need to hitchhike into town to find something to eat for supper."

"I'll be there." Feeling somewhat better, I checked on my drying clothes before calling Suellen and Kate. Everyone encouraged me to keep going. I didn't think about quitting because I refused to give myself permission to flirt with the idea. It was just hard to believe in myself, but self-doubts were a sure way to foster negative attitudes and feed depression. Quitting was sure to follow. Lum had been right, hiking without a partner was a lonely business, but I was committed to my goal and myself.

Gray skies threatened rain while the fellows and I gorged on pancakes, cheese omelets, hash browns, and coffee. Breakfast meant closure for more thru-hikers. Crash would stay ahead. Thomas and his dad were going home. I was used to good-byes.

On the way to my room, I recognized a fellow from Canada who was slack packing a woman. He waved and came to the door. "Nice to see you again. Remember me? Stanley. Need a ride? His accent was warm and willing.

"Yes, I need to get to the Post Office and then back to the Trail. I'd love a ride!"

"My car is out front. I'm ready when you are," he smiled. Trail Magic is miraculous. At the Post Office Stanley waited in the car while I went in to repack my backpack. I wasn't prepared for the support that awaited me.

My stepmother Gloria and I had never been particularly close. I had moved south before she and Daddy married. During trips home I usually drove to Vermont over the Connecticut River from my mother's house in Keene, New Hampshire, to visit them in Putney. Gloria and I kept in touch for a year or two after Dad's sudden death in 1986; but as the years went on communication, had diminished to mere Christmas gift exchanges. For the last several years, little effort had been made by either of us to stay connected, until I decided to hike the Trail. I had sent Gloria a copy of my flier and the newspaper article. She immediately sent a donation and a letter telling me how proud Daddy would have been. I was touched, but had not a clue how vital Gloria would become to my success. As I stood in the Bland Post Office on that cold, dreary April 21st, I was not prepared for what the postal clerk handed me.

"I'm thru-hiker, Ellen Wolfe, here to pick up my mail."

"You must either be someone really special, have a lot of fans, or both. I haven't seen this much mail for a thru-hiker in a long time." The clerk handed me a stack of letters, the maildrop box, a box from Campmor with a lighter sleeping bag that I'd ordered while at Hot Springs, a box from Kate, and a box addressed from Putney, Vermont.

I carried my treasures to the counter. I started with Kate's box. She'd sent a bag of the Trail mix and a hand drawn Trail map. "You can do it Mom! You are almost half way there!" She'd drawn a map in handwriting familiar only to a mother. I got long letters from Suellen, Mom, Suzanne, Judy, American Cancer Society in Knoxville, and Mr. and Mrs. Earl Nash. As I read each card I felt more committed and grounded in the faith that my friends had in me. But none touched my heart like the contents of Gloria's box. It was only the size of a living room couch pillow, but it was packed solid. Wrapped in tissue paper with notes attached to each item were: bath oil beads, chocolates, gum, crackers and cheese, lip balm, energy drink, cookies, Vermont cheese, handy wipes, pencils, pens, tiny pads of paper, carob covered almonds, bubble bath, baggies, Kleenex, a journal, hard candies, Tic-Tac breath mints, mole skin, Band-Aids, tape, hair elastics, fig bars, peanuts, protein energy bars, shampoo, skin lotion, postage stamps, cookies, dried fruit, vitamin C, candles, stamped addressed post cards, tea bags, and, last but not least, pictures of Daddy, their home, her dog, and New England in all four glorious seasons. I was overwhelmed.

"Go Girl! Go!" the card read. "I'm so proud of you. I'm thinking of you every step of the way. Your father is with you, too. He would have been so proud of you. I can't wait for you to get to Vermont. Love, Gloria." I could hardly believe what I'd spread across the counter. I touched the items one after another while popping carob-covered almonds, fig bars, and apricots in my mouth, as I tried to grasp the authenticity of Gloria's support.

I stuffed the food in my pack and placed the gifts that were too heavy to carry in a box with the mail, my winter sleeping bag, long underwear, used Trail maps, and journal notes to send back to Tennessee. My next stop was Catawba, one hundred and thirteen miles or one week away. Keeping the weight of the pack down was essential. I put the pictures in baggies and carefully slid them in the top of my backpack.

Just as I finished, Stanley came in to see how I was getting along. "I'm sorry it has taken me so long. You wouldn't believe all the cool things I got from my step-mother." I babbled like a child on Christmas morning all the way to the Trailhead. The drizzling rain had become a down-pour. Stanley helped me pull the pack cover over my backpack, wished me well, and drove away. Watching him disappear reminded me of friends leaving me in the woods. With a lump in my throat, I recalled Suellen walking me up the Trail out of Hot Springs, and departing. Time after time friends, family, and total strangers appeared, supported me, and deposited me back in the woods. Symbolically their actions represented their faith. If I doubted myself, they did not. The contents of Gloria's blessed box weighed as promises not pounds on my back. She believed in me, and with Daddy's spirit my faith was renewed.

After the rain ended, the terrain of gradual ups and down in a still leafless deciduous forest allowed me to clip right along. Suddenly, up ahead I saw a large pack protruding over the top of a small frame. Not wanting to startle the hiker, I announced my arrival. "Hi there, coming around."

Turning around, a middle-aged woman looked up and smiled from under a soggy raincoat. "Hi, how are you doing?"

"Just fine, I'm glad the rain stopped. You going far?"

"To the next shelter. I'm Sylvia."

"It's nice to meet you. I don't see many women. I'm Wolf Woman, thru-hiker from Tennessee. You hiking alone?"

"No, there are two more women, a young man, and a dog up ahead. You'll pass them in a minute. When did you start?"

"March first. And you?"

"We're section hikers out for a week. We'll get off in Pearisburg. I'm with a friend from Vermont and her sister from New York City."

"Vermont! I grew up in Vermont. Where abouts?"

"Brattleboro, near the Connecticut River."

"I can't believe it! I grew up in Westminster, Vermont. My dad lived in Putney. Just today I got a care package from my stepmother who lives there. Do you know the Harlow's that own the Harlow Sugar House? They make the best maple syrup."

"Yes, I know them. Dot's from Brattleboro, and knows them better. Why don't you join us for lunch on the ridge?"

"Thanks. Talking to Vermont women will be special Trail Magic. I'll tell them I detained you." We pulled on our packs that we'd let slip to the ground. My feet flew at the thoughts of meeting more women, especially from Vermont. Approaching another hiker trudging up the hill, I announced. "Hi, coming around you."

"Hi there. Where are you hurrying off to?" asked the second smiling woman I'd seen in less than an hour. Gray hair wisped around a soaked, blue sweatshirt hood.

"I'm looking for a woman from Vermont. I'm Wolf Woman"

"I'm Barbara, from New York. My sister, Dot is up ahead and Sylvia, behind, lives in Brattleboro. I guess you met Sylvia? You're not hiking alone, are you?" The questions were always the same. I was thinking of hanging a sign around my neck that read: "Left Springer Mountain, March 1, Wolf Woman, from Cookeville, Tennessee. Yes, I'm hiking by myself." That sounded more positive than "hiking alone".

"I know hikers. Most of them are guys. I've met Sylvia. She's not far behind."

"It's dangerous to hike alone, but I am impressed. You're making good time! Dot and I have been section hiking for twenty-five years."

"What dedication. Now I'm impressed! It's great to meet women hikers."

"Dot has done many of the sections you're heading into and can tell you what to expect. I'm sure you'll catch them and do join us for lunch."

"Thanks, I'll do that." I was off again in search of the third woman hiker of the day, and the second Vemonter. Minutes later I spotted two people and a dog sprawled in the middle of the Trail. "You must be Dot," I said dropping my pack.

"Sure am, and this is Nathan, a family friend. And you?" The woman asked.

"I'm Wolf Woman, originally from Vermont and I know the Harlows.

"What a coincidence. I grew up in New York City but moved to Brattleboro. I teach kindergarten and live with my son Michael. What do you do?" Slipping to the ground, I told Dot about quitting fourth grade teaching, my college job, and my children. We were swapping school tales when Barbara and Sylvia joined us. Lunch was a feast. They had enough food to feed an army. I shared Gloria's treats. As we ate, we talked of our love for Vermont and the stress of raising children. Barbara was married to a psychiatrist and juggled substitute teaching with tending to her twenty-year-old boys. While they had not come with her, their friend Nathan had tagged along. Dot supported her adopted African American teen-age son who had learning disabilities. Michael had been with her since infancy. His needs usually kept her close to home, but family friends were caring for him while she was on the trail. Sylvia's story as a breast cancer survivor confirmed my incentive to walk for a cure.

At Jenny Knob Shelter, I climbed the bank to the creek for water. Dot and Nathan soon rounded the corner. Dot plopped her backpack down and told me Trail stories until Barbara and Sylvia arrived. In no time we had our belongings spread over the three-sided structure until it resembled a girl's dormitory. Seeing woman's clothes was comforting. We shared food, tasks, and advice, as women have done throughout the ages. At dusk we climbed into our sleeping bags, with Nathan in the middle of the group, and talked long into the night. I savored the nurturing camaraderie of my gender. As our voices grew weary, Barbara propped herself up and called softly over Nathan's snoozing head, "Call me when you get to the ranger station at New Jersey 23. I'll come get you. Here's my number."

I fumbled for my flashlight. Shining the light on a page in my journal, I wrote down the number. "OK," I whispered. "I'll do it. Good-night." I wasn't sure what she meant. I wouldn't be in New Jersey for a month. Barbara was teaching again after taking two years off to care for her aged parents. Both had recently passed away. She could get real busy. When I relaxed in the moment and stayed with the process, Trail Magic happened, this time womanly magic. Connecting with people and allowing them into my experience was significant to the journey. I walked alone in body, but not in spirit.

I was almost asleep, still tasting Gloria's treats and memorizing Barbara's phone number, when a hiker strode into camp. "Oh, dear! Looks like the shelter's full." A tall, thin, dark headed hiker stood leaning on walking sticks and staring at our array of belongings. I suspect we looked more like a pack of gypsies than hikers.

"We can move over," mumbled Dot. "Nathan, move over this way." She nudged the sleeping teenager as she scooted closer to me and I backed against the wall. "You are Trail Trooper, aren't you? I've been following your process on the Internet. I'm a section hiker and keep up with the thru-hikers on the net. I'm a Vermont Trail volunteer too. My club built the Spruce Peak Shelter."

"Yes. Thanks for moving over. I hiked thirty miles today and I'm exhausted. I ran out of water and started seeing mirages."

"You should take care of yourself." Dot admonished Trail Trooper for doing marathon mileage until she'd talked us both to sleep. April 21st was the first and only time I'd see Trail Trooper. A married police officer from Virginia with two children, he was doing the Trail in four months for a charity. Although the Trail grapevine later indicated that he had yellow blazed or skipped sections of the Trail, including sections of the White Mountains, he went down in the records as the first hiker to finish the Trail in 1997.

Trail Trooper was gone when I got up the next morning. The women joined me for breakfast. Under a cloudy sky we took pictures and promised to be in touch. "Call me, don't forget," Barbara said, giving me a hug.

"I will," I promised as a lump rose in my throat. The women carried tents and planned to camp a few miles down the Trail. I headed for Doc's Knob Shelter, twenty miles away. Difficult as it was, I was learning to walk away from positive experiences, knowing if I kept moving more awaited me down the Trail.

Kimberling and Dismal Creeks were beautiful. I was glad not to have to carry much water. Festive flowers flourished along the forest floor. Deer darted out of the deep woods. Squirrels scampered in the leaves. A rabbit romped across the Trail.

Hiking twenty miles a day made it seem as though a million years passed. Continuous days and nights passed without seeing a single soul. Consequently, as I struggled up a steep climb, just past Wapiti Shelter, I was startled to see an elderly man sprawled in the Trail with his gear spread everywhere. At first I thought he might be hurt, but immediately I felt uncomfortable. There was no way to get around him without speaking. "Tough climb, isn't it?" I said, keeping eye contact as I picked my way around his worn equipment.

"Aint no hill. Any hiker oughta be able to do it. Where you headed?" he snarled.

I ignored his comments and didn't reveal my night's destination, "To Katahdin."

"I mean for tonight? Where you going tonight. When'd you leave Springer?"

"March first, I'll go as far as I can and then get off the Trail."

"So you're a thru-hiker. You aren't making very good time. Better hurry if you're going to make it to Maine before it snows. I'm section hiking to Pearisburg, but I've been to Katahdin and Springer. You won't make it, if this little hill's giving ya trouble."

"Like you said, I need to hurry." I moved quickly without turning my back on him until I was a safe distance away. He didn't move but exploded in an earth-shattering laugh that sent chill bumps down my spine. My adrenaline raced and my body went into overdrive. I doubled my strides over the hill. I wanted to put as much distance as possible between us. He would know I couldn't get much further than Doc's Knob Shelter, still eight miles away. I'd gotten such a late start, I wasn't sure I could make it. Woodshole Hostel was up ahead but Dot said it wasn't open. "It is a great place, but it's still too early. There'd be signs in the shelters and on the Trail if it was open."

Even though the energy in Virginia was very eerie, meeting the weird character was my first uncomfortable experience with people. Posters of the two women who had been murdered near the Trail in the Shenandoah National Park a year ago that month were everywhere. Just before my encounter with the unnerving character, I had passed the Wapati shelter that had also been a murder location in the distant past. Turning the experience over in my mind, I kept moving. My heart pounded so fast that my feet raced but I doubted I'd reach the shelter before dark. I tried not to feel guilty about enjoying a leisurely breakfast with the women, but thoughts that I should have gotten on the Trail earlier haunted me. The air was warm, but the sky looked like rain. Getting way off the Trail was an option.

But my feet kept moving. They moved until I stopped fabricating scenarios and allowed Trail Magic to happen. In the distance I saw a paper attached to a tree. I ran, my backpack flopping up and down. OPEN WOODSHOLE HOSTEL— Take Sugar Run Road - Follow posted signs. "YES! Thank you, Trail Magic," I said to all of nature. The spirit of the Trail was with me. Sugar Run Road was less than a mile away. Deep breaths rose and fell with the rhythm of my steps as the frantic anxiety dissipated.

Roy and Tillie Wood had settled the homestead at Woodshole Hostel while Roy was studying elk area. In the early 1940's, the couple had built a bunkhouse and opened the hostel to hikers in 1986. In exchange for a minimal fee or work, hikers could spend the night, eat breakfast, and enjoy a solar shower in warm weather. Roy's recent death had not stopped Tillie from opening her home to thru-hikers. Tillie's trusted friend High Pocket from North Carolina, arrived in early April to ready the place for her arrival and welcome the early hikers. As a 1989 thru-hiker, he loved swapping hiker stories with the younger hiking generation.

Seeing no car other than a dilapidated 1963 Mercury-Comet that I assumed didn't run, I was not surprised no one came to the door. The bunkhouse was also empty. Climbing a ladder above the open front room, I found rows of mattresses separated by low partitions. A light bulb hung from the ceiling and a switch attached to a pole meant electricity by which to write. Hiker equipment was spread on one mattress. I climbed back down the ladder and began pulling food out of my backpack on the braided rug.

"Ah, you scared me. When did you arrive? You can eat in the house. Would you like me to fix you a cheese sandwich?" A young man with a gentle face and short pony tail stood over me.

"You mean a real grilled cheese sandwich? That would be great. I can make it as soon as I change clothes."

"You don't have to. I'll have it ready when you come in to meet High Pocket. My name is Rain." The young man extended a hand.

Grasping his hand, I explained, "I knocked on the door and no one answered. I'm Wolf Woman. You'll really make me a sandwich?" Now I was the one in shock.

"Sure I will. Wolf Woman! It's good to finally meet you. I've been hearing all about you. You were hiking with your daughter back in Georgia, right? Aren't you the one hiking for breast cancer? Broken Road and Pilgrim were just through here and were wondering if I'd seen you. Having any trouble hiking alone?"

"Kate was with me for six days." I ignored the question about having trouble. Things had been fine until today. The experience with the strange character was over. "You going all the way too?" I asked.

"Yeah! I'm Katahdin bound. I left Springer the end of January. I don't hike very fast and take a lot of days off. I'm in no rush. We'll visit in the house. High Pocket will wonder what took me so long. He'd sent me out to see if hikers were here. I'll tell him you'll be right in. Oh, and I'll have your sandwiches ready."

"Thanks a lot! I'll be right in."

I sat in disbelief. Whenever I accepted the process and I let go of worry, Trail Magic happened. In dry clothes, I headed across the lawn and in the front door. High Pocket stood slowly from a table in the cozy kitchen. He offered me a strong weathered hand and motioned for me to sit. "The fire feels so good. I'm so glad you're open."

"Rain just put those signs up this morning. We aren't officially open until Tillie gets here the end of next week, but I let hikers stay to help me get ready for the season. Rain here, he's been a great help. He's a real fine young man. You a thru-hiker?"

"Yes, I left Springer March first and hope to climb by the first of August."

"You're making good time. Having any trouble?"

There was that question again. Concern for trouble on the Trail was evident. Rain set two cheese sandwiches, a tall glass of milk, and sliced tomatoes in front of me. "I can't believe you cooked my supper! Thank you. As to having trouble, I hadn't had any until today. I met this strange guy in the middle of the Trail." I shared the story of my encounter. "I don't know what I'd have done if you hadn't been open."

Rain shared a similar version. "I ran into the same guy going south two days ago. He stopped me and laughed real weird at my equipment. He said if I didn't hurry and get to Katahdin he was going to get me. I don't know what he meant, but he sure scared me."

"You're both safe. Sounds like a local. He'll probably move on by the time you get back on the Trail." High Pocket's words were comforting. There was nothing to do but enjoy the safety and fellowship of the evening and let go of the fearful afternoon.

The conversation turned to talk of people Rain and I knew. High Pocket told stories of the cabin's history. We visited until High Pocket got up and unfolded a cot in front of the stove. The kitchen was the only room with heat. Rain and I started to leave.

"Wolf Woman, you can take a shower. It is a little nasty in there. Hasn't been cleaned since last year, but the water is plenty hot."

"I'd appreciate that. I'd be happy to scrub the bathtub. Do you have any soap?"

"Look under the sink," High Pocket suggested. I found a scrub brush covered with mouse turds and a rusty can of cleanser. High Pocket was reading when a clean woman with scrubbed feet emerged from a clean bathroom with a scrubbed tub. "Nothing like a hot shower at the end of a day," he smiled.

"I feel like a new woman. Thank you. Before I go, could I use the phone to call my Mom? Today's her birthday. I'll use my calling card."

"Go right ahead." The phone rang and rang. Mom didn't believe in using an answering machines. I was probably more disappointed at not being able to connect with her than she would be at not hearing from me. "There's plenty of work to do if you want to stay. It is supposed to start raining tonight and rain all day tomorrow."

"Thanks, but I need to get back on the Trail." Suddenly I remembered I was trying to let go of outcomes. "Maybe I'll stay. We'll see what the weather does. Good night and thanks for the shower and supper." Rain stopped reading when I topped the ladder.

"You planning to work tomorrow?" I asked as I spread out my sleeping bag.

"I wish I could but I need to get back on the Trail. Every place I stop I think it is the best place I've been, but I love it here best. High Pocket reminds me of my grandfather. I was in Damascus a week working on a roof and thought that was the neatest place, but Woodshole is better. I've been here several days helping High Pocket get the water fixed. Everyone I was hiking with is way ahead. Are you staying?"

"I'm going to wait and see what the weather does," I said with sigh of resolve to keep my motto.

I'd no sooner fallen asleep then cracks of thunder woke me. Rain as loud as pelting bullets ricocheted off the tin roof above my head. The wind sounded like roaring engines as it ripped through the treetops behind the loft. Yellow lightening scattered flashes as bright as the bulb had been that now dangled black in the dark cabin. I thanked the powers-that-be that I wasn't hunkered under a tree in the woods and was safe from both a brusque human being and the brutal forces of Mother Nature. I was also glad Rain was sharing the cozy loft with me. I still couldn't believe his thoughtfulness. It was easier to believe the roof would keep the storm on the other side of the bunkhouse, than it was to believe a perfect stranger would make me a grilled cheese sandwich. The Trail was teaching me to accept the goodness of humanity. "Sounds like Mother Nature is telling me I need a day off," I said, raising my voice above the storm.

"Me too," came a wide-awake response from across the room. Picking up my pen I journaled between flashes. *April 22: Today's nearly twenty mile hike took me away from three delightful women, past a really weird guy, and to Rain and High Pocket at Woodshole Hostel. I'm safe from the storm, full of home cooked food, and clean. Life could not be better or more full of opportunities to respond to ever increasing experiences to trust the process. Happy birthday Mom, wherever you are.*

After one of High Pocket's famous egg and biscuit breakfasts, Rain and I took a bedroom and cleaned it from stem to stern. Mice had made nests and left tracks in every conceivable corner. We dusted, vacuumed, shook rugs, and washed floors. The work was a welcome change and made me grateful for my long absence from housework. When the chores were done we piled in the old Comet (that ran after all) and High Pocket took us into Pearisburg. We bought the ingredients to make ravioli, salad, and brownies. Rain's mother had won the Pillsbury Bake Off in 1955, as had his grandmother many years before, and could make brownies worth hiking to a maildrop for. For supper Rain tried his hand at his mother's accomplishment. Hiker, Double Bacon Cheeseburger, joined us.

Working with Rain and High Pocket felt like a family. High Pocket had doted on us as if we were his children. "I'm so proud of you two! You've worked so hard. I wish you'd both stay here and help me all season. Tillie would put you to work." I smiled. I felt privileged to have cleaned her bedroom. "But," High Pocket continued in his soft Southern drawl, "Katahdin is waiting for you and you must go climb her." Rain and I hugged the older man's neck. His words of encouragement spoke volumes we would need in the days to come.

The rain had stopped in the night. Rain had hiked the section to Pearisburg, and High Pocket was taking him to the Trail crossing in time to hike to the next shelter before dark. He offered to take my pack and meet me in town. I appreciated the chance to slack pack the ten-mile section. The sky was dark but my body felt light as I flew along the Trail. Shortly before noon, I popped out on Main Street and found Rain and High Pocket waiting in the rain at the Rendezvous Motel. Rain and I decided we needed a Subway sandwich before leaving the dear old man who had become a grandfather to both of us. We ate slowly. After hugs and promises to write, we walked into the rain.

Rain and I hiked together until we came to the Shumate Bridge over the New River. As I watched him dodge the speeding traffic on Highway 460 and enter the woods on the other side, I thought of the juxtaposition between the name of the river and its age. The river is the second oldest river in the world, next to the Nile. Because it flows north into the Ohio River before emptying into the Gulf of Mexico, the early pioneers named it New. All the rivers north of this point flow into the Atlantic Ocean. The Appalachian Trail crisscrosses creeks, streams, brooks, ponds, and even reservoirs constructed behind concrete dams. Water running from mountain tops travels hundreds of miles farther than I would before reaching its destination. Although gravity moves it through crevasses and gullies, water often cuts its own path. I don't have to forge my own way. My path is marked. I depend on maildrops and stores for food. But water, too cold to bathe in and too dirty to drink without purification, is critical to my survival.

Watching the New River flow beneath me was an experience in trusting the intricate balance between land and water. I felt a sense of pride to be part of the dance. Sonia, in the movie *Mindwalk*, describes this dance of life as self-organizing, self-maintaining, self-transcending and self-renewing interconnecting patterns. Staying conscious of my interdependence with land and water gave me faith.

# Chapter 7

## *"Thru-hikers add to the ambiance"*

### (Central Virginia) Pearisburg to Waynesboro

Built in 1995, the natural hewn logs of Rice Field Shelter still looked new. "Feels good to be back on the Trail. Too bad the cold weather came with us." I greeted my Trail family. A cold wind added a nippy chill to the dusk hours.
"I wish I was back at High Pocket's," Rain grumbled as he pulled on a fleece hat.

"We missed seeing you at the Pearisburg hostel. Where did you stay?" Pat was always concerned about me.

"I had a great time at Woodshole Hostel." I shared my experiences, including my encounter with the weird guy, as I cooked supper.

"I ran into the same guy," said a young man with sandy colored hair. "I don't think he was a thru-hiker, although he said something about hiking Katahdin and Springer. He was pretty weird. By the way, I'm Snail."

"Nice to meet you. You thru-hiking?" I asked.

"Sure am. I left when there was still snow on the ground. I'm not in a rush. How 'bout yourself?"

"I left March first. I'm Wolf Woman. Aren't these Virginia Trails great?"

"They're a piece of cake after the Nantahalas," Snail said.

Leaning against the back of the shelter with his sleeping bag pulled up over his shoulders, an older fellow had been quietly listening. "Dragon's Tooth will be tough, and the climb over the Priest is no stroll in the park; but Virginia is the place to pick up mileage before you hit the Whites. They say the Pennsylvania locals have sharpened the rocks on the ridges into fine points! It's good to meet you, Wolf Woman. I've been reading your journal entries. Not many women hike this alone. I go by Tacoma." Smile lines around his dark eyes and a weathered face let me know he was a veteran of the Trail. Gathering knowledge from those who had walked the walk was helpful, even if the news was disheartening. Tacoma lapsed back into silence.

"I'm Cowpenski from Pennsylvania and I've heard so much talk about those rocks that I'm going home and soak my feet when I get there."

"Is there no way around them?" I wanted to avoid the rocks if possible.

"All I can say is, I hope you've got another pair of boots broken in." Tacoma added as he pulled on a fleece hat and zipped up his sleeping bag.

"High Pocket says the elevation isn't bad. It won't be like scaling cliffs in the Whites. We'll be picking our way over rocks for a hundred and twenty miles north of Duncannon. They're embedded in the ground like daggers. But," Rain continued, "High Pocket says the Shenandoah National Park is a piece of cake!"

Ron handed his wife a cup of coffee. "I've heard the Trail crosses the Parkway about fifty times. I'm looking forward to seeing deer and not having to carry as much food because there are restaurants near the Trail."

Cowpenski had heard rumors too. "I hear the shelters are either real close or far apart and that the rangers are stricter about a shelter schedule than in the Smokies."

Feeling both fear and excitement, I added, "No sense speculating and worrying about the unknown."

After food sacks swung from the rafters, silence fell over the seven occupants of Rice Shelter. I twisted and turned, trying to get comfortable on the hard floor. Two nights on a mattress had spoiled me.

So, the Trail ahead would be both easy and hard. The future held frightening and exhilarating challenges. The strange character probably wouldn't show up again, but would there be others? Would I be able to climb sheer cliffs? I was no mountain climber, polished athlete, or even a proficient hiker. The search for answers haunted me. Struggling to find comfort in more than my sleeping bag, I lay in the dark realizing that civilization offered no more guarantees than Trail life. Movement would bring meaning.

The day was cold, dry, and sunny as we headed out for Bailey Gap Shelter the next morning. Red barns, green grass, and black paved roads dotted the rolling Virginia farm below the ridge crests. Between the crests were open valleys void of trees.

While I was walking through one of these fields, the sun suddenly disappeared and a huge black cloud settled overhead. Sinking lower and gathering speed, the sky looked as though it would swallow me up or explode. I looked for a cave or a ditch but found neither. After tucking the pack cover across my backpack, zipping gaiters over my boots, and buttoning up my rain jacket, I had barely reached the woods when huge, hard hail balls were hurled from the sky. Ricocheting off my head, the hail hit the ground transforming the Trail into a sea of frozen ice marbles. Deafening wind roared through the trees. All around, limbs crashed to the ground and branches snapped. The ground looked like a sea of glacier chips. I calculated each step trying not to fall on the slippery glassy ground. About the time I had decided that the roaring in my ears and the pounding on my head would last forever, the blackness lifted and the sun reappeared. I felt weak as I gingerly picked my way over the hail. Sweating under my layers I glanced at the sky. As I lifted my head to pull off my jacket I gasped in terror, "Oh, no! It's coming back!" I jerked my arms back in my soggy jacket. I looked within for comfort.

No sooner had I pulled my raincoat on than a second attack of the ice balls pelted earth. Hovering like a huge black vulture circling its prey, the cloud swirled into a black whirlpool. Deafening wind swallowed the silence. I walked slowly, and sang softly, "When you walk through a storm, hold your held up high...."

Surviving the first attack gave me strength to endure the second. But knowing what to expect didn't lessen the pain of the hailstones beating on my head, nor silence the roaring wind. The experience reminded me of going into labor for the second time. The first successful birth gave me experience, not relief. Like the first storm, the second lasted no more than ten minutes and stopped just as abruptly. Wondering if I had walked out of the storm or if another would return reminded me of debates between my parents as to whether the thunderstorms that roared through the Connecticut River Valley returned, or new storms follow previous ones. Cautiously, I walked on.

The climb through thick rhododendrons up to Bailey Gap Shelter was trivial after the hailstorm. I found Rain, Snail, and Cowpenski eating and basking bare-chested in the late afternoon sun as their shirts dried on low branches. The fellows had gotten soaked, but hadn't seen hail. I'd stayed dry. After chili, rice, and beans, I crawled in my sleeping bag. Snail was about to follow my lead when Rain suggested. "Let's hike by moonlight."

"Moonlight? I don't see a moon." Snail was clearly skeptical.

"It'll be fun. I did it once in Georgia. Once your eyes adjust to the darkness, you can see the Trail. Want to join us, Wolf Woman?"

"No, thanks. I'm a morning person, not a night owl. How do you know there'll be a full moon?" I, too, questioned the logic.

"It's about time for one," Rain said glancing at the sky. "It's warm, the sky is clear, and the stars are out. Are you game?"

"Sure, why not? We can always camp if we decide to stop." Snail looked nervous.

As Cowpenski and I zipped up our bags, Rain and Snail waited. Their legs swung impatiently as they watched the horizon for a glimmering go ahead from the moon. I was nearly asleep when I heard Rain whisper. "Let's get going. We have flashlights if the moon doesn't come up."

"Are you sure?" Snail straightened up from a nap.

"Yeah, let's do it. See ya, Wolf Woman."

Fully awake, I was suddenly aware that my hiking companions were leaving and in total darkness. Motherly instincts waved red flags of concern. "Are you guys sure this is a smart thing to do? The Trail may be full of debris and mud after the storm. Maybe there'll be a moon later in the week."

"Nah, we've waited this long, let's go." Rain was determined.

"Be careful. Leave me a note in the next shelter so I'll know you're okay. Do you need extra batteries? "

"You'll probably catch up tomorrow. We have plenty of batteries. Thanks." The tiny lights looked like fireflies darting among their dark silhouettes as the hikers picked their way up the rocky bank behind the shelter. I, too, dug out my flashlight. *April 25: Happy 24th Birthday, Kate. If you were here I'll bet you'd join the guys for an adventure of night hiking. I'm too much of a skeptic to think night hiking is all that advantageous. I wish you'd been with me during the hailstorm today. I can just see you running around catching the ice balls as they fell. Now that it's over the experience was pretty cool. No comparison to our time together in North Georgia though. I miss you.*

I didn't have long to wonder how the guys had managed. About three miles up the Trail I found them at Wind Rock talking to campers and munching on cheese sandwiches that hadn't come out of their packs. I joined the group hoping for a handout. When no one offered me one, Rain handed me the rest of his sandwich.

"Thanks," I inhaled the sandwich in one bite. "Did the moon ever come up?"

"It came up at midnight. By that time we were sick of dealing with the rocks. We slept off the Trail until these people arrived this morning. When they got food out we decided to visit them. Today we're headed to Twin Oaks Grocery in Sinking Creek Valley on VA 42 and then to the church pavilion. Want to stay with us?"

"Sounds like a more sensible plan than last night's, but the Handbook says hikers can't stay there anymore."

"The older books say you can. If we have a problem we'll find a barn. Meet us at 5 o'clock on the road."

"I'll be there," I said as I headed down the Trail. The newness of hiking had definitely worn off. I was ready for an escapade and was glad the guys wanted to include me. They were about the age of my son or my college students, and I was old enough to their mother, but their company created a diversion from empty shelters and lonely dinners. The Trail led me through rustling waist high grass, down a hill, past an old oak barn, through a swamp, over a stile, and onto the road. Two tenths of a mile to the right stood the Green Christian Church. Perched on a hill behind the church and a house sat the covered pavilion. No one appeared to be around. I dropped my pack on a picnic table and snacked on Trail mix. Within minutes Rain and Snail rounded the corner with arms full of brown paper bags. I ran toward them at the sight of food. "Let me help. What did you get? Did you have any trouble getting a ride?" I babbled like a child.

"You won't believe the Trail Magic. A guy picked us up, took us to town, and brought us back to the Trail! We're having rice, bean and cheese tacos, and strawberry shortcake. I got you grapefruit juice." Lowering his voice Rain asked, "Seen anyone?"

"Thanks for the juice, how sweet. I haven't seen a soul. If someone comes, I'll ask permission because look at the sign, 'No Overnight Camping'."

"Surely they'll let us eat before kicking us out," Snail said hopefully. And that we did. We cooked and ate until we were stuffed. A cold breeze blew up when the sun dropped. We pulled on fleece shirts and stood around conjuring up plans in case we were asked to leave. Pacing around to warm up, I walked to the back of the pavilion and absentmindedly turned the knob on a small block room attached to the pavilion. The door opened. Except for dust, dirt, and dead insects, the tiny room was nearly empty. "Hey you guys, look at this! A place to sleep."

Rain and Snail peered over my shoulder. Feeling a sense of urgency, I got the boys moving. "There's a broom. I'll sweep; you guys move the gear. Let's get in here before anyone comes. Look! A light switch! Electricity! We'll be in high cotton tonight!" I grabbed the broom while the guys gathered up the equipment.

The dead bugs and spiders went out the door, but the crickets were quite upset with having their home disrupted. They hopped erratically around the concrete floor to escape the broom. The space was barely wide enough for us to spread out mats, but we were so ecstatic about being out of the cold and out of plain view that cramped quarters were inconsequential.

As we settled in, Rain announced. "I'd like to eat at the Old Home Place in Catawba. They're open Thursday through Sunday and Catawba is still thirty-one miles away. People at the store told me we could catch a ride to Catawba from VA 621. So tomorrow we could eat at the restaurant and stay at the Catawba Hilton near the general store. The next day we could leave our packs there, hitch back to VA 621, and slack pack back to the hostel. You two want to join me?" Rain was a planner.

I was skeptical about losing time, but after figuring the mileage, I said, "Count me in." Snail gave us the high sign.

"You guys are sweet to include me. Now I think we need to see if light shows underneath the door before we get too excited about having electricity. I'll go out, you guys turn on the light, and I'll check the edges."

Turning off the light, I slipped back out into the chilly air. Snail shut the door and turned on the light. I checked the cracks. "Tight as a drum," I announced as Snail let me in. We settled down on the cold concrete with chirping crickets and stray spiders in our damp dwelling. We were in hiker heaven. That is, until we heard a car pull in the driveway. We looked at one another, held our breath, and silently marked places in our books or journals. We heard voices, then a door slam shut. If anyone had opened the door, they would have seen three wide-eyed thru-hikers lying side by side like animals prepared for slaughter. As if the tattered belongings would save us, we tightly clutched our sleeping bags and books across our chests with white-knuckled fists as we tried to look innocent. We waited and listened. I broke the silence. "Looks like we're safe."

"I'm out of here first thing!" Snail declared. Rain and I agreed. Picking back up our books or journals we read and wrote while crickets pounced on our sleeping bags like house cats. I was the last one to get drowsy. Like a good mother, I got up and turned out the light, feeling triply blessed for the company, full stomach, and light. *April 26: Today I met two middle-aged couples from different states who section hike together. I was impressed that older folks hike rather than vegetate in front of television sets. They loaded me up with snacks. This journey has so much to do with taking risks, facing fears, and making decisions. Rain and Snail have added an exciting dynamic. Rain is twenty-two and very resourceful and bright. Snail is twenty-six and very sweet. Thanks to them, I drank grapefruit juice, ate strawberries, and am sleeping with crickets.*

Snail left before daylight. Rain and I were close behind. Looking nonchalant we eased out the door, down the grassy bank, and onto the road. We didn't breathe until the Trail entered the woods. We agreed to meet at VA 621 at noon.

I arrived at the road first. It had been raining on and off all day. Another deluge hit as Rain and Snail came out of the woods. "Only one car has come along this dirt road in the half hour I've been here." I didn't feel positive about the plan.

"Let's start walking. I think the turn off to VA 311 into Catawba is only about a mile," suggested Rain.

"At least we'll stay warm. I've gotten cold walking circles in this parking area."

At the road we turned right and kept walking. Hiking on pavement made our feet very sore. I felt blisters forming under the moleskin on my heels. It was 3:30. The restaurant closed at 6:00. Only four cars had zoomed passed us in the first hour. The odds weren't good anyone would pick up three, soaked hikers. "I'm going to wait five more minutes and then I'm going to a likely looking house and ask for a ride," I announced.

"You're going to do what?" Rain wanted to know.

"What is a likely looking house?" Snail asked.

"A house with a truck in the yard that looks well cared for. Houses with nice yards indicate people who have respect for nature, maybe for us. We need one with evidence of kids. Older folks might not be as willing to get out in this kind of weather."

"I can't believe you'd dare do such a thing, but we need a miracle. Looking for a likely-looking house will take our minds off the rain." Snail shook his head in disbelief.

We walked on. The houses had huge yards and were far apart. Most didn't have trucks, looked too shabby, or just plain didn't feel right. Finally I saw it. "There's our likely looking house." A swing set stood in an attractively landscaped yard. There was evidence of remodeling and most important, an empty pickup truck stood waiting. "Wait here." Leaving my companions dripping in the road, I hustled up the driveway, on the porch, and knocked. A man with a broad smile opened the door.

"Sir, I'm a thru-hiker and I wonder if you would please give me, and ah, my two buddies a ride in your truck to the Old Home Place. We've been walking for hours and the restaurant closes at six. We won't make it without help. We'd appreciate it."

"Sure, it's several miles to town. Let me get a coat. Go ahead and hop in."

"Come on guys! Old Home Place, here we come!" I hollered.

Hunkered down out of the wind, we imagined melted butter on mashed potatoes and juicy fruit cobbler instead of freezing rain streaming in our mouths as we whizzed down the highway. In the parking lot we thanked the man, retrieved our packs, and stared at the restaurant. Well-dressed people lined the porch. "I didn't know this place was so fancy. Do you think we should go in looking like this?" asked Snail, looking down at his soaked, dirty clothes.

Rain looked as surprised as Snail and me, but had an answer to defend his idea. "We'll stick out like a sore thumb, but Wingfoot says the management welcomes thru-hikers because they add to the ambiance. So here comes today's dose of thru-hiker ambiance, Rain, Snail, and Wolf Woman!" We laughed at the effect our ambiance would have on those sitting near us as we set our packs under a porch around back and got out our sandals and money. We left our boots on the front porch and hung our fleece on the pegs far away from the door in hopes the dripping water wouldn't cause anyone to fall.

After making noble efforts in the bathrooms to dry our faces and look presentable, we were seated (to our horror) in the middle of a dining room full of elegant people. The family style meal was a flat rate for all you could eat. Dining with two vegetarians, Snail consumed the whole platter of roast beef and Southern style chicken. Rain and I kept our waitress busy replenishing the table with bowls of real mashed potatoes, crisp Cole slaw, hot rolls, sweet baked apples, and fruit cobbler, as puddles formed under our chairs.

Being in such close quarters revealed, even to us, our desperate need for a bath. We tried to remember to pull our arms to our sides when people passed or the waitress returned. When we no longer could hold another bite, we slipped out of our puddle-filled chairs. No one said anything derogatory, but the cashier seemed very eager to take our money, and none of us remember her saying, "Hurry on back!"

Back out in the rain, we walked to the General Store. The Catawba Hilton hostel was a larger block building than last night's but had no electricity. Joining two young hikers, we sprawled on our sleeping bags, too full to do anything except dream of mashed potatoes and cobbler.

My eighth maildrop brought letters from Suellen, Gloria, Kate, Judy, Deb, and the Equity Center. After reloading my pack and storing it at the Catawba Hilton, I put food in my raincoat pockets for a twenty-mile slack pack day over Dragon's Tooth. I caught a ride to the Trail before Snail and Rain woke up. Even though the Trail was full of boulders and thick mud, I moved free as a bird without the pack. Hiking was definitely an exercise in calculation. Having to monitor and adjust because of changing Trail conditions reminded me of trying to predict a nursing baby's schedule. Those days were twenty-plus years ago and today I had twenty-plus miles to hike by dark. Spring flowers, singing birds, and spectacular scenery made the effort worth it.

The sun hovered on the horizon behind me as I swung open the door to the Hilton. "I made it!" I gasped. "I'm glad the days are longer or I wouldn't have gotten here before sunset. Climbing Dragon's Tooth was really something, didn't you think?" I looked down at Rain and Snail. "How come you guys never passed me today?"

"Busted," Snail laughed. "We woke up too late to do the whole twenty miles so we only made it to VA 620 and then we came back."

"Will you be able to do that ten miles and still make it to Troutville tomorrow?" I didn't want to lose my hiking partners.

"No, we're going to skip them. Guess you'd call that yellow blazing. Personally, I don't know how you keep going day after day with hardly ever a day off. I need a day off at least once a week," Rain sounded defensive.

I didn't know who was supposed to feel guilty, but I knew I didn't. I was walking every step to Maine. "Guess I'm driven, but I have to finish and get back before school starts. There is a difference between people with unlimited time and those on a schedule. Everyone has to walk his or her own walk. It doesn't matter to me if you skip the section. I'm just glad for the adventure and your company. I suspected something was up when you didn't pass me. Hey, have you guys eaten?"

"No, we waited for you." Rain had fired up his stove by candlelight and boiled water for rice and beans. I contributed fig bars, tea bags, and humus. Snail had bought bread and cheese in the store. "We met a guy today who is willing to slack pack our gear to a motel in Troutville tomorrow. He will pick up the packs at 5:00 in the morning. Do you want to share the cost of a motel room? I don't know about you, but I am past due for a shower, clean clothes, and a day off.

"I won't take a day off, but I need to shower and wash clothes. Count me in."

Losing my companions clouded the excitement of slack packing. Slack packing was restful, even though I was doing long mileage. Fearful we would oversleep, I tossed and turned all night. At 4:30 a.m., I woke Rain and Snail. We rolled up our bags by flashlight and hoisted our packs into the waiting car. Back inside, we slumped against the wall. Shivering in the chilly morning air, we waited for daylight, trusting our packs would be at the Comfort Inn when we arrived twenty-one miles down the Trail. The trade-off for sleeping in a building, home cooked food and slack packing meant trusting the process.

McAfee Knob is an anvil-shaped slab of rock jutting out into space. Farther up the Trail, the stony flat ledges of Tinker Cliffs offered another of Virginia's best places to take photographs. We took advantage of the brilliant sunshine and clear air as we ate and rested. Rain was expecting traveler's checks and his mother's brownies in a maildrop, so he and Snail picked up their paces after our break. I was hiking at nearly three miles an hour but still couldn't keep up with their pace. I didn't mind, hiking without a pack meant I didn't have to concentrate as much on my feet, and my mind was free to wander. I wasn't sure whether my thoughts moved my feet or my pace kept me thinking.

Black highways spread among sprawling green farmland with spotted black and white cows, and stacked red silos above Troutville's snarled traffic. Being in town was overwhelming, but walking into the motel room was a culture shock. Showered and in clean clothes, the guys lounged in front of the television munching chips with salsa and guzzling Coke like they knew no other life. I couldn't believe the transformation and only recognized them by their voices. "You made it!" Snail greeted me at the door. The room smelled like cologne advertisements in magazines.

"We waited for you to go eat. There's plenty of hot water. Want one of Mom's brownies?" Rain handed me the box. I took one, knowing I could easily eat them all.

"Thanks. These are almost as good as the ones you made at High Pockets," I said with a grin. "I'll eat another after supper."

Fragrant and fresh in a clean tank top and shorts, I asked, "Do I look as unlike a thru-hiker as you guys?" My dripping wet hair hung unbraided for the first time in days.

"You look good enough to go to Shoney's," laughed Snail. "First time I've seen your hair down, looks good," he added with enough of a compliment for a fellow half my age. Pulling on dirty fleece jackets, we headed to the hot food bar. After eating, I walked to the truck stop laundromat. The guys returned to watching television.

Truck stops are not safe places for women, especially alone at night. But I needed to wash. I walked into the laundromat dressed in a sleeveless T-shirt and shorts with nothing underneath. The lid on the last machine in the row of four was up. I layered my clothes around the tub, poured in the soap, closed the lid, and jumped on top. Pulling the data book out of my pocket, I tried to look occupied while keeping my sixth sense tuned in to the five burly men who were engaged in trucker talk between the door and me. I sat undisturbed until my clothes finished washing. Climbing off the machine, I pulled the clothes out and carried them to the dryers located near the men. As I shut the dryer door, four of the men left the room. The one remaining man looked at me and said, "There's plenty of room if you want a seat, Missy."

"No, thank you." My hand trembled as I fished coins out of my pocket. Looking down at the handful of silver, I saw I only had one quarter. The man noticed my dilemma.

"I have quarters if you need some," he offered, holding out a handful of change.

I didn't want to set myself up to make conversation. Neither did I want to be rude or leave my clothes. Pulling a dollar bill out of my pocket, I held it out. "I'll buy four."

"Sounds like a fair trade," he said, reaching for the dollar and placing four quarters in my hand.

"Thank you," I said, hoping that was the end of our need to communicate.

"You traveling far?"

I answered in as noncommittal sentences as I could. "I'm a thru-hiker on the Appalachian Trail.

"Yeah, I see hikers when I come into town. You're brave to be hiking alone."

I wondered what made him think I was hiking alone but I'd didn't want him to know it was true. "I'm with two guys and I know lots of hikers."

"How far is it up to Maine, anyway? And what made you wanta hike?"

"It's 2,160 miles. I've wanted to do it since I was a kid," I answered.

"What'd ya do for training? You got some mighty, strong legs. You must be quite a sight in the gym." I huddled near my dryer, ready to grab my clothes and run if necessary. The man stayed seated.

"Not much, I swim and run."

"Ah come on, you don't get your good looks and big muscles from floating around a pool. Bet you're quite a number in a bathing suit."

I said nothing.

"How'd you get outa work, Missy? Did ya leave yer ole man with the kids?"

I didn't want him to know I wasn't married but that I did have grown children so maybe he'd think I was older than he might presume. "My children are in their twenties and on their own. I took a semester off from teaching college." Then adding, "It's important for people to do the things that mean something to them. People need goals and the opportunity to see them through. We only get one go-round at life you know."

The sharp edges of the man's countenance softened. His burly attitude changed. Somehow, I didn't fear him quite as much. "Yeah, you're right ma'am. I'm right proud of you. Not many women dare get out here and hike a dream. Doubt I'd be much good at mountain climbing, but I've always wanted to bike across America. I read something about them turning old railroad beds to bike Trails. You reckon I could bike one?"

"Sure you could. Do you have a bike?" I was eager to get the attention off me.

"No, I'm on the road and in these truck stops week in and week out. Suppose I could get one, though. Heck, ya got something lady, about life and all.

Mine's not been full of too much good. Maybe I oughta think about doing a few things different."

I wasn't sure if he meant he'd done a lot of bad things or just hadn't done much of anything worth writing home about. I didn't care to find out. My dryer had stopped. I quickly packed hot clothes into a sack. The man silently watched me with a pensive look on his unshaven face. Somehow I got a feeling that talking about my determination to carry through with my dream had a positive impact on this burly truck driver.

As I headed for the door he opened his mouth. "Good to meet ya, Missy. You just may have inspired me to take to the trails on a bike instead of always taking to the road in a truck. Hey, that was almost poetic, don't ya think, Teach? Glad to talk to you. You done me some good. Probably done you some good too. Be careful now, especially when you stop in these here trucker places." He paused. I reached the door and he continued. "There's a lotta truckers out there that sit in laundromats waiting for ladies like you to come along. You watch out for them kind, ya hear?"

"I will," I said as I moved through the door.

Out of eyeshot, I stopped short. The whole time I'd been in the laundromat he'd never once moved to put clothes in or out of any of the machines. None of the machines were occupied when I left. I turned to catch a last glimpse of him. He sat in the same seat, waiting. Wondering what he was waiting for made chill bumps run up and down my spine. The somber look on his face as he stared at the washing machine I had used told me I'd been blessed with a double portion of Trail Magic. Trail safety for sure and just maybe the opportunity to turn an unsavory character into a cross-country biker.

Safe in the motel room, I told Rain and Snail about the experience. I'd only met Rain a week ago but we had gotten very close. I crawled in bed not wanting to think about leaving them, but eager to be out of town.

After breakfast at Shoney's, I pulled on my backpack. "I don't know how you do it! You're one of the most determined women I've ever known. I'm real glad to have been part of your experience." Snail hugged me real big.

"I need to keep going. Let me hear from both of you after we make it to Katahdin. Thanks for being good to me." I hugged the sweet young men.

"It's been fun." Rain encircled the pack. "I'll never forget sleeping with the crickets. Keep adding ambiance to restaurants!" Thinking of chasing crickets around the block room and leaving puddles under the table at the Old Home Place eased the awkwardness of walking out of a motel with a backpack on. There was no car to get into and it wasn't time to go home. Out on the highway a tractor-Trailer roared by, blowing his horn. Chill bumps ran down my spine. I didn't try to hitch a ride back to the Trail. The fast pace and fears of town stops confirmed the Trail as home. I only had enough daylight left to hike the ten miles to Wilson Creek Shelter. Only Cowpenski joined me. A full moon spilled warm light into the shelter. I smiled, grateful to be alive.

The next morning after hot cereal, nuts, and dried fruit, I headed for Bryant Ridge Shelter, twenty miles away. Wood sorrel, trillium, spring beauties, May apples, and lady slippers colored the forest in pinks, whites, and green. Because I was hiking north into cooler climates, I'd been seeing May apples make their annual appearance ever since leaving Georgia. Although it was late April, frost still occurred at high elevations. Spring flowers drooped pitifully under soggy withered leaves. Between Wilson Creek and Bryant Ridge Shelters, the Trail crossed the Blue Ridge Parkway eight times. Incredible views of the one hundred miles that remained before entering the Shenandoah National Park beckoned me. I seldom passed people except when an increase of hikers let me know that weekends had arrived. Rhododendron bushes and flaming orange azaleas were company enough.

Built in 1993, the Bryant Ridge Shelter was a memorial to the AT hiker, Nelson Garnett. Facing a bubbling creek, the shelter's three levels included sleeping platforms, an upper level, and a covered porch with a picnic table. Heavy iron hooks for packs and prongs for food sacks hung from the walls. An attractive rustic box housed the journal and hiker information. A plexi-glass window in the roof provided views of the trees and sky. Melodious birds, a gentle wind, and a soothing creek were my companions. Longer days gave me more time to journal. *May 1: I'm on a roll to get to Harper's Ferry by May 15th, half the distance to Katahdin, in half my time. I know I can do it. My under teen mileage days have mushroomed into twenty. The pack is an extension of my body, even when it's full. I feel naked when I take it off. The weather and terrain changes still create fear. About the time I establish a rhythm the grading changes and rock climbing or mud slopping slows me down. Gratitude for my ability to endure fluctuates with a deep unrest that I won't finish. The AA program encourages alcoholics to build sobriety one day at a time. I'm building success one step at a time. I've been hiking sixty-two days. March first seems long ago. Most frightening is the thought that the trip will end. This simple nomad life is more suited to my natural rhythms and tempo than the rat race I left.*

After filling water bottles and taking a sponge bath, I headed back across the creek and up the steep Floyd Mountain. On the top I met my fourth group of Trail volunteers busily cutting downed trees and trimming undergrowth in preparation for summer. I was not looking forward to sharing shelters with hordes of scout troops and whiny kids. I'd learned the importance of freedom and choices. Being able to stop, take pictures, rest, and eat when I wanted were luxuries I would never again take for granted.

On the grassy summit of Apple Orchard Mountain, I took off my pack and flopped on the ground without asking anyone's permission or approval. I stared up into the clear blue sky. The privilege of being free to indulge in a moment of stillness was as precious as the moment itself. I was free from the pressure of attending to the expectations of others. Only the passing hours dictated when I needed to move.

Looking over the 4,225 foot summit, the highest point until I would climb Moosilauke in New Hampshire, brought back memories of taking breaks with children who were sure they were at death's door because they'd climbed a hill. Memories of watching the Connecticut River diligently form the boundary between Vermont and New Hampshire flowed through my mind as easily as the clouds drifting on the winds over the slow moving James River in the valley below. The scraggly apple trees dotting the hillside reminded me of the orchard I played in as a child. These aged craggy trees were making just as noble an effort to produce fruit as the old trees used to in the Connecticut Valley Orchard. Apple Orchard Mountain was a special landmark in the twenty-three mile hike to Matts Creek Shelter. Vermont poet Robert Frost's words nudged me to my feet: "I have miles to go before I sleep."(67).

The trail continued to cross the Blue Ridge Parkway until it left Petites Gap and headed to the Big Cove Branch. Then the terrain changed from open fields and deciduous forests with mountain views to scrubby forests in thick rhododendron thickets. As the Trail wound round and round the narrow mountainous trail in an effortless but endless manner, I understood what slabbing meant. For ten miles dusty chip-like soil flew up from under my feet. Finally the Trail descended. The faster it dropped, the faster my feet flew into the gorge and the deep creek crevasses. I was anxious to strip down and submerge my tired body in the deep indentations in the rock. I'd only passed one group of students and expected to have privacy. That is, until I spotted movement up ahead. Two people I didn't recognize! "Hello, coming around you." A man and woman turned and faced me.

"How do you do. I'm Wolf Woman. Ya'll headed to Matt's Creek Shelter?"

"Yes, we're Annie and the Salesman. You thru-hiking?" asked the woman.

"Yes, I started at Springer March first."

"We thru-hiked in '93. My wife and I are out for a week. Then we're headed to my daughter's graduation and then Trail Days in Damascus. We've hardly seen any thru-hikers this year. It'll be nice to visit with you at the shelter." The man adjusted his pack. "Come around us. You seem to be on a roll."

"Thank you, see you at the shelter."

I wasn't going to be alone, but visiting with past thru-hikers could be useful.

A footbridge over inviting pools led to the shelter. I prepared supper while I waited for Annie and the Salesman. Chatting about the cold baths, they crossed the bridge ten minutes later. I was in the middle of cooking, so they were first to soak in the frigid, exhilarating water. An hour later I lowered myself in the natural bathtub, gasping as the water flowed over my middle. It was delightful and stimulating. I soaked away the grime of the Trail as I thought of Suellen, who hates dirt as much as I love it. Today was her birthday and I wished she were here. I'd gathered feathers and tree bark to send her. I lingered in the pool until the water froze my hind side and shivers to ran down my back.

Annie and the Salesman were also vegetarians. "I get my protein from humus, polenta, and bean flakes that only need to be soaked in water. I doubt if I get enough vegetables though."

"We dried vegetables in a dehydrator and mixed them with rice, pasta, or dried beans. That's about the only way to get a good variety," Annie explained.

"The chair of my department gave me dehydrated vegetables to keep me going between stops," I said.

Annie laughed, "Just keep going, that was our motto. You were smart to start early. We hiked from April until September and it was real hot. Sweat poured down our faces all day and all night. The mosquitoes were terrible in New England."

"I grew up in New England with the pesky devils and know how bad they are."

"You're moving right along and your gear looks good. You'll make it." The Salesman's encouragement was good to hear.

"I think I see someone coming!" Annie gazed down the Trail.

"Hey, I saw him at a shelter and in the forest fire back in the Smokies."

"Wolf Woman! You're making good time. Good to see you!"

I jumped up and gave the fellow a hug. "Where is the girl you were hiking with?"

"Hallybop and I hike some sections alone and some together."

"Wasn't that snow beautiful at Peck's Corner?" I asked.

"What snow? We didn't see any snow. I remember it being so cold we stayed in our sleeping bags until the sun was high and then we built a fire."

"You missed quite a sight." I was sorry they'd missed the snow but the experience had been so spiritual, I hardly wanted to talk about it.

"My name is Ed. you've got a nice hike along the creek to the bridge tomorrow."

"Sounds nice," spoke up Annie. "I love following water and sleeping by it."

"Speaking of sleeping, I could use some of that," the Salesman yawned.

"Me too, good night." I said, crawling into my bag. Darkness fell over our secluded spot and the creek lulled us to sleep.

Rain beating on the shelter roof and pelting in the creek made it difficult to get out of bed the next morning. Heading out behind Annie and Salesman, I left Ed deep in his sleeping bag as I had in the Smokies. Seeing people I'd met on the Trail put the journey in perspective. I was halfway though Virginia. In four days I'd be in the Shenandoah National Park. While my feet moved up and down the mountains, the days also moved. The days, the Trail, and my progress moved as one. Today they moved in the rain.

The James River signifies land that was once claimed by northern Iroquois tribes. After crossing railroad tracks, the slow-moving river gracefully wrapped the valley in a dark ribbon of lace between towering mountains. As I walked on through the storm I imagined raindrops racing down the mountain to join other raindrops on their way to the ocean. I imaged the raindrops enjoying the freedom of flowing over the land after being hurled thousands of feet through the air. Just as water's movement depends on the shape of the land, so had the dynamics of my companions changed.

As raindrops drip off tree limbs, trickle down embankments, or stream off rooftops, they parallel thru-hikers as they scramble down banks, slide under cliffs, and step over boulders. Just as I am deterred when I stop in towns, take a day off, or spend time on mountain tops, water too, gets sidetracked when it mingles in puddles, gathers on flower petals, or stands in rock crevasses. Whether side tracked or rerouted, both water and thru-hikers depend on movement to reach their destinations. Standing impedes progress for both. As raindrops splashed on my head, I splashed my way to The Wildwood Restaurant and campground off U.S. 501 near Big Island, Virginia.

I'd mailed a box of supplies from Catawba to the campground. After crossing the bridge, road signs listed familiar cities. I was disoriented and had not a clue which way to go. After thirty minutes of hitch hiking, a car with a well-dressed man at the wheel stopped. "Sir, could you give me a ride to the campground?" I asked, scrutinizing his appearance. The car's interior was clean and I didn't see evidence of alcohol.

"Sure. Hop in. It's a mile or two down the road. A bit too cold to be camping, isn't it? You a thru-hiker?" he asked as he helped drag my dripping pack onto my lap. I felt safer when my pack was near me. I could get to my mace and knife if I needed them.

"Yes. I left March first." I gave strangers as little information as possible.

"You're not hiking alone, are you? You know two women were murdered in the Shenandoah National Park last year?"

"I heard, I'm just stopping to get a maildrop."

"Here you are. You be careful. It is not safe to hitchhike around here. The papers are full of stories about some crazy attacking children and women on Route 29."

"I'll be careful. Thank you for the ride." I hoisted the pack up on my shoulders.

"Mind what I said, now."

Chill bumps ran up and down my spine as I walked to the restaurant. Talk of the last year's murders was still prominent conversation in Virginia. Unfortunately, the incident created bad publicity for the Appalachian Trail. The women were not thru-hikers and had been camping off the Trail.

The store looked closed. I knocked, anyway. Remodeling was in process but no workers were in sight. As I turned away a woman opened the door. "May I help you?"

"Yes, I'm a thru-hiker. Do you know where I can pick up a maildrop?" I asked with full confidence that it had arrived.

"Try up there on the hill at the campground office."

"Thank you, Ma'am."

In the small office sat an older fellow behind the counter watching television and eating a sandwich. "Can I help ya?" he asked, never taking his eyes off the program.

I repeated my question. With his eyes glued to the television, he got up and walked behind the corner. "This you?" he asked handing me a box.

"That's it!" I said, "Thank you. Mind if I load up my pack here?"

"Go right ahead. You hiking alone? Not safe to be doing that ya know! Women getting shot left and right out there." A commercial had come on the television.

"I have people to hike with." I said curtly, hoping to cut off further disheartening comments. Murders left and right were a bit out of context. The man opened his mouth to say more but his program returned and he lost his train of thought. I detest television but for once was grateful for its invention.

After loading up I headed for the door. "Thank you."

"Hurry on back," the man said never taking his eyes off the screen.

The first place I was hurrying to was the deli across the street. "I'll take two vegetarian sandwiches, that's vegetables with cheese no meat." I said to the girl behind the counter. After twenty-seven years of being a vegetarian, I'd learned it was necessary to define a vegetarian sandwich. While I waited for the sandwiches, I went out to the gas pumps to wait for a vehicle headed in the direction of the bridge. A battered truck pulled up to the pumps. "Sir, would you mind giving me a ride to the Trail?"

"Reckon I could do that. Toss your pack in the back. I'm heading that way as soon as I put some gas in this ole rig."

Tossing the pack over the tailgate, I went to get my sandwiches. Back out at the truck I stuck the sandwiches in the pack and climbed in. The man got in. He didn't say a word. The silence was strange but spared me a lecture. The man stopped the truck where the Trail entered the woods. I thanked him, retrieved my pack, and walked into the woods.

It was ten o'clock. I had twenty miles to hike to Brown Mountain Creek Shelter. The rain had stopped. The Trail wound easily over short knolls, low ridges, and narrow valleys. The fields were full of cows, creeks, and craggy trees. Majestic pines grew among smooth rocks. The scenery was beautiful and diverse. As I topped a particular hill, a chorus of zealous frogs greeted me with an explosion of spring. A deep blue pond, glistening with bright yellow lily pads, masked the croaking harmonious melody. Knowing the timid creatures stop when they sense danger, I tiptoed, my boots squishing in the muddy ground. As I suspected, they stopped singing when I reached the pond. Mystified by how frogs instantly stop at once, I imagined a thin reed attached to a leg of every frog in the pond. At the sign of danger a sentinel frog tugs on the string signaling the frogs to stop singing. As I enjoyed the beauty and my sandwich, I wondered if the frogs were getting tangled up in their emergency reeds while they swam about waiting for me to leave. The longer I pondered the ceasing of the symphony, the sleepier I got. The day had turned warm. I headed down the Trail.

After a short road walk, the Trail led me up a stairway and over a dam. The water pouring over the dam came from a deep lake tucked between two mountains. For the next six miles I followed the bubbling frothing creek that fed the pond. Deer leaped across the Trail and birds twittered in the trees. Even a rabbit hopped across my path. As dusk drew near, my daily anxiety returned. The days were getting longer, but so were my expectations to hike longer mileage. Every day I feared I wouldn't reach the shelter before dark. Every day I made it, but every afternoon the doubts returned. Today was no different. As always, I kept walking and as always, the shelter appeared. A backpack hung from the rafters. "Hello." I announced my arrival.

"It's me, Chief."

"Chief, what a surprise. It's good to see you. Where's the rest of the gang? I can't believe I caught up to you. I've enjoyed your journal entries. Seen Ron and Pat?" I couldn't stop asking questions. I hadn't seen Chief or any of my other Trail family since March 25 in Hot Springs. It was May 3rd and two states later.

"Stork and Lynx left this morning in the rain. I hate hiking in the rain so I stayed to wait it out and fell asleep. When I woke up it was too late to start today. Broken Road and Pilgrim are a day or two ahead. I think the Derbys are behind. Stryder is way ahead." Chief flicked cigarette ashes off the edge of the shelter. Earphones dangled from his neck and a deck of cards lay beside him. I couldn't imagine carrying the weight.

"I'm going to the creek and wash up before it gets any chillier." Out of eyeshot, I stripped down and washed up. The water wasn't as cold as Matts Creek. I rinsed out my green shirt and underwear with the hopes they would dry by morning. If they didn't, it wouldn't be the first time I'd put on wet clothes and worn them until the sun or my body heat dried them, or until sweat made them so wet it didn't matter whether they had dried or not. I put on my only spare shorts and shirt. Back in the shelter with purified water, I cooked macaroni and cheese and broccoli soup to eat with the sandwich.

Chief told me he had shin splint trouble. I gave him some Aleve. "Montebello should have medicine. I'm picking up a maildrop there."

"Where are you staying in Montebello?" Chief wanted to know.

"I don't know. Surely, there'll be a pavilion. Want to join me?

"Maybe, I'll see how I feel in the morning. Thanks, Wolf Woman."

"Good night." A soothing creek put me to sleep for the second night in a row.

Reaching up in the rafters the next morning, I pulled down damp clothes. After breakfast I left Chief snoring in his sleeping bag. The scenario reminded me of earlier days when I would leave before the others, only to have them fly by me later in the day. I was part way up Cold Mountain before Chief strode by me and announced his leg wasn't any better. He scoffed at the idea of putting wet leaves down his socks.

Seeley-Woodworth Shelter was near the Trail so I decided to sign the journal. Leaving my pack on the Trail, I flew down the short trail around the front of the shelter, and stopped short. A hiker was curled up asleep. "Chief, are you all right?"

"My leg got bad coming down those hills and hurts like hell. I'm staying here tonight. I'll hitch a ride from Montebello tomorrow into Waynesboro."

"I'll carry some of your gear if you want to get to Montebello today. Take some more Aleve."

"Thanks for the medicine, but I'm staying here. Maybe I'll see you in town tomorrow." Lighting another cigarette, he rolled over, blowing smoke into the rafters.

"I hate to leave you here. Do you have enough water?"

"Yeah, plenty, thanks. I'm okay. See ya down the Trail."

"Okay, be safe." I didn't want to leave him alone and injured, but there was nothing I could do. The guys appreciated my motherly touch just so long, then I could tell they wanted me to turn it off or get over it. However, we were comrades. On way the back to the pack, it dawned on me what a solo experience hiking really is. It is one thing to say, "walk your own walk," and it is quite another thing to do it, especially when you are injured, or even wet, lonely, or scared. Where was the gang when Chief needed them?

But what could they have done? His situation was not life threatening. Had his buddies been here, they too probably would have gone on. Thru-hikers must take responsibility for themselves whether they walk with companions or not. Opportunities to trust one's judgment present themselves daily. How hikers react to situations often determine whether thru-hikes are completed. Chief's injury showed me not to take a single step for granted. I, too, had been set back by shin splints. I hoped Chief would overcome the challenge and keep going.

Coming to a rough dirt road that looked like a tractor path, I wondered if it could be the road to town. I'd seen rough roads that were Trail intersections, but this was a bit too primitive. Looking at my watch, I figured I had another fifteen minutes, or a half a mile, before I'd reach the road. I kept going although I had not a clue whether I'd made the right decision. Standing was not an option.

Motivation moved me forward, yet again.

Fifteen minutes later I came to a gravel road that didn't look much different from the last one, but a rough, wooden AT sign lay on the ground. The Trail continued across the intersection. The Handbook warned that traffic was not likely. The road was full of rocks and potholes. After a snack, I headed down the sharp incline. I walked for an hour. My legs and feet ached. Walking on gravel was harder than the Trail. At the fish hatchery I looked for someone to give me a ride. It was Sunday and the place was deserted. By the time I reached town I vowed if I ever thru-hiked again I would not use Montebello as a maildrop. Walking two miles to the Post Office was ridiculous.

The store and gas station also served as the office for the Camping and Fishing Resort. I dropped my pack on the porch and went inside. Wood floors creaked under my heavy boots as I wandered aimlessly about the attractive store. "May I help you, Honey?" came a thick Southern drawl from behind the counter.

"I'll take a slice of cheese, please, ma'am, a couple of muffins, and this quart of grapefruit juice. Everything looks so good."

"You hiking alone, honey?" asked the woman as she rang up the items.

"There's a hiker coming in behind me." I was glad I'd seen Chief. Maybe I wouldn't get a lecture about the dangers of hiking alone.

"I wonder if there might be a pavilion or shed I could sleep under? I don't have a tent and need to spend the night so I can pick up a maildrop in the morning." I didn't mention money hoping to avoid the fee of a campsite.

"We aren't open for the season and the pavilion up on the hill is locked but there is a porch. We don't usually put up hikers." The woman pointed out the door.

"That's perfect! I'll be quiet and not make a mess. Thank you so much. What time do you open and do ya'll have a phone?" I was so excited I could hardly contain myself. "You are so kind!"

"The phone is on the porch. We open at 8:00. Don't tell anyone I let you stay."

"I won't! Thanks again." After buying two more muffins and a cup of coffee, I headed to the phone. Checking in with Suellen was always first on the list. An eternity passed before her voice broke in to the incessant ringing.

"Suellen! I'm in Montebello and will be at Auntie Sue's in two days." "Are you all right? How's your leg? How is the weather? It has done nothing but rain here for days. Everyone's asking about you. Your dog Lars misses you. He quit eating. The vet says he's depressed. It sure is lonely around here." The sound of her voice brought back the secure life I'd exchanged for walking day after day and spending night after night in the elements. Minutes earlier I had been ecstatic about sleeping on concrete floor. Now it didn't seem so luxurious. I could be home in a real bed. But if I were, I wouldn't be where I'm supposed to be.

Calling home boosted my moral, but distracted my vision. Staying in the moment was vital if I hoped to climb Katahdin. I called Auntie Sue to tell her I'd be in Rockfish Gap on Tuesday, May 7th. I looked forward to my first day off in two weeks. My last shower was eight days ago. The Shenandoah foothills glistened in the sunset as I sipped soup, water from a spigot, and munched muffins.

At 8 o'clock sharp, I was at the Post Office. I was five days ahead of my schedule and another box waited me at Auntie Sue's, so I left a box of supplies at the store for her companion, Waverly, to pick up. I would be at Rusty's hostel off the Blue Ridge Parkway by nightfall. With muffins, grapefruit juice, and coffee, I joined the only customer at a table. "Sir," I asked when the customer and the clerk came to a break in their conversation, "I wonder if you could give me a ride back to the Trail?"

"Sure, but you'll have to show me the way," he said pleasantly.

"I will," I promised, not mentioning how bad the road was and hoping his vehicle would make it up the hill.

Just as we were leaving, Chief came in, limping badly. "I'm catching a ride to Waynesboro. Coming down that hill nearly killed me." After buying cigarettes and candy bars, Chief retreated to the porch. No one questioned the road conditions.

"Ready to go?" asked the man.

"When you are," I answered, holding my breath and hoping he wasn't driving a sports car. I thanked the woman and followed the man to a small pickup truck. I breathed a sigh of relief as I pushed the pack past toolboxes and boards hanging out the tailgate.

"See you down the Trail. I hope your leg gets better." I called to Chief.

"Thanks, me too." Chief said miserably. I never saw Chief again.

"Take that road to the left and go straight." I could have walked faster but walking two miles straight up hill was wasted energy. I had eighteen miles to hike. With every dip in and out of the potholes came loud scrapes from under the truck.

"This isn't a passable road, and this truck hangs low," the man said nervously.

I didn't say a word. We were still moving and we weren't stuck.

"Can I turn around at the top?" he wanted to know. I was about to answer when we heard a terrible crash. "Oh, no, there go my tools!" gasped the man.

"I'll get them. Maybe it was only boards." I said, glad for a chance to ignore his question. I jumped out of the truck and ran around to the back. Tools and boards littered the road. I gathered them up.

"I can't go any farther, but I don't see anywhere to turn around. Is there a place at the top?" He asked again.

"I don't know," I said in all honesty. "But I would think so. There's not one here, so we may as well keep going." We got in and resumed our snail's pace up the hill.

"I see the top," I announced excitedly.

"I don't see a turn around. I'll have to back all the way down to the fish hatchery. This truck doesn't back well." The man was clearly disgusted. Lighting a cigarette, he brought the truck to a stop. I got out and retrieved my pack. I was about to hoist it on when I noticed tire marks into the woods.

"Sir, I think you can turn around here. I'll help you."

"All right," he said reluctantly. I set the pack in the woods and coached him into the ruts. After much maneuvering the truck was headed downhill.

"Thank you. Sorry to cause you trouble," I called after him. As I put on my pack I thought about all the problem-solving opportunities I was getting. Staying calm and aware was vital. Making it to Rusty's Hostel before dark was my next challenge.

For north-bounders, climbing the Priest is preparation for climbs in the White Mountains. Going north is easier than south but the switchbacks are monotonously never-ending. I didn't notice; the name of the mountain made me think of my father, Emerson C. Priest, Jr., known as Pete. Daddy would have been a fun companion. He would have grumbled a lot, but lovingly. He would have wanted to stop and have a snack at every turn and would have stuck his fishing pole in all the streams. Daddy would have wanted to shoot the deer and catch the bears. He was a carpenter and would have remodeled all the shelters. Hikers would have appreciated that, but if I wanted him to climb Katahdin with me, I would have to ask him to meet me in Maine. Daddy loved jawing with people too much to be bothered with time. He would have kept everyone up late telling stories. As I started up the Priest I took a deep breath, allowing Daddy's spirit to gently push me.

The soft contour made the mountains look like hills. However, I knew they were toothpicks compared to what was ahead. Priest Mountain got its name because a huge vertical boulder rests on top of a horizontal boulder at the summit. Towering up into the sky, the posture of the upright boulder resembles a Priest in black robes, guarding hikers as they walk by. The space felt awesome, sacred, and ceremonial. I focused my camera on the massive rock and sent a silent "thank you" to my father and the spirit of the Trail for answering the dream of a ten-year old child. Because of Daddy, more than my dream had come to fruition. I was comfortable in the natural world.

Beaver dam excursions were one of my fondest childhood memories. Sitting quietly next to Daddy, my chubby legs would fall asleep as we watched beavers build dams. As a child I didn't know what an impact the motivated creatures would have on my future. Every twig, branch, and movement was necessary to their goal. While stepping through swollen creeks, washed out gullies, and mud-filled sections, I thought of the motivated furry creatures. Gloria was right; Daddy would have been proud of me and Katie was right, I was driven and motivated. Thru-hikers had to be.

Rusty's was near mile marker 13.6 off the Blue Ridge Parkway. From Maupin Field Shelter I was told to take the fire road to the Parkway, turn left and walk one mile to the fenced driveway. I arrived at Maupin Shelter at nearly dusk and couldn't find the fire road. I was tempted to stay for fear of being stuck in the woods after dark, but I wanted to see Rusty's. I continued, almost jogging, two more miles down the Trail and came out onto the Parkway. I started jogging. I reached the road as the sun reached the horizon. Ten minutes passed before a car came down the road. I flagged it down and a man rolled down a window. "Sir, do you know where a hostel called Rusty's is?" I could smell alcohol on his breath. His eyes looked wild. The inside of his car was a mess.

"No honey, but we'll find it. Hop in."

"No thank you. I just thought I'd ask, " I walked way.

"Hey come back here! I thought you wanted to get to Rusty's. Get in the car."

I ignored the man and walked slowly down the road. If I returned to the woods I feared I'd be trapped if he came after me. "Get back here Missy! Don't be afraid. I won't hurt you. I'll take you to Rusty's." He followed me in his beat up vehicle.

I walked along the grass. Another car came up behind the first man's car. I ran back. A younger man rolled down the window. He had long dirty hair and an unkempt beard. I wouldn't have trusted him but I needed help. "Sir, do you know where Rusty's hostel is?" Smoke poured out from under the hood of the car.

"Lady, I've heard of Rusty but my car is over-heating. I gotta get to a gas station."

"Please wait until another car comes. If this were my car, sir, I'd let it cool down a bit before driving any farther. I have water you can put in the radiator, after it cools off." I talked slowly, trying to stall the man with the fuming car. Meanwhile the man in the first car was doing his own fuming as he yelled obscenities and accusations that I'd run off with another man.

"I need to get going, lady. A bottle of water ain't goin' to fill the radiator." He was about to say more when a car came up the Parkway. Yelling, I ran in the road. The car screeched to a halt. "Having trouble ma'am?" asked a third single man.

I repeated my request, as I smelled for alcohol. A Bible lay on the seat and child's car seat was fastened in the back. The man was well dressed. "Yes ma'am, I know Rusty well. He does a great service to hikers. Hop in. He lives around the corner." I glanced back as we drove away. The two other men were leaning against their cars looking like sheep that had lost their shepheards. "You a thru-hiker?" asked the driver.

"Yes, I left March first from Springer."

"You're making good time. I haven't seen many hikers so far this year."

"I guess it is early," I mumbled as I searched the woods for a chain link fence. "How much further is it?" The man looked safe, but I felt very uneasy. "I thought it was just around the corner? It seems as though we'd been traveling for miles."

"We are almost there. Don't worry. The gate won't be open and you'll have to walk from the driveway." At mention of gate, I felt better. But we kept driving. My heart raced and my stomach felt sick. I concentrated on how I could get out of the car. Just about the time I was ready to scream, "I'm going to throw up," the man stopped the car in front of a gate that read "Rusty's."

"Here you go," he smiled.

"Thank you," was all I could stammer as I stumbled out. My heart was still racing as I walked across the yard. Hikers greeted me. Stork was the only hiker I knew. We relived our night with the skunk on Blood Mountain, March third. Some hikers were section hikers but most were thru-hikers who had been ahead of me. Some people, including Phoenix, a woman thru-hiker, I recognized from the journals. The atmosphere was relaxing. I leaned my pack against a wall and flopped on the couch. I was safe. I sat and said nothing. The hikers respected my need for space. In the kitchen a woman prepared hamburger meat to cook on an outside grill. In the yard hikers played cards, read books, and cooked meals. The tension flowed out of me in the peaceful atmosphere.

Rusty was a small man whose hair had once been red. He owned a large chunk of land that bordered the Park. As a backwoods Virginian, he valued simple, rustic living. His hostel attracted young folks who often stayed for weeks. He loved signs. Signs lined the driveway and the property. The words *Hard Time Hollow* sprawled across the side of a barn in big white letters. The main house had a kitchen, bunk room, sitting room, living room, and a porch. An elaborate privy covered with signs and pictures was accessible by a long ramp. Food was kept in a springhouse. Gardens, compost piles, and old machinery dotted the land. Full of old relics and antiques, the house used kerosene, battery, and solar lights and was heated with wood. Rusty told me to help myself in the kitchen. The offer sounded appealing until I discovered mice tracks everywhere. The food was old, moldy, or stale. Settled on the couch with my Trail food, I heard slack pack plans to Rock Fish Gap being discussed. "Is their room for one more?" I asked.

"Sure, have your gear ready to go by eight." I didn't know the hikers, but trusted the process and that my pack would be waiting at Howard Johnson's where I could retrieve it at the end of the day.

The next morning, with Trail mix in my waist pack and full water bottles, I climbed in the car. Arriving at mile marker 13.6 reminded me of last evening's fearful episode. I hurried into the safety of the woods. Rockfish Gap, the official entrance to the Shenandoah National Park and my ride to Auntie Sue's, was sixteen miles away. Waverly would pick me up. Making it to Auntie Sue's house was a major milestone. I'd been counting down the days.

# Chapter 8

## *"Follow me for water!"*

### Shenandoah National Park through Maryland

My Auntie Sue and her companion Waverly had made the largest single contributions to my breast cancer campaign. They graciously opened their home to me so I could slack pack the Shenandoah National Park. Reports of the unsafe character on Route 29 and a general feeling of unrest after last year's murders contributed to my decision not to stay in the shelters. After sixty-seven days on the Trail, I had looked forward to home-cooked food, showers every night, and a familiar home at the day's end.

Delicious odors floated from the kitchen as I opened the front door. "You made it! You're really here!" Auntie Sue threw open her arms and I scooped up my five foot two inch Aunt before dropping the backpack. "You poor thing! You look so tired. Do your feet hurt? Put your things down. Dinner is ready" Exuberant energy and natural generosity bubbled out of this creative, little woman. Looking up, I caught sight of a colorful hand made banner hanging across the front hall. *Welcome Home, Hiker Girl!* Evidence of Auntie Sue's artist talent and her years teaching kindergarten looped and swirled in rainbow colored lettering across a long strip of school butcher paper.

"Oh, Auntie Sue, I love it! It's so like you. It's beautiful. Almost makes me miss elementary teaching, but not quite. These Trails are so easy it doesn't feel like I'm hiking nearly twenty miles a day. My last bath was in Troutville, one week ago today and a hundred and twenty-eight miles back down the Trail. It doesn't seem possible." I jabbered as I pulled off filthy boots and peeled off rotten socks.

"A bit ripe!" Auntie Sue grimaced as she gingerly picked up the socks by their edges. "Let me have your clothes. I'll get you something to put on so we can wash everything. I bought you special bubble soap and lotion."

"Oh, Auntie Sue, you're so good. I can't believe I've made it this far. It's still a long way to Maine, but making it to your house is a special milestone." As bubbles filled the Jacuzzi, reassurance bubbled up within. Others' faith in me built faith in myself.

Smelling sweet instead of rotten, I sat down to a mouth-watering cheese tofu casserole, salad, and homemade bread. "The guys on the Trail are so sweet, Auntie Sue. I haven't had any trouble with any of them. They are respectful and kind. I even shared a motel room in Troutville with Rain from Pennsylvania and Snail from Georgia. I had one bed, Snail had the other, and Rain slept on the floor. They took a day off. I kept going."

"How about your equipment and your feet? Is everything holding up all right?" Waverly was more concerned with logistics than with people.

"Everything is fine. I'm sick of Trail food but I have plenty. I'd like to leave a box of supplies to pick up on the way back down, including my water filter and tent. The pack feels like part of my body but I'm getting blisters again. My feet stay sore and my toenails are getting black. Not carrying the pack for a while should help. I'm worried about the rocks in Pennsylvania and the cliffs in the White Mountains; but my knees, back, and ankles are fine." I put down my fork and breathed a sigh of contentment. "Thank you for the delicious dinner." After clearing the table, we washed clothes. Everything I needed for five months barely covered the bottom of the washing machine.

Auntie Sue had arranged for a substitute at school for the following day. She drove me to the Blue Ridge Mountain Store so I could fill my fuel bottle and get new boot liners. Two Gulps was in the store. I'd hadn't seen him or his companions since April 9 th at the Vandeventer Shelter. Running into thru-hikers off the Trail was delightful Trail Magic. After buying moleskin and masking tape, and having a nice lunch, Auntie Sue and I spent the rest of the afternoon lying in the sun.

Feeling renewed the following day, I loaded up with vegi-burger and cheese sandwiches, fruit, and chips, and headed for Loft Mountain Campground, twenty-seven miles down the Trail. The weather called for rain, but I didn't care. For the first time in over two months a hot shower and a dry house waited at the end of the day.

Eight miles down the Trail I passed the official sign to the Shenandoah National Park. Few people were on the Trail, but deer were everywhere. Their soft brown eyes showed no fear as they darted across the Trail. Tamer than the ones in the Smokies, they stood still as I moved close for photographs. Hiking the well marked, low elevation Trail was literally a stroll in the park. Sixteen times between Rockfish Gap and Loft Mountain Campground the Trail intersected with the Blue Ridge Parkway. Late in the afternoon rain began to fall. At the campground a gate crossed the road leading to the Parkway. The campground was not open but I spotted a telephone. As I fumbled in my pack for phone numbers, the decision to let someone know where I was felt confining yet comforting, and very out of character "Waverly, this is Ellen. There's a gate across the road."

"I was afraid that might be the case. It's at least a mile walk to the bottom. There's a gas station you can wait at."

"I'll be there. Thank you." It felt nice to depend on people. Merging my schedule with the outside world was new behavior after operating alone for two months. However, I needed this break. I needed to hear people tell me I could make it to Katahdin and that I was not crazy to do it alone.

As I stood under the awning of the vacant gas station, deer tested their bravery at my presence. A car full of excited children straining to see the deer slowed down and parked. In the front seat a woman held a camera up to the foggy windshield. The deer nibbled grass and drank water from puddles forming on the asphalt. Apparently not satisfied with taking pictures through glass, the woman pulled on a raincoat and stepped out into the pouring rain. Keeping her camera focused, she stepped cautiously toward the deer, no doubt expecting them to flee. Suddenly the deer moved, but not as I, the woman, or the family expected. Rather than run away, the deer moved toward the woman. Keeping the camera focused, the woman stepped backward toward the car. Slowly she backed up until she was leaning against the car. Looking like a fugitive, she continued to take pictures as the deer moved in close enough to touch. They sniffed as they circled the car, rubbing the big metal box that had parked in their backyard. The children screeched with delight. I was so captivated with the scenario, I hadn't seen Waverly's car pull up.

"Haven't you seen enough deer?" came a familiar voice over the partially cracked window of his Lincoln Continental. As he turned the car around, I glanced back at the woman who still stood against the car, her family held hostage by the herd of deer.

"What you are doing is quite something. Look at those ridges. You have walked all the way across them in two days. You should be proud of yourself. I know your body can make it. Just don't let yourself get depressed. Discouragement will be a bigger enemy than physical pain." I knew he was right.

The next morning, Waverly had me on the Trail by the time a beautiful sunrise filtered over the Blue Ridge Mountains. Big Meadows Wayside was thirty-three miles away. Just past Ivy Creek Overlook I came face to face with a big black bear. This bear was more alert than the one I'd seen on Pond Flats. The instant we made eye contact the big fellow disappeared.

All morning the sky had been getting black. A blasting wind ripped through the gap. As a flash of lightening hit the Trail, I caught sight of a blue blaze leading to a shelter. Having watched numerous storms blow up and pass over quickly, I hoped this one would do the same. For thirty minutes I sat in the shelter, I wrote in the journal and watched the sky. About the time I decided the rain was going to last longer than I wanted to wait, the sun popped out and the sky cleared. Weather Trail Magic happened again. It was already 1:00 p.m. and I'd only covered fourteen miles. Lewis Mountain campground was twelve miles away. The hot spots on my heels were turning into blisters. Pain shot up the backs of my legs. I pulled up my socks, tightened my bootlaces, and readjusted the moleskin. Nothing relieved the pain. I popped Aleve and kept walking.

Coming around a bend, I heard voices. The campground was full of campers and tents. I hitched a ride to the Harry F. Byrd Visitor's Center on the Parkway and called Auntie Sue from the lodge. I was asleep in a rocking chair by the fireplace when Waverly's voice jolted me back to reality. "Ready to go home?" I jumped up, but excruciating pain stopped me. Slowly, I limped to the door.

"What's wrong?" Waverly asked taking my pack.

"I don't know. My heels are hurt terribly. I can't wait to get in the car and take off my boots." After carefully peeling off my socks I discovered both heels had blisters the size of half-dollars. "I can't understand what's doing this. I had blisters in March, but I thought my feet had toughened up. I can't walk if this keeps up." I was close to tears.

"Hand me a boot." With one eye on the highway and one hand on the wheel, Waverly took a boot and peered inside. "Here's your problem. Look inside the other boot. You don't have any cushion or padding left in these heels."

I looked inside and saw nothing but the hard outer leather of the boot. The padding was gone. The lining was gone.

"Oh my word! My feet have chewed the insides out. Can we stop somewhere and find something to pad them with? I'll have my second pair sent to a maildrop."

"Where do you suggest?" Waverly turned off the Parkway and onto Route 29.

"Let's try that Kroger's. If we don't see anything we could try a drug store." I had no idea what I was looking for. Limping in my sandals, I wandered up and down the isles. From down the isle I heard Waverly chuckle. "Do you think these would work?" He asked. Waverly had stopped in front the boxes of sanitary napkins, Tampax, and panty liners.

"Yes, that's it! What a great idea! I'll use sanitary liners to fill in the backs of the boots." Exploding in laughter, we cackled hysterically until I thought we were going to be asked to leave the store. Waverly laughed so loud I thought he was going to collapse. "I'll have to change my panty liners everyday, in my boots that is."

I called my sister Susan in New Hampshire and asked her to send my second pair of boots to my twelfth maildrop in Boiling Springs, Pennsylvania. I had sent the boots to New Hampshire because I didn't think I'd need them until I got to New England. Letting the fluid out of the blisters took the pressure off and eased the pain. After soaking them, I smeared my heels with antiseptic cream and bandaged them. I packed liners in my backpack and put three in the heel of each boot.

After an egg and cheese omelet, I tossed the backpack into Waverly's car and hugged Aunt Sue good bye. "This visit has meant so much. Thank you for your support."

"You'll make it if you believe you will. We're so proud of you. Take care of those heels." My heels hurt but my boots had padding and new boots were on the way. The problem had a solution. Blisters wouldn't stop me. Waverly would take my pack to Thornton Gap so I could slackpack the last twenty-six miles of the Park. I was only five days away from Harper's Ferry.

The Blue Ridge Mountains were gentler with wider views than the shorter more dramatic views in the Smokies. The road and the Trail followed the same contour through the mountains, unlike the Smokies where only by hiking can the summits be reached. The terrain was so easy that it was hard to tell whether I was hiking mountains or gaps. However, the stroll turned out to be one of the biggest challenges of the trip.

Coming around Hawksbill Gap, I thought I saw milkweed seeds floating in the wind. It couldn't be snow because I was at less than four thousand feet and, it was May 10th. Leaves had filled out the trees and flowers covered the ground. The flakes had to be some kind of smog, pollen, or dust. However, they looked more and more like snow as they swirled around me. Catching a flake, I was horrified to discover it was snow. I got out my camera and snapped proof that I had walked through snow in mid-May.

The snow danced in the air as if it, too, wasn't sure what to do at this time of year. Within thirty minutes the flakes became a blizzard. The air was so thick I could see only yards in front of me. Snow covered the ground and clung to the trees. I had on my long underwear top, a fleece pullover, and a raincoat, but my legs were freezing in shorts. The wind howled and whipped at my raincoat like sails on a ship tacking on the open ocean. The snow fell so hard it was difficult to stay on the Trail. Trudging along, I tried to recall happy moments of playing in the powdery whiteness. Today however, the snow presented danger to my bare legs, scantily clad body, and my peace of mind. I tried to hurry but the Trail was now full of treacherous rocks. For an hour I inched along, trusting I'd make it to Thornton Gap before dark. After many self-talks and a vivid imagination, I began to enjoy the biting wind as it stung my cheeks and knees, delight in the soggy flakes landing in my eyeballs, and appreciate the roaring wind ricocheting in my ears.

At the Skyline Drive Service Road I heard voices. Horses were being led into a barn. The big animals looked more like spotted leopards than black riding horses. I heard someone call my name. "Wolf Woman, isn't this fantastic? I just love it! Can you believe this snow?" It was Magot. I hadn't seen her, Daddy, or Stick-in-Face since the Nantahalah Outdoor Center in North Carolina one month ago.

"Magot! Where did you come from? This is amazing, that's for sure."

"I stopped to get some hot cocoa in the lodge." Magot bounced in front of me.

"It sure is good to see you. I hear Daddy went home with a broken thumb. Where's Stick-in-Face?"

"He's way up ahead. I was up with him until my parents came and hiked with me for a few days last week. They said I don't have to hurry and finish or worry about working this summer. Now I can slow down and enjoy nature.

"Virginia is so beautiful," I said struggling to keep up. "It's too bad a blight is killing the trees. I met a man from Woodstock, Vermont yesterday who is

**111**

down here studying the trees. The Trail runs behind his land. He gave me his phone number."

"That's great. The motels up north will eat us alive."

"So will the mosquitoes, which is one reason I'm glad to have his address." At Mary's Rock, Magot stopped. I headed down the hill. As the elevation decreased, the air became warm and the wind stopped blowing. By the time I reached the Thornton Gap parking lot the snow had melted off my clothes, visibility had returned, and not a speck of snow lay on the ground. It seemed as if nothing unusual had happened on the mountain that afternoon. My flaming red, icy knees knew better. I wondered if they looked anything like Rudolph's nose after he'd been leading the sleigh on Christmas Eve. Just as Rudolph leads his pack of reindeer, I wondered if moving in front of Magot meant I was moving in the lead of the 1997 thru-hiker pack? This journey to Katahdin was by no means a race; in fact I had no idea what Annie meant when she asked me at Matt's Creek who was in lead this year. I never had participated in competitive sports. In elementary school I used to hide in the bathrooms during recess because it was embarrassing to be chosen last on kickball teams. Walking, running, or swimming alone was far less stressful. However, hiking 2,160 mile alone was no small feat, and hardly free from stress or risk. Being the first woman to reach Katahdin had not been a goal, but I recognized fewer and fewer names in the journals, and none were women. While, reaching Katahdin was a walk, not a race, I began to wonder if I would be the first woman to finish in 1997.

After picking up my pack at the lodge, filling water bottles, and using the bathroom, I headed to the shelter less than a mile away. During my four days in the Shenandoah National Park, I had walked through two thunderstorms, one blizzard, and now sunshine. The first, second, and third peaks of the Hogback were the steepest climbs of the Park's one hundred and six miles. My pack was down to thirty-five pounds, but it felt heavy. Four-tenths of a mile after mile marker 20.8, the data book indicated I would come to water. After walking for longer than I thought I should have, I slipped off the pack and sat on a log at the side of the Trail to check the data book. I was so intent on studying that I didn't see a man coming from the direction I was headed.

"Are you lost?" asked a man with a ponytail, daypack, and a wide brimmed hat.

"No, but did you pass a stream?"

"You passed the water back at the corner," the man pointed up the Trail.

"I didn't see any water. I'll just go on. There'll be water soon. Thank you." I looked down at my book. I didn't want to contradict the man, but something about him made me uncomfortable. I'd have seen water if there'd been some.

"It's right there. Get your water bottles. I'll help you fill them with the best water on the Trail. I live in the valley and come up here once a week to do a ten-mile walk. I had lunch at the stream today. Come on," the man urged. It was one o'clock in the afternoon and it didn't make sense that he'd eaten lunch here and was already coming back from the opposite direction. However, he was too persistent too ignore.

"I don't want to leave my pack," I said looking for a reason not to go.

"No one's going to bother your pack. You can see it from the Trail. There isn't any one up here anyway." The man started up the Trail. "Come on!" He said sharply. I followed at a safe distance. There was no water at the corner.

"I guess it's around the next bend. It's not far. Come on, we'll find water."

"I'm going back to the pack." I announced.

"Look!" the man said, gruffly and sounding agitated. "This is a watershed area. See how the land dips out there? There's water out there. Follow me out here." The man headed off the Trail into the thick woods.

"Come on!" he kept saying. "Follow me, I said! Come on!"

Acting as though I was intent on following, I took tiny steps, pretending to trip over the underbrush. "I'm coming. You go ahead and find the water. I'm coming. I'm right behind you. It's hard to walk without my walking sticks."

The man kept going. I let him think he was leading me until he was far enough in the woods that even if he ran after me, I would be able to get back to my pack and get my can of mace before he caught me. After a few minutes without a word I turned and ran to my pack, put it on and ran down the Trail. Eight-tenths of a mile later the Trail intercepted the road. As I hiked across the parking lot, a ranger pulled up behind me. Rolling down his window he called, "You a thru-hiker? Doing okay?"

It seemed strange a ranger would pull up just now. I walked to the car. "Yes Sir, I left March first from Springer. I'm doing fine, I guess."

"Good! The Park has such a bad reputation after the murders last year that I like to check in with the hikers. I saw you cross the Parkway earlier. You're making good time. No problems, huh?" The ranger questioned me again.

"Well I'll tell ya, I just ran into a weird guy who said he was a local and tried to get me to follow him into the woods looking for water." I told the ranger the whole story.

"You think you could recognize him?" he asked.

"I'll try."

The ranger stepped out of the car bringing with him a brief case. He took out a folder of large black and white photographs. I looked carefully as he flipped through them. "Tell me if you recognize him," the ranger encouraged.

"That one, that looks like him!" I said excitedly. "The man I saw had a wide brimmed hat on so I wouldn't have seen the balding head, but I recognize that thin, pointed chin and the eyes. He had a ponytail so that hair length is right. I can't be sure of course. I hate to condemn anyone."

"If you're right, you've helped us find the local whose been causing trouble in the Park. If I hurry I might catch him on the other side of the mountain. Thanks for your help. Be careful." The ranger jumped in the car and sped away. I never found out why the man was wanted. But I did know Trail safety had been with me.

Voices made me nervous as I approached the Tom Floyd Shelter. Easing my way up the wide porch of the spacious log shelter, I found two men stretched out looking at maps, another man resting on the bench, and two more men setting up tents. "What a nice shelter," I said, using a neutral topic as I slid off my pack.

"Sure is. Should be a nice sunset, too. You hiking far?" asked a middle-aged man with sandy hair as he put down his map.

"I left Springer March first. And yourself?" I asked as I pulled off my boots.

"There's nine of us from a church fellowship in Ohio. We get together for a week twice a year to do a section of the Trail. We split into two groups so we won't fill the shelters, and can leave cars at both ends. I'm the pastor. Welcome!" He extended a hand.

"Nice to meet you." I grasped his hand. "I'm Wolf Woman from Cookeville, Tennessee. I was nervous to see so many guys here after a rather unnerving encounter this afternoon." I shared my experience. "I couldn't believe the ranger actually had a picture of the guy and that he was wanted." Discussing the events took the fear away.

"Sounds like a close call," commented one of the men, with a deep sigh.

"You're very brave to hike alone. Why are you out here?" The pastor posed the question. I told them about my childhood dream to hike the Trail, my move South, and of my breast cancer campaign. "I've held on to the goal waiting for the time to hike."

The pastor put down his soup cup, "That's a quite story. You're a remarkable woman. Not many people have the patience or insight to accomplish long term goals."

"I'll say!" chimed another fellow. "It takes a lot of nerve to be out here in the first place. Never mind for five months. I look forward to our trip each year, but I'm ready to get home by the time the week's over. I couldn't stay out here without support."

"Oh, I have lots of support! I couldn't do this without my friends and family. I call home every time I get off the Trail, get lots of mail at my maildrops, and have connections for places to stay." I explained how I had used Auntie Sue's house as a base while slack packing the Park. "This trip is teaching me how important people are from a perspective I wouldn't get in civilization. At home I took relationships and community for granted. I never stopped to realize how much I need people until I left them. The paradox of going on this solo adventure is that it has taken me hundreds of miles away from everything and everyone familiar to develop a sense of dependency for people. I mean, you'd think since I'm responsible for my schedule, entertainment, safety, and all my emotional, spiritual, physical, and mental needs, that I wouldn't need people. But..." I paused to make sure I was hearing what I was about to say. I knew if I kept talking, I'd risk moving out the self-confident shell I'd built around my feelings. "I haven't found that to be true. The trip has become a series of inter-connecting, interweaving experiences with people. I'm not just moving through the Appalachian Mountains, I'm moving through the wilderness of my soul. Which I've found can be a very lonely place. Doing the Trail has become the catalyst to move me from thinking I am the biggest loner in the world, to decid-ing that people are important to my wellbeing. I'm an introvert. I can entertain myself and need lots of time alone; most thru-hikers are. But being alone for five months is a bit extreme, a bit of an obsessive compulsive expectation, don't you think?" I looked at the pastor. My fearful experience had made me needy for an empathetic ear. I wasn't much of a churchgoer but in the presence of Christians, complete with a Pastor, it felt safe to spin my thoughts.

While I'd been venting, we'd all been preparing supper. All the men were self-contained. "How we are preparing this meal is an example of what you are saying," the pastor responded thoughtfully. "We all have our own supplies and the knowledge of how to cook, but doing it as a community makes it so much more fulfilling. If any of us need anything, from borrowing salt, holding a water bag, sheltering a stove from the wind, or just plain lending an ear, we are here for each other." As he spoke, I watched him steady a pan of water on a stove while his buddy stirred rice into boiling water.

"You're right." I smiled as I sipped soup.

"You're an inspiration to us. It takes a lot of guts not only to be out here for weeks but to have awareness and insight into the reason for your journey."

I missed Auntie Sue and a shower but it felt good sleeping in a shelter again. I picked up my pen to journal by flashlight. *May 11: Today my journey has led me away from a manipulative wanted man, to sharing the shelter with three Christian men. It has been quite a day of testing boundaries. The weather, too, has gone from blizzard-like conditions of yesterday to temperatures too warm to zip up my sleeping bag tonight. Changes are part of every day on the Trail. There is never a dull moment in this solitary experience. I do the walk-ing, the people make the memories. How I relate is my choice. I'm reminded of President Kennedy's words, "This solitary work we can not do alone."*

Crawling out of my sleeping bag, I headed to the privy. Back on the porch, I primed the stove and boiled water. The guys joined me. As the men sipped coffee, I picked up my backpack and I bid them goodbye. At the bottom of the porch steps I stopped. My heart pounded. I needed something totally out of character. Knowing that if I analyzed the need, I'd dismiss it as irrational and ridiculous. Pack and all, I walked back up on the porch. "Did you forget something?" one of the men asked.

"No. I mean, yes," Looking at the man who had said he was a pastor, I asked, "Did you say you are a pastor?"

"Yes."

"Would you have prayer for me before I go?"

"Yes. I'd be glad to." The men removed their caps and formed a circle around me. The pastor looked me in the eye and asked. "Tell me your first name again."

"Ellen," I said "Ellen Wolfe."

The pastor began. "Dear Heavenly Father........," It had been a long time since I had heard a prayer. I couldn't remember when I'd ever asked anyone to pray for me and I didn't hear every word the pastor said in his standard sincere prayer, but I felt the connection with stability, security, and safety. There didn't need to be a reason for wanting prayer. My need was spiritual with no regard for religion, gender, or geography.

"Thank you," I struggled to contain the tears in my eyes. Reaching up, I gave the pastor a hug. Without another word I walked off the porch and blinked my way into the woods. Relationships with men were not easy, but here on the Trail connections with them seemed comfortable. In the last twenty-four hours I'd nearly been accosted by a suspicious character and spent the night with a minister.

A couple of miles down the Trail my mood shifted from sadness, to sheer joy as I hiked through the beautiful wildflowers in the National Zoo compound. Lady slippers, trilliums, wood anemone, Virginia blue bells, showy orchids, and wild columbine filled the woods with incredible color and variety. The whole seventeen miles to Dick's Dome Shelter resembled a long colorful pathway daintily decorated for an outdoor wedding. The trees contributed a soft image as tender new buds filled in the sky above trickling creeks. Brilliant blue bells, violets, wood sorrels, and lily-of-the-valley colored the creek banks. I was so busy identifying flowers and taking pictures that I nearly missed the sign leading down the two-tenths of a mile blue blaze Trail to the shelter. On the bridge, I heard the loud laughter of men. So far I hadn't walked in on any drinking crowds. There was always a first time.

"Welcome! Come on in. Are you alone?" A man asked. Three men sat around a picnic table. I didn't see any sign of alcohol as I dropped my pack.

"I know lots of thru-hikers." I was ready with my usual line of defense.

"I didn't mean to intimidate you. It's just that this shelter is small and we would put up a tent if you were with a group. We have hot water if you need it."

"This shelter is a weird shape." I wondered if whoever had built it stopped to think how bodies were going to fit in an octagon. "Thank you for the water. I'm beat. I hiked eighteen miles from Tom Floyd Shelter."

"Tom Floyd? I'll bet you saw the other half of our group. We're with a bunch of fellows from our church in Ohio."

"Yes! I stayed with them last night. They were real nice."

"You're brave to be out here alone. You start at Springer?"

"Yes sir, left March first."

"You're making good time. I've got a bunch of food left you are welcome to." The youngest of the three guys handed me a bag full of gorp, M & M's, raisins, and nuts.

"Looks great! I'll take anything you can't use," I stuffed the food in my food sack and hung it in the shelter.

"Let me make some room for you in there." The older man rearranged their sleeping bags and I spread mine out. I crawled in my bag and looked up at my food sack swinging low with the weight of new gorp. Sighing, I wondered if I would ever trust the process. Today's Trail Magic had spared me the assumption that I was walking into a drunken brawl. The laughter had been nothing more than three old cronies, crowing like barnyard roosters at their own silly jokes.

Spring flowers covered both sides of the Trail and creeks splashed across my path as I hiked my last nineteen miles of Virginia. In the afternoon it began to rain. I was soaked by the time I reached Bears Den Hostel. Walking up on the porch, I knocked. A tall, dark headed woman opened the door. "I'm a thru-hiker and would like a bunk."

"I'm sorry, we don't open until 5 o'clock. There's a hiker room around back you can wait in," the woman said pleasantly.

I was too cold and wet to sit around for an hour. "Ma'am, I'd be happy to work in exchange for a bed. If you'll give me a minute to change, I'll do whatever you need." I preferred working to sitting around, and if I could get out of paying the $12.00 fee I'd be that much happier. The woman eyed my bedraggled appearance.

"Yes, I can use some help. Leave your boots on the porch. The bunkroom is to the left. Would you like some hot tea before I set you to work cleaning bathrooms?"

"Yes, Thank you."

The front room had reading material and a fireplace. The twenty-bed bunkroom had mattresses with sheets, blankets, and pillows. Everything was neat and tidy. Owned by the Appalachian Trail Conference, the hostel offered kitchen facilities, a laundry, Coleman by the ounce, and a freezer full of pizza and ice cream. I peeled off my wet clothes and put on a dry but identical outfit. Gathering up the soggy pile, I followed my nose to the spiced tea. "Sit and enjoy the tea while it's hot. My name is Betsy."

"Glad to meet you. I'm Wolf Woman. Thank you. This hits the spot."

"Glad you like it. When you finish, the washing machine is at the bottom of the stairs. Here is a bucket and rags to wash down all the shower stalls and bathroom walls. The floors need mopping, too. This cabinet needs to be wiped down and rearranged.

"I can do that right now. Rearranging reminds me of organizing a classroom."

"Are you a teacher? My husband and I took this job after I retired from teaching."

"I used to teach elementary school. Now I teach college." I told Betsy about my career change and raising money for breast cancer. When I finished my tea I put my cup in the sink and headed off to do my chores. After stripping the dirt off the shower walls, I stripped off my clothes and hopped in. Leaning against the wall, I let the hot water run over my body. I could have stood forever if my growling stomach hadn't coaxed me out. Wonderful aromas filled the kitchen. A guest from Australia had arrived with all the ingredients to make a vegetable stir-fry and rice dinner. I perched on a stool and waited for my frozen pizza to heat.

"Betsy tells me you're a thru-hiker. That's very admirable. I don't think I could be one. What do you eat?"

"I eat things like Trail mix, dried fruit, pasta, rice, and soups. Easy things, that get very boring."

"I've made more than I can eat. Would you like some?"

Finally! The question I'd been waiting for. "Yes! I'd love some! Home cooked vegetarian meal is more than Trail Magic, it's a miracle."

A man who worked in the area and an older gentleman who worked at the Conference Office joined us for dinner. I asked the conference worker if he minded taking my pack in to Harper's Ferry in the morning. "I'd be happy to. Have it in the van by 8:00. It will be waiting for you when you arrive." After eating two plates of stir-fry plus the pizza, and ice cream, I bade everyone good night and headed to the bunkroom. Eating vegetables on brown rice, sleeping under blankets on a bed, and sending my pack to Harper's Ferry in a van was a perfect way to celebrate my last night in Virginia.

At the crack of dawn, I was on the Trail with only raincoat and fanny pack tied around my waist. The rain was over and the sun was out. I passed up going to the Blackburn Trail Center and only took a few minutes to check in with the journal at the David Lesser Memorial Shelter. In terms of actual miles, Tagg Run Shelter in Pennsylvania was the halfway point in 1997 between Springer Mountain and Mt. Katahdin. However, Harper's Ferry, 85 miles shy of Tagg Run is traditionally considered halfway. For me reaching Harper's Ferry and hiking the meager two miles of West Virginia was more than just a psychological halfway point. It was proof that I had learned to trust white blazes. I'd seen enough Trail Magic to know all I needed to do was believe I'd make it to Katahdin.

During the planning stages of the trip my mother had been told that Janet

Ady, the daughter of her best high school friend, Pat McDermott Clarkson (originally from Massachusetts, currently from California), lived near the Trail. The night before I'd left, I checked my e-mail for the last time and a message from Maryland popped up. "My mother tells me you're hiking the Trail. Please stay with us when you pass through. I work in Harper's Ferry and can pick you up at the Conference Office. Janet." At the hands of old-fashioned caring mothers, and at the fingertips of modern technology, Janet and I connected and none too soon. She included her address and a phone number. I responded by e-mail, mailed her my itinerary, and reached for the telephone to connect a real voice with the gracious invitation. "Ellen! We're proud of you and want to be a part of your walk for breast cancer." I promised to call when I got close. While at Auntie Sue's I'd left a voice message on her answering machine that I'd be in Harper's Ferry on May 14th and would be on the front porch of the conference office.

Founded in 1747, the quaint residential village was dominated by the Harper's Ferry Historical Park. The Shenandoah and the Potomac Rivers merge in town. Walking over the footbridge and down the C&O Canal is as significant a landmark as is walking up the steps of the conference office. "I'm Wolf Woman. I left Springer March first."

"I'm glad to meet you. We've been looking for you. We'd like to take your picture and have you to sign our register." Back out on the porch, I posed in front of the door. As I waited for the Polaroid snapshot to transform the blurry image into a clear replica, I wondered if hiking the Trail was transforming my own blurry image into a more authentic and genuine human being. Knowing the same number of miles I'd walked remained in front of me, I felt like I had truly arrived at mid-life. By flipping through the 1997 thru-hiker photograph album, I discovered I was the forty-third person and first woman to arrive in Harper's Ferry. Stryder was the forty-second. The Appalachian Trail literature, maps, and books gave the trip a sense of cohesiveness. Along with my maildrop, a box from Gloria, and letters from Suellen and friends, I also received a package from someone in my distant past.

In the 1930's in Winchester, Massachusetts, a suburb of Boston, George Barboro and my dad, Pete Priest, grew up with one house separating them. Because Daddy was an only child and George never had any brothers, they were as close as real brothers. George was one year ahead of Daddy in school, but they were inseparable. George was often invited to Cape Cod for vacations at Pete's grandmother's beach house and Pete spent equal time with George's family. As best friends, they stayed close into adulthood. When my father enlisted in the Korean War and later George was drafted, they stayed in contact. When the war was over, college routed George to New Hamphire and Daddy moved to Vermont. George was the best man at my parents' wedding. Although caring for a family took priority in both men's lives, they often visited in each other's homes.

As children, my brother, sisters, and I affectionately called him Uncle George. He could spin a tale almost as believable as Daddy. With an undergraduate degree in biology, Uncle George made a career of working for the Upjohn Pharmaceutical Company. As a child, I was not interested in his knowledge of the latest medicines. His visits meant he would bring "boo boo" pencils. Uncle George could instantly heal cuts, scratches, and bruises with the magic touch of a "boo boo" pencil. With his red, blue, yellow, or green pencils, he would draw neat circles around the areas in question and fill in the wound with a little spit. The injury would instantly disappear. I was up in years before I learned "boo boo" pencils could be bought anywhere and that filling in wounds with colored lead might not have been so wise. However, Uncle George was so convincing that we accumulated as many injuries as we could before he arrived. By the time his visit ended, we looked like clowns at a circus, dressed in rainbow spotted skin.

Uncle George visited frequently until my parents divorced in 1964 and my mother moved my brother, sisters, and me to New Hampshire. I didn't see him again until 1986 at Daddy's funeral in Putney, Vermont. Our reunion was melancholy, but "boo boo" pencil experiences from the late 1950's had left colorful traces of memories.

Gloria had sent George a copy of my flier and the newspaper article. He called Gloria and said, "Pete would have stood behind her. What can we do to help?" In February Uncle George had sent me a donation check for my breast cancer campaign and a check to buy good boots. A few days after receiving the checks I was working on the computer when the phone rang. With my attention still on my work, I said "Hello."

"If Pete went up stairs and George went up stairs, then Pete came down stairs and George stayed up stairs but Pete wanted George to bring him up a drink of water, who would go up and who would come down?" The absurdity continued until I shrieked, "Uncle George! Is it really you?"

I wasn't accustomed to men calling the house, especially men with thick New England accents, but it didn't take long to recognize whose voice was on the other end of the line. The silly nonsense joke sounded so much like daddy." Uncle George! How good to hear your voice." I was so excited I could hardly stand it. "I did what you told me to do and bought good boots. I've waterproofed them and broken them in. Thank you so much," I reported like a child to a parent.

"I'm proud of you. I hope you get two pair."

"I did. I've bought one pair and used your money to get a second."

"I have mole skin and clothes you can use. I'll have maps ready for you when you get here. I've hiked all over the Whites and will help you get through them." As we talked, Uncle George told me how rugged the Trails were, how

**120**

Up above the clouds in the Smoky Mountains. *(photo by Ellen Wolfe)*

Suellen, David, Wolf Woman, and The Blue Snail *(photo by Judy Madonia)*

Wolf Woman and The Blue Snail at Neel's Gap *(photo by OAB)*

OAB and Wolf Woman at Spring
Mountain Shelter. *(photo by Lum)*

Leaving Hot Springs on Easter.
*(photo by Suellen Alfred)*

Halfway point
sign in VA.
*(photo by Roy)*

Rocks in the
trail in PA.
*(photo by
Mapman)*

Lum in Mahoosuc Notch. *(photo by Ellen Wolfe)*

Wolf Woman and Stryder in
Vernon, New Jersey.

Uncle George on Moosilaukee
in the White Mountains.
*(photo by Ellen Wolfe)*

A trail rainbow in Vermont. *(photo by Ellen Wolfe)*

Wolf Woman on a logging road in Maine. *(photo by Suellen Alfred)*

Wolf Woman at Saddleback Mountain. *(photo by Jesse McIntire)*

A moose in Andover, Maine. *(photo by Suellen Alfred)*

Crossing the Kennebec River. *(photo by Down Under)*

Spaulding Mountain lean-to. *(photo by a fellow hiker)*

Reaching the summit of Mt. Katahdin and my goal. *(photo by Orion Thompson)*

Climbing off of Mt. Katahdin. *(photo by Orion Thompson)*

unpredictable the weather in the White Mountains can be, and how much he wanted to help. Bringing the conversation to a close, he added, "By the time you get to the halfway point, you'll need a little boost. Look for a package at Harper's Ferry."

Now, weeks after the phone call, I sat in the conference office opening a box that contained two pair of L. L. Bean wool socks and two pair of sock liners. As I touched the clean wool to my cheeks, I could feel the faithfulness of friendship. Although over ten years had passed since Uncle George had lost his best friend, the socks I held in my hands were a testimony that true friends are always there for one another. Forty years had passed, since "boo boo" pencil days, but Uncle George again would not let me down. He would be to me everything Daddy would have been.

I added his box to my stack and carried everything to the porch to wait for Janet. It was significant that my mother's and father's best childhood friends should enter my experience as I began the last half of the trip. Accepting adult support by way of my parents was accepting my need of an extended family. In the days when people lived in clans, tribes, and close-knit communities, children were the responsibility of the whole village.

As I had in Nolichucky when waiting for Linda after leaving a message, I hoped Janet would come. I had just begun to worry when a car pulled up and stopped. A tall, thin woman with soft brown hair got out and hurried around the back of the car. I jumped off the bench, ran to the road, and into her open arms. "So, you must be Janet!"

"Yes, I got your message and hope you didn't worry"

"No, I'm used to sitting and trusting that people will come," I chuckled at the truth I was beginning to believe.

"I tried to get away from work sooner but we were swamped. Let me help you with your things." Janet picked up the boxes and letter pile as I hoisted the backpack into the car.

We chatted as though we had known each other for years as we headed out of the quaint town. At the house, ten-year old Laurel, six-year old Merrill, and Janet's husband Piers greeted me. After a shower I enjoyed vegetarian pizza, salad, and garlic bread while the family enjoyed bear and deer stories. When the pizza was gone it was time to do homework. Being with a family brought back memories of juggling homework and chores with family time. I'd planned to get back on the Trail with the pack but Janet wanted to help me slack pack. A nineteen-mile hike would bring me out on Zittlestown Road at Washington Monument State Park.

"I'm glad to have a part in your walk for breast cancer. You are doing such a wonderful thing. My friend Judy Zeck writes for the *Middletown Valley Citizen* and wants to interview you for an article. We want to join you on the other side of Washington Monument Park," Janet's enthusiasm was uplifting.

121

"Great, the half-way point is an appropriate place to write another article." After dropping the children off at school, Janet dropped me off in Harper's Ferry. I quickly moved through West Virginia's two miles of Trail and headed into Maryland's forty-one miles. I wore my gaiters to protect myself from poison ivy that grew in the Trail. At the Dahlgren Backpacking Campground, the only campground on the AT, I stopped to use the bathroom and scrawl in the journal. *"Stopped to use the bathroom just to be sure I still knew how to sit, after squatting for the last two and a half months. Wolf Woman."*

Maryland's highest mountain, Mt. Quirauk, is only 1,880 feet in elevation. Knowing millions of people in the hundreds of cities between Boston and Washington, D. C. live only a few hours from the Trail was very humbling. Every mile I hiked north got me further away from southern humidity and into a northern dry climate. Through Maryland and West Virginia I hiked a three-mile-an-hour pace.

At the replica of the Monument in D. C., I sat and watched the clouds float across the wide expanse of blue. Something inside was shifting too. Though rocks, cliffs, and the wilderness of Maine were ahead, I sensed I would make it. The loneliness of not seeing anyone for days or sleeping in shelters full of strangers had been interrupted by opportunities to slack pack and stay with friends. After leaving Janet's, I would only have one night in the shelters before staying with Helen Walker in Carlisle, Pennsylvania. I was through the adjustment period, out of severe weather, and had learned to trust the process. As I munched on crackers and cheese I believed I'd become Trail hardened enough to face the challenges ahead. I would climb Katahdin, come high winds or flooded footing! Wandering around the park, I saw a phone booth. "Janet. I'm at Washington Monument."

"I won't be able to come for an hour but you're only two miles from our new house. I'll tell you where the key is." I had walked nineteen miles and wasn't enthralled with the idea of more hiking, but I needed to use the bathroom.

"Great!" Janet gave me directions. A car came down the road as I hung up. I stuck out my thumb. The man stopped, and I hurried to the car.

"Sir, I am a thru-hiker and need a ride to a friend's house."

"Sure thing." Soon I was resting in Janet's brand new house.

After taking Merrill to school the next morning, Janet, Laurel, and I headed down the Trail. Time passed quickly as we told stories, including a few tales about our mothers. Judy and her son joined us. Judy interviewed me for the article. Weeks later, Janet sent the May 29th article to a Connecticut Post Office. I was amazed at how positive I sounded. She quoted me as saying, "Whatever happens I can get through it. Rain eventually stops. Hailstorms don't last forever. The weather warms up. Whatever happens, I will hike through it." I might not have sounded so positive if I'd known how bad the mosquitoes, mud, and mountains were going to be.

At the bridge the women and children left. Janet would pick me up on Old Forge Road at six o'clock. She assured me she'd find the road so I could hike 28.8 miles. At the border between Maryland and Pennsylvania in Pen-Mar Park I studied the sign indicating the miles north and south. Seeing the Mason-Dixon Line reminded me that war grievances had had no direct impact on my life until I married a southerner. Seeing my first flaky white birch trees brought tears to my eyes. The white bark joined white blazes, leading me home.

# Chapter 9

## *"Oh, my feet hurt!"*

### Pennsylvania

On May 16th I entered Pennsylvania and began counting road crossings, but unmarked gravel roads appeared more often than the data book indicated. I tried timing my hiking rate between crossings, but Trail conditions made calculating impossible. After crossing more roads than I could keep up with, the Trail deposited me in the middle of a park full of children. Two yellow school buses were parked near a block building that I hoped was a bathroom. As I neared the building, a hiker came out and continued up the Trail. After using the facilities and filling water bottles, I curiously picked up my pace behind him. I caught up to the hiker when he stopped to get water at a creek. "Might you be Wolf Woman?" He asked as I approached.

"Yes, how did you know?" Now I was really curious.

"News travel fast. You left March first and are hiking for a charity, breast cancer, right? Your daughter hiked with you in Georgia. You've been leaving surveys in the shelters for women thru-hikers. Good to meet you. I'm Roy."

"Good to meet you. I can't believe you know all that. You thru-hiking? Have you seen Stryder, Broken Road, Chief, Pilgrim, or Monarch with the dogs?"

"Stryder's up ahead a day or two. The other guys are a few days behind. I haven't seen anyone with dogs. Where are you headed for the night?"

"A friend is picking me up at Old Forge Road," I answered looking down at Roy's bare toes sticking out of heavy leather sandals. "You always hike in sandals?"

"Yes, I get around the rocks easier with sandals and my feet don't get as tired. This is the sixth time I've been on the Trail. I've started at both Springer and Katahdin. I hike until winter sets in. Then I flip-flop, or hitch-hike to the other end, and hike to the place I got off. I've never done a complete thru-hike, but hope to this year."

"Seven is a spiritual number meaning completion. Maybe this is the year to do it. You don't work?" Living on the Trail sounded intriguing.

"I'm retired. I don't create bills on the Trail."

"Retired? You don't look old enough to have retired!"

"I invested well doing construction in Florida. You teach, right?"

"The Trail grapevine sure is accurate! I'm amazed. Yes. I've just changed careers from elementary to college teaching. I don't take a lot of time off because school starts in August. I didn't know I was making good time until people started telling me."

"You use the journals and hikers read them. They are a good way to keep up with where hikers are and get news of places to get off to stay and eat. Not all the changes make it to the *Handbook* or *Companion* before they go to print. Journals, or registers, inform hikers of closed stores and new ones. Here's Old Forge Road. I'm going on to the next shelter. See you up the Trail," waved Roy.

"Be careful. Thanks," As I watched Roy disappear I marveled at the idea of hiking the Trail over and over, especially in sandals. Knowing what to expect would get boring. The element of surprise and the exhilaration of seeing new places would be missing, although it would relieve the anxiety of hiking without a deadline. Nature always changes, but there wouldn't be as much reason to trust the process. Right now I trusted Janet would find me before darkness filled the white birch and pine forest.

Pennsylvania reminded me of home, of course depending on whether home was north or south of the Mason-Dixon. Tennessee and Vermont were a long way from Pennsylvania. If Janet never came, I didn't even have a clue where the nearest town was.

Just as I'd picked the last M & M's out of my Trail mix, a car rounded the bend in a cloud of dust. Janet waved and blew the horn. I breathed a sigh of relief. Janet hugged me as I climbed in. "I'm sorry I'm late. I hope you haven't worried. I can't believe you knew which road to stop at. I drove all over the place looking for you. What would you have done if I didn't come?" Janet was more panicked than I.

"Oh, I don't know. I would have thought of something. I wasn't worried, yet anyway. I trusted you, and the process."

At nine the next morning Janet had me back at Old Forge Road. "I've enjoyed being with you. Thank you for everything." As I hugged Janet, I spotted a white blaze shining like a white omen in the sun.

"Don't be in a hurry. This is not a taxi service. Let me take your picture. It's been such an honor to be part of your experience. I'll send a copy of the article to a maildrop. Hiking the Trail to find a cure for breast cancer is incredible." Janet took a picture.

"Let me take one of you. It's cool we're friends because our mothers were friends. I didn't know my mom had such good taste in people," I laughed as Janet handed me the camera. I tried to imagine what my mother had been like in high school as Janet smiled.

"The Trail is calling. I have twenty miles to hike before dark. Thank you, again. I'll keep you posted." I picked up my sticks and walked into the woods. Janet waved until I was out of sight. Through blurred vision I waved back, remembering good-byes to Linda, Judy, Suellen, and now Janet. My destination was hundreds of miles farther than theirs, yet they always drove away. Hiking though Pennsylvania would bring me two hundred and thirty-two miles closer to my goal.

A few miles down the Trail I found Roy was gathering water from a stream near the Quarry Gap shelter. "Great day to hike," I called.

"Sure is! I see you got your pack back. Where you headed for tonight?"

"I don't think I'll get any farther than Birch Run Shelters. And yourself?"

"Same place. I don't put in as many miles a day as I did a few years back. I just need to get to Katahdin before October."

"October! It would be incredible to have that much time. I'm so driven. I'd probably hurry even if I had all the time in the world."

"I stop in all the towns and get to know the people. Everyone has to hike their own hike and has their own reasons for being out here. I wondered when you'd catch up to me. I started in February. Most of the folks who started in the early spring have zoomed by," Roy said with a laugh.

"I know what you mean about hiking your own hike. Everyone has agendas, goals, and expectations. I've wanted to do this since I was a kid. My life finally came to a place that I could. I can't imagine not finishing."

"With a positive attitude like that, you'll be with the less than ten per cent who finish a thru-hike in one season. Every year over two thousand hikers plan and prepare to make it to Katahdin, but somewhere along the way ninety percent of them pack it up and go home. It would be interesting to know what snaps when people decide they've had enough. Research reports injury as the lowest reason people quit. What would send you home, Wolf Woman?" Roy looked at me seriously.

"Loneliness. I'm surprised I am saying that, though. I'm such a recluse. I have close friends, but I don't exactly run with a pack. I enjoy hiking alone; however, meeting people has been more important than the scenery. I never looked for a hiking partner because I didn't want to be locked into someone else's agenda. Hiking with someone and needing support from home are different. Looking forward to maildrops keeps me going. Number eleven is coming up. Nature wouldn't be reason enough to keep me going through days of rain, snow, or freezing weather. Beautiful days are a rarity and thru-hikers don't sit around waiting for black clouds to go away. What keeps you coming back going after the experience lost its newness?"

"Being free and in nature. I love it out here. Life is so simple and uncomplicated. Hiking is stress and responsibility-free. I only have to worry about myself. I've been on the Trail so many times that I know where the rough places are and don't do long mileage when I know it's going to be tough. When it rains, I stay put. Time is not an issue. As complicated as it gets is finding water before dark."

Roy made hiking sound so simple. I didn't find it quite that anxiety-free. "Maybe setting unrealistic expectations is what separates those who finish from those who don't. If quitting was an option, I'd say goodbye to seeing Katahdin; but I never think about quitting, even when the Trail and weather are terrible. In

Georgia I resolved to walk through every situation, no matter how difficult. A fast thru-hike is better than none."

"Looks like you've walked and talked yourself to the Birch Run Shelters. Instead of one large shelter, Pennsylvania shelters are often two small ones." Several people sat around a roaring campfire and more people sat in the shelters. "This place looks packed. Hiking through Pennsylvania may be tough for you without a tent. Many of the shelters are built close to roads and locals frequent them. Anybody can use them, although thru-hikers are supposed to have priority. I'm going to pitch my tent by the creek."

Two teen-age boys had their gear spread all over the second shelter. "Room for one more?" I asked pleasantly, as I dropped my pack and untied the top.

"I guess so," grumbled one of them. "Move your stuff over," the boy who had spoken snapped at his buddy.

I ignored their disgust. "You fellows local?" I asked, trying to make peace.

"Yeah, up the road a piece," the first boy mumbled without looking up.

"This is the first time I've seen two small shelters instead of one large one since I left Springer Mountain." I hoped by mentioning Springer they wouldn't consider me an intruder. The plan worked.

"You thru-hiking? Lady, did you say Springer? Ain't that where the Trail starts?" The boy who had spoken first asked.

"Yes, I left March first. I've been on the Trail for two and a half months. I should climb Katahdin by the first of August."

"Holy shit! That's a long time." Both boys stared at me in disbelief.

"Yep, I'm doing it alone, too. Awfully nice of you to give me some space," I added, spreading my sleeping bag along one third of the shelter. "Company was the last thing you fellows wanted, huh?"

"You take all the room you want lady. Going all the way, that's awesome!"

The boys' attitudes had changed. They found it unthinkable that a woman would hike to Maine. "Holy shit, that's amazing," they were still saying as I walked off to get water and join Roy and the campers around the fire. The local folks shared their food and treated us like a royalty. Roy had told me that from Pennsylvania north, thru-hikers are treated with a great deal of respect. Being a thru-hiker, with the promise of making it to Katahdin, was not something to be taken lightly.

Rain woke me the next morning. Across the clearing Roy pulled down his tent, packed up, and left. Shelters were more convenient than tenting. "Alone again and another day of rain," I thought as I eased out of my sleeping bag, trying not to awaken the snoring youth. Within ten minutes I, too, was on the Trail munching Trail mix from my waist pack, as I did every two hours.

The Pennsylvania Trails reminded me of sections in Virginia, though not as refined and lush. Road crossings, parks, towns, and campgrounds were as numerous as pinegroves, fallen chestnut trees, and fields of fragrant flowers. In the first thirty-eight miles, I crossed roads twenty-one times. Grove Furnace State Park is where hikers traditionally eat a half-gallon of ice cream and receive a special "wooden spoon" as a prize for accomplishing such a feat. Tempting myself with a killer headache from cold ice cream was not on my list of things to do, but buying grapefruit juice was worth the stop. The rain stopped by the time I reached the park. Roy had spread his tent out to dry on a picnic table and was enjoying snacks. As I left the store I noticed a map of the area. Carlisle was only a few miles from the Park. I hurried to a pay phone. Helen's daughter said she was sure her mom would come get the pack so I could hike the thirteen miles to Whiskey Springs Road pack-free.

After gulping down my juice, I said goodbye to Roy and skipped down the Trail. I stopped at Tagg Run Shelter, the 1997 exact halfway point, long enough to turn to another chapter in my journey at this landmark by signing the journal. Now I'd really count down the miles to Katahdin rather than adding them up.

The Trail descended steeply to the two-lane paved Whiskey Spring Road. At the bottom I didn't have a clue of which way to go. A car pulled into the narrow parking area and a young couple got out. "Excuse me, could you tell me which way to Carlisle?"

"Down the road to the left a few miles. You hiking the Trail, need a ride?"

"Yes, and I'd appreciate it. I need to get to a friend's house."

"We just wanted an excuse to get away. My girlfriend here wasn't crazy about climbing that bank anyway." The young man put his arm around the girl and she giggled. "How far you hiked? How many miles is that Trail? You got directions?" I showed him Helen's address before answering the questions.

"I know my way around. Do you want to call her?" He handed me a car phone.

"Good idea."

I dialed, but Helen wasn't home. After asking at several gas stations and touring the town, we finally pulled up in front of Helen's condo. "Thank you so much," I said, climbing out of the back seat.

"Good luck and happy hiking!"

I knocked on the door, but no one answered. Sitting on the front porch, I waited for the next piece of my journey to unfold. Thirty minutes later a car pulled up. Helen and her daughter jumped out. "How did you get here? No wonder you wanted a break from carrying this pack. It's heavy."

Helen hugged me "I met two really nice young kids at the parking lot and they offered to give me a ride. Thank you for getting the pack."

"Come right in. I can't imagine hiking all day for so long. I couldn't do it. I'm real proud of you, though, and glad I can be part of your process," Helen gave me a hug.

"It's not for everyone, but it's definitely for me."

"I told my colleagues at Messiah College about your campaign, and everyone is impressed that you're really out there walking the Trail. Your mission is a miracle."

"As of today I'm halfway to Katahdin. I couldn't think of a better way to celebrate than taking a bath, eating a good meal, and visiting with a friend."

By 7:30 the next day, I was back at Whiskey Springs Road. Helen was in a hurry to get to the university for a workshop, so there was no time for lengthy good-byes. As she sped away, it occurred to me what tremendous faith my friends have in me to leave me in the woods and trust me to know what to do. They didn't always understand, but they always supported me. My five-month pilgrimage was definitely not something anyone talked me into or even suggested. It originated within me. However, never once had anyone doubted I could do it. Through their belief, I was learning to have faith in myself. Glancing up, I passed a white blaze on a twisted tree. The white rectangular stencil mark symbolized self-reliance. The wilderness was schooling me in trust. Trail experiences in sustenance and nurturing would carry me beyond Katahdin.

The Trail had been routed through Boiling Springs, PA in 1990. It felt odd following the white stenciled blazes on telephone poles and buildings on my way to pick up my twelfth maildrop. "Good morning! I'm thru-hiker Ellen Wolfe, here to pick up my mail." I said to the postal clerk.

"We've got plenty for you. When did you leave?"

"March first."

"You're moving right along. Happy hiking," the clerk smiled as he handed me letters from Suellen, Judy, Deb, Linda, Kate, Mom, Beth, Donna, Janet, and another box from Gloria. I carried them across the street to the Appalachian Trail Office.

"What a stack! Got anything good to eat?" Roy called from the porch railing.

"I'm sure I have more food than I know what to do with. I'll be in Port Clinton in four days." After picking out what I needed, I offered the rest to Roy and other hikers. I put a new plastic liner in my backpack, clothes bag, and food sack before adding rolls of film, toothpaste, mailing stamps, toilet paper, and food. In Gloria's box I found more Tick Tacs. Gloria put them in every box so the rattle would remind me of her support. I ate her snacks as I read my mail and wrote on the stamped post cards I'd sent to myself. I packed the items to carry and boxed the rest with journal notes and used handbook pages to mail back to Tennessee.

Darlington Shelter was only eleven miles away. After a long road walk through the traffic, construction, and over bog boards, I reached I-81. "Wolf Woman! Trail Magic over here!" Roy waved to me from the backyard of a house a few yards off the Trail. I cut through a thicket and joined him and others. "Help yourself to water and cookies. The lady who lives here is making us sandwiches. I'll tell her to make you one when she comes back."

129

"Great! How'd you chance upon this Trail Magic?"

"We were passing by and she hollered at us to come get food."

"One more, I see! You like peanut butter?" a pleasant middle-aged woman asked. "We like to feed the thru-hikers because we think you deserve it for making it this far."

"I love peanut butter. Thank you," I said, dropping my pack.

The woman went in the house. I chugged down as much water as I could hold and filled my bottles. After eating enough peanut butter sandwiches to give me energy all the way to Maine, I followed Roy down the Trail and picked his brain on how to slack pack in Maine.

"It will be tough to slack pack in the wilderness but you can get maps from the guard shacks showing the logging roads. You'll just have to figure out where the Trail entrances are on the roads. Before the wilderness you can slack pack from the Pine Ellis Hostel in Andover. Paul and Irene Trainor cook great breakfasts. Carry as light a pack as possible through Mahoosuc Notch and plan on two or three hours to get through the one mile of boulders in the gully. There's no place on the Trail like it. It's dangerous, especially in the rain. There are places you'll have to take off your pack and crawl through small crevasses. The gully flows with water so don't let go of your pack or walking sticks or they may disappear. Your adrenaline will be racing so fast you won't even know you are doing the Mahoosucs. You'll make it. Monson is the last town before the hundred-mile wilderness. There are no roads, stores, or people but plenty of water, woods, and if you are lucky, moose. Be sure to stay at Keith Shaw's."

"The wilderness sounds wonderful and Mahoosuc Notch sounds scary. But, I'll do whatever it takes to climb Katahdin." We stopped to listen to the city sounds.

"In Maine you'll only hear nature. From here to the Whites the Trail will be a piece of cake, then the real climbing begins. Hikers often quit in the Whites because it's so rough and the weather can be so bad. You're nothing but a lightening rod if a thunderstorm hits, so get off the ridge if you see a storm coming. Here's the shelter."

"Thanks for the advice." Dropping my pack, I got out Gloria's snacks. The peanut butter sandwiches were gone already. I ate all the time even though I'd lost a lot of fat. No one joined us at Darlington. After a meal of humus, bread, and spaghetti, I got out my journal. *May 19: The weather is finally hot. I hate humidity, although it's nowhere near as hot as it is down South. Leaving Springer in March was perfect. Cold as it was, I'd rather be cold than hot. I should be finished before the heat of August hits New England. Everything about the trip is going the way it's supposed to. This supplex shirt is too hot. I'll get a cotton teeshirt in Duncannon tomorrow. What incredible Trail Magic to get slack packing advice from Roy. He even put notes in my Handbook and data book. I'm nervous about the cliffs and rocks. Knowing women have made it gives me courage.*

Under a crystal sky, we stopped at Hawk Rock three miles above Duncannon to watch the Susquehanna River move through the valley. I imagined Iroquois standing on the very spot prior to 1736, when they inhabited all the land as far as I could see. Just before descending into the city, we were slowed down by boulders across an exposed rock-strewn mountainside. "This is just a taste of the Trail after you leave Duncannon. About the time you think you're back on smooth ground, a whole section of rocks shows up to give you more stone bruises. You won't be totally free of rocks until you climb Katahdin, but Pennsylvania is definitely the worst. Ouch!" Roy kicked a boulder. Looking at his bare toes, I decided boots weren't such a bad idea after all.

In Duncannon, Roy headed to the Doyle Hotel to have a beer and to find Vagabond. I found a telephone to call my son David for his twenty-first birthday. I felt guilty at not being home to celebrate with him. Fellows on the Trail had tried to reassure me that David wouldn't want his Mom around on his big twenty-first anyway, and that a check would suffice. I'd given Janet traveler's checks and asked her to send him a birthday check from Maryland. But that wasn't the same as being home to sing. David wasn't home. I left a message on his answering machine, the kind only a mother would leave. After chugging down a quart of grapefruit juice, devouring a huge deli sandwich, and stocking up on crackers and cheese, I headed down the street in search of a place to get a sleeveless cotton shirt. The weather was finally hot.

Spotting a corner variety store; I slipped out of my pack, dug out money, leaned the pack against the store, and walked in. I was relieved to find a table of shirts just inside the door. Being in close quarters reminded me that I didn't smell particularly decent to be shopping. Oh well, I needed a cooler shirt and for a few minutes of thru-hiker's scent, the clerk would have a few of my cents. Six dollars to be exact. After stuffing a large purple shirt in my pack, I continued up the street to the hardware store on Market Street for Coleman fuel. Crossing the Clarks Ferry Bridge Street led me out of Duncannon. Town stops and roadwalks were a frustrating stab in the natural rhythm of wilderness living, but without fuel and food, life in the woods would be impossible.

In the woods I peeled off my sweaty green shirt. The sun felt warm on my bare breasts. I would have stretched out for a sunbath if I didn't need to hike ten miles before dark. After a steep climb, the Trail leveled off at an elevation of 1,250 feet. From the crest, incredible farmland views looked like patchwork quilts. Already rocks filled the path and poison ivy crept between the rocks. I pulled on my gaiters to prevent exposure.

Peter's Mountain Shelter with its open porch and ample space is called the "Hilton of Pennsylvania." I heard voices as I rounded the corner. "Vagabond! I haven't seen you since Stecoah Gap in North Carolina, over two months ago. I can't believe I've caught up to you! Roy is at Doyle looking for you."

"Good to see you, too. Think he'll come up here tonight?"

"He probably will when he finds out you aren't in town." I turned my attention to a hiker who was quietly eating. "I'm Wolf Woman. I don't think we've met." I extended a hand to the hiker with a graying beard. "You thru-hiking?" I asked, sitting down.

"Sure am. I'm Buddha Jim. So you're the famous Wolf Woman! I wondered when you'd catch me. I left back in February and was ahead of everyone for a while, but now hikers who left in the spring are zooming by."

"Buddha Jim! I've been reading your journals all the way from Springer!"

"I hike slow because I meditate as I walk." Buddha Jim and I were discussing Trail spirituality when Roy came zipping around the corner.

"Vagabond, you rascal! Where you been, man? They told me at the Doyle that you'd been through town earlier today, so I hoped you'd be up here. Today was some kind of election and they weren't opening the bars until after the polls closed late tonight. I see you made it too, Wolf Woman. You get a shirt and some Coleman?"

"Sure did. Thanks for asking." It felt nice knowing the guys cared. The Trail had the sense of community. Roy and Vagabond were connected. I had connected with a vegetarian who was doing the Trail in search of spiritual sustenance. And all of us had connected none too soon. Darkness was filling the corners of the cabin-like shelter with a soothing blanket of protection. Vagabond shared the water he'd hauled up from the scant source over the hill. Roy had warned me water would be scarce in Pennsylvania. Scouting for water and scooting over rocks were new challenges to monitor and adjust.

At daybreak I was on the Trail before the guys. A clear sky promised a good day to hike the eighteen miles to Rausch Creek Shelter. At Shikellimy Rock overlook Buddha Jim caught up to me. "Being out here is truly freeing. Life up here is foreign to most people down there. Do you think the people in the valley wonder what kind of people walk the ridges above their communities?" Buddha Jim gazed into the valley.

"I figure folks who like to hike get up here from time to time and the rest may not be aware of the Trail. Do you feel like you are invading their privacy?"

"Sometimes, especially when I hike through private land. This Trail is far from total wilderness. I wish I could live off the land and stay in the woods."

"So do I. I used to know edible wild plants in the Smokies. But plants change with the regions and the climate. There's no way I could keep myself alive." I picked a blade grass and tossed it back down. "Even though the Trail is overused, it's still awesome."

"Definitely. I dread going back to civilization. The trip is half over for both of us. I love feeling the earth's rhythms. There is such value in walking for months and months. You are probably right about the folks down there. They may be oblivious to the Trail and don't know what they're missing. Awareness is the key to living."

"You're right, and I'm aware we've sat here for an hour," I pulled on my pack.

"I hike alone most of the time. Having someone to talk with is a nice change." Buddha Jim smiled as he got up. The soil under our feet was black like coal. Buddha Jim explained we were seeing evidence of the coal beds, building foundations, and old earth works from the mining operations that once thrived in the valley communities. Huge pine trees towering over a perfectly smooth roadbed led to the shelter. A wide creek followed the Trail to the beautiful rock Rausch Gap Shelter. A circular table was fastened around a straight pine tree in front of the shelter and water ran from a pipe into a trough. Buddha Jim and I settled in with two retired gentlemen and Drifter, a thru-hiker whose journal entries I had been seeing since Springer. After a pot full of noodles, lentil chili, and fruit roll-ups, I journaled until dark. *May 21: It seems like I walked farther than 17.7 miles today. I hate hiking through towns, but the experience brings perspective to the trip. I couldn't wait to connect with David on his 21st birthday and Suellen, but neither was home. I was depressed when I left town, but meeting Buddha Jim has cured that. The Trail never fails to give me community. Today has been pleasant, windy, and insightful as I listened to Buddha Jim talk about how meditation impacts his thru-hikes.*

I initiated the topic as we headed down the Trail the next morning. "It seems relationships develop easier in the woods than they do in civilization because thru-hiking is such an intense short experience. Thru-hikers need each other in more precise ways than people do back home. These rocks would be worse if I was stumbling over them alone." By flinging my walking sticks between the rocks, I tried to cushion my steps. We were making good time, even though fist-sized rocks covered the path. Talking helped pass the time, but didn't do anything to stop the sharp-pointed rocks from piercing the bottoms of our aching throbbing feet. My toenails were getting infected and hurt as much as my feet.

"Talking helps, but I'm not concentrating as much on where I'm walking."

"We don't have a choice." My sticks clacked with every step.

"Oh yes, we do. We can sit down and not go anywhere, or turn around and go back," Buddha Jim continued the debate.

"True, but I'm going to Maine. Sore feet or not, I'm going forward."

"We have choices. We can pace ourselves and concentrate more on what we're doing or we can fly through here, get bruised and get over it faster. The rocks are here for a reason. They challenge our faith and give us a reason to look beyond what's in front of our face and under our feet. What do you think about as you walk?" Buddha Jim asked.

"I think about people I've met and wonder where everyone is. It's odd that so many people are on this narrow space of land and yet we see so little of each other. Knowing people are out here is encouraging."

"Are there lessons in these rocks?" asked Buddha Jim as he kicked a rock.

"Every conquered obstacle toughens me for the next. Every challenge with the environment connects me closer to the earth. Trials put the trip in perspective. Whether we climb mountains, ford rivers, or walk on pine needles, we connect with the earth. We also aren't given more than we can handle. Today we aren't slowed down by slippery bog boards, gooy mud, thick fog, or soaking rain. And one more thing, these rocks are terrible!" Buddha Jim understood.

"With balanced perspective, expectations, and attitude, we'll learn the lessons of the Trail and find spiritual connection with the environment. Here's 501 Shelter!"

"I say, thank God, Goddess, the Universe, Higher Power, and Trail Magic!"

501 Shelter, located off PA 501, is an enclosed building with bunks, tables, and a skylight. Roy, Drifter, and Vagabond were relaxing with peanut butter and honey sandwiches. Buddha Jim sat for a minute and then announced he was going on to camp. I was at a far less needy place than I had been in Southern Virginia when Luvtuhike had walked on. I accepted the news and didn't try to change it. Trusting the process, not hanging on to it, was powerfully freeing. Hikers come and go, and serve their purpose in my journey, just like rocks.

"Thanks for the insight."

"I'll see you up the Trail," Buddha Jim turned and walked out the door.

"We're not far from town, are we? Why don't we hitch in for something good to eat?" I was definitely tired of Trail food.

"There's not much traffic out there and no one would pick all four of us up." Roy spoke from experience. "The last time I was here I stood for an hour and finally gave up."

"Then I'll go and bring back pizza for all of us."

"You don't have to, but it sure would be nice. The town is five miles to the right once you get to the road" Roy handed me a couple of dollars.

"You guys have been good to me and hitch-hiking is easy. If I don't get a ride after a few minutes I'll come back." I buckled my fanny pack around my waist.

"It's nice having a woman around when you're hungry." Vagabond handed me a couple of dollars.

"Count me in if your going after pizza." Drifter gave me his contribution.

With a pocket full of money, I headed to the road. On a gravel-pull off I saw a car parked with a woman at the wheel. I approached the car and asked, "Would you mind giving me a ride to town so I can get supper for a bunch of thru-hikers?"

"I have an appointment at six across the street, but it's too early to go so hop in."

"Great, we'll have time to go and come back. Hikers call this Trail Magic." In less than an hour I swung open the shelter door. "Supper's on the table. Come and get it."

"How did you do that so fast?" Roy asked picking up a piece of pizza. "What'd you do, hold up traffic?"

"Thanks a lot, Wolf Woman," said Vagabond, taking a bite. While enjoying my share, I explained the evening's Trail Magic.

"This shelter has a caretaker who lives in the house next door. I'm going over and see if he has any ice cream for sale. Anybody want some?" Roy ate more ice cream than anyone I'd ever known.

"I'll take one, and if you don't mind, ask the caretaker if there's any chance of slack packing into Port Clinton tomorrow."

When Roy returned loaded down with ice cream, he announced, "Have your pack ready at 5:00 a.m. and it will be waiting for you at the pavilion when you get there."

"Yes! Five o'clock is early but I've done it before, I'll do it again." After giving my pack to the caretaker I returned to my bunk and shivered in the cool morning air until dawn. Barely able to see the Trail, I headed out for another day of walking on rocks. Not having the pack took some pressure off my feet, but the freedom from the weight tempted me to go fast which just wasn't possible. I couldn't dodge the jagged rocks that stuck straight up.

I caught up to Buddha Jim. He passed the time by telling me about his girlfriend coming to pick him up in Port Clinton for the weekend. Thirty minutes before the Post Office closed Buddha Jim and I walked into the sleepy town of Port Clinton. "Have a good rest of the hike. You'll be way up the Trail by the time I get back on Monday. I'll think of you tripping over rocks while I soak in a hot tub, drink coffee, and eat salad."

"You'll be stubbing your toes while I'm sailing along in New Jersey." I laughed.

"Ah, that's the truth," waved Buddha Jim. The clerk handed me the second pair of boots, socks from Uncle George, a letter from Gloria, a letter from Suellen telling me Lars was eating again, a map from Kate showing how far I'd come, the newspaper article from Janet, and news from Judy. I cherished my support!

At the counter, I wrote postcards. "I'll see you in Maine real soon." I wrote to Suellen. Little did I know that two months from that very day, July 23, I would climb Mt. Katahdin. In only four days I'd be in the Delaware Water Gap at my fourteenth maildrop, and soon I'd touch New England soil.

After sorting out the food I'd need for the next four days, I prepared a box to send home, including my old boots. The new boots felt firm with real lining instead of sanitary liners. I stacked my mail and walked to the pavilion where my pack waited.

Passing a phone booth, I called Suellen. Hearing her voice and her words of praise and enthusiasm warmed my heart, soul, and even my sore feet. As I hung up, Barbara popped in my mind. I wouldn't be in New Jersey for a week.

Preparing myself that she might not be home, had forgotten, or was too busy to come, I dialed.

"Hello." A New York accent reached my ears after only two rings.

"Hello. Is this Barbara? This is Wolf Woman. Remember me? I met you in Virginia near Pearisburg. I was ..."

Barbara's thick Brooklyn accent cut me off. "Wolf Woman! Where are you? Of course I remember you. How could I forget?"

"I'm in Port Clinton. I'll be in the Delaware Water Gap in four days. You said..."

Barbara's enthusiasm interrupted me again, "I didn't expect to hear from you for a couple more weeks. You're moving fast. The school knows not to call me to work when you get here. I've told everyone about you! Call me from the Delaware Water Gap and I'll come get you. How are your feet? Those Pennsylvania rocks are terrible aren't they?"

"My feet are sore, but I just picked up my second pair of boots so they should feel better tomorrow. I'll call again. I'm looking forward to seeing you."

I stared at the receiver, oblivious anyone was passing by. "Is everything okay? You eating at Helen's?" the section hiker I'd met at the pavilion asked.

"Yes, everything is fine, just fine!" I could feel myself glowing all the way down to my sore toes. "I'm going to ask the legendary Helen to make me the biggest salad she's ever made, and cook me a huge plate of her famous fries."

"May I join you?" the young man grinned.

"I'd be glad for the company." Company was important. An hour later, stuffed to the gills with every vegetable Helen could find, I stretched out on a mat I found in the pavilion. In the darkness I watched silhouettes move in the dark shadows created by the street lamp, I felt restless. I tried to blame the fact I couldn't sleep on the freight trains that clattered over the track behind me, but I knew better. I was in shock that Barbara had not only remembered, but had planned on meeting me. I didn't know why she wanted to be part of my experience, but I accepted this one thing I did not want to change.

In the morning I joined the guys at the 3 C's Restaurant. While I was walking to the Post Office with Vagabond, Helen's big car whizzed by with Roy seated in the back. I felt sad, but not crushed to watch him disappear. I'd hiked with him more than anyone so far. He was taking a day off and I probably wouldn't see him again. His advice would be valuable, but I could let him go. It was time again to walk my walk, alone.

There was no escaping the rocks between Port Clinton and Eckville Shelter. I calculated, contemplated, and considered every step but they poked, punctured, and pierced the bottoms, tops, and sides of my feet. I vacillated between trying to hurry and slowing down. Stranded in the middle of Pennsylvania, halfway between where I'd started and my destination, I felt trapped by the hard, jagged chunks under my feet. My boots didn't fit between the rocks and often got stuck. I tried walking in the woods, but the excruciating rocks were every-where. If I'd thought crying would make the rocks go away, I would have spilled enough tears to float to Katahdin. Resting only prolonged the ordeal. I concen-trated on naming people I'd met, listing the items in Gloria's boxes, and reliv-ing my adventures, until I landed on another rock.

After what seemed like days, the Trail led me to Hawk Mountain Road and the Eckville Hiker's Center. The bunks, a porta toilet, water, solar shower, and picnic tables were a welcome sight. "Pilgrim! You've cut your hair!"

"Yep! I cut the top off. I knew you weren't far behind. Seen Broken Road?"

Pilgrim's hair had been a thick mass of shoulder length waves when I'd seen him last in Nolichucky on April 3d. He'd shaved the top and left it long around the sides. It looked like Bozo the Clown! "No, I haven't. Have you seen Chief, Tacet, or Stryder?"

"Tacet went to Trail Days and Chief is way behind." As we shared news, I pulled off my boots. Two section hikers, and Map Man who had done the Trail from Springer to Duncannon in 1996, were back to make it to Katahdin and joined us for supper.

"Map Man is a neat name. I used to do the geography bee with my elemen-tary school kids." Map Man was tall and my age.

"I study cartography in Idaho. I hear you are hiking for breast cancer. I am a survivor of leukemia and admire your work."

"Thanks. Being out here must be especially rewarding for you."

"I'm lucky to be alive. Making hiking plans occupied my mind during treatments. I'm planning to hike the Pacific Crest Trail after I finish the AT. Maybe I'll hike for leukemia. How did you set up your fundraiser?"

As I explained my campaign, Map Man and I discovered that neither of us drank alcohol or ate meat, and that both of us dreaded another day on the rocks. Hiking together to Bake Oven Shelter would make them more bearable.

Heavy black clouds, socked-in fog, and drenching rain dampened our spirits and the rocks as we set out the next morning. Telling stories passed the time but they didn't soften the pain. About noon Map Man had a brilliant idea. "I hear there is a restaurant off PA 309. We deserve hot food."

"Sounds good to me. I'm starving. This Trail mix in my pocket is nothing but mush," I pulled out a bag of rainbow colored peanuts and raisins, and soggy M& M's.

Soaked to the bone and freezing cold, we reached the Blue Mountain B & B. The proprietors let us hang our raincoats in the kitchen to dry. "This is not the first time I've made puddles in a restaurant." I shared the story of adding ambi-ance to the Old Home Place with Rain and Snail. "It's hard to believe how far I've hiked."

"Restaurant breaks on rainy days are Trail Magic," Map Man concluded.

I agreed. With our stomachs full and bodies warm, we pulled back on water-logged boots and cold packs. Three miles down the Trail I stopped to shake rain out of my eyes and gasped in disbelief. I stood face to face with huge chunks of pointed rocks.

"Does the Trail go over these?" I asked, not wanting to believe the white blazes were stenciled in the rocks along the cliff edges.

"I'm afraid so. Go slow and be careful. You want me to lead or follow you?"

"You lead. I'm so glad you're with me. This is the scariest thing I've done yet." Climbing the Cliffs and peaks of Bear Rocks in the pouring rain was not going to be easy. As I watched Map Man pick his way over the cliffs I noticed that his walking sticks were a hindrance. I collapsed my poles and stuck them in my pack. With my free hands, I was able to grab the rocks when I started to fall. By concentrating on equally distributing our weight, keeping our center of gravity low, and securing each step before making a move, we made it through the tortuous section. Vacillating between saying encouraging words and utterly discouraging groans left us drained. I didn't think the shelter would ever appear. The last mile took all the strength we had left.

"I see it." With revived energy, we hurried down the blue blazed Trail. Behind the shelter, we stopped short. The sound of voices and smell of marijuana drifted from the shelter. Facing two soaked thru-hikers was no doubt as disheartening for the five young guys we found sprawled in the shelter smoking pot, as it was for us to see them. Without a word, they moved over. Map Man and I changed into dry clothes behind the shelter before settling in. With altered minds, the guys asked us what had prompted us to do a thru-hike. After today, I wasn't so sure myself. Answering questions put us all to sleep.

In the morning Map Man and I changed back into wet clothes. In the early days of my trip, I would have feared hypothermia wearing wet clothes but the sky was once again clear and the air reasonably warm. We smelled smoke as we approached George W. Outerbridge Shelter. At the shelter we found two hikers enjoying breakfast around a roaring campfire. Noticing they had huge bags of gorp, we decided it was time to take a break. We joined the campers and grumbled about how tired we were of our food.

"Here," one fellow said, handing me a gallon-size bag of gorp. "We're out of here as soon as we clean up and that'll be one less thing to carry."

"Wow! Thanks!" I pulled out a baggy, filled it and handed it to Map Man.

"Ready to do some hiking now that we are through yogi-ing?" I asked, grinning at Map Man. The hikers looked up at me quizzically, but Map Man knew yogi-ing meant the good natured way thru-hikers ask for food without actually begging.

"Thanks for the food and fire. My shirt is nearly dry," Map Man waved.

Munching on new gorp helped us forget about our sore feet. Above Lehigh River and PA 238 we could hear traffic from the Pennsylvania Turnpike tunneling under the mountain. Map Man was stopping to rest for a few of days.

"Thanks for the support over Bear Rocks. Maybe I'll see you up the Trail." Good-byes were getting as common as greetings.

"I was glad you were there for me too. I'll look forward to seeing your articles."

"I'll send them. Take care." I gave Map Man a quick hug. I didn't watch my most recent companion walk away.

After crossing the bridge over Lehigh River, I lost sight of the white blazes. Totally frustrated I walked up and down the road. There were blazes on the bridge so the Trail had to be on this side of the river. The cars wouldn't stop. I missed Map Man. The ridge above PA 248 was a jumble of huge boulders. I knew the Trail was up there but I couldn't find the entrance. Glancing above my head, I finally saw a lone white blaze shimmering in the sunlight. There was no way I could get to the blaze from where I stood. Walking up the road I found an unmarked Trail leading off the roadway. A few yards up the Trail, I saw a blaze. I'd heard the Trail was poorly marked in Pennsylvania, but I didn't know it would be this bad. Climbing over the boulders in fifty mile-an-hour winds was a challenge. Grateful it wasn't raining, I took off my pack and pushed it over boulder after boulder until I reached the top. The scenery resembled the Western Badlands. A zinc-smelting plant had destroyed the vegetation. Life was barely returning to the barren wasteland. The terrain was strikingly different from that in the Southern states and far less fertile. Purple wild flowers clustered in the dusty clearings and pale moss grew in the parched soil. Short thick hedges grew close to the Trail. What the state lacked in vegetation, it made up for in rocks.

Voices and a barking dog welcomed me to the Leroy A. Smith Shelter. A woman gathered a small beagle up in her arms as I approached. An older man stood by the table cooking supper. "Welcome! You thru-hiking?" asked the man as I dropped my pack.

"Yes, I'm Wolf Woman."

"I'm Bob and this is Sally Beagle. You know Grasshopper, don't you?"

"Grasshopper! I can't believe it. Remember me? Kate and I met you on the March first. I've enjoyed your journal entries and smiley faces."

"Sure I remember you! Stryder has kept up with you."

"I haven't seen Stryder since Harper's Ferry. Where is he?"

"He's over the hill getting water." Grasshopper pointed in the direction of the stream. "He'll be glad to see you!" Grasshopper gave me a hug.

"This'll be like old home week. Pilgrim told me at Eckville Shelter that you left the morning I arrived. You've been a day or two ahead of me for weeks. I've been reading about Sally Beagle, too." I looked at Bob, the proud owner of the dog lying in Grasshopper's arms. "Where is your dog, Bailey?"

"My parents came and got her in Virginia. Here comes the water boy."

"Wolf Woman! Where'd you come from?" Stryder hugged me.

"Springer Mountain, same place you came from; and now I suppose you want to know where I'm headed?" Laughing, I hugged the gangly young man.

"It sure is good to see you. How you doing on the rocks?"

"Awful! Look at the boots I got in Harper's Ferry." They were full of holes. He wore lightweight boots that weren't as tiring as heavy ones, but were no match for rocks.

"Want some water? We have plenty." Grasshopper asked.

"Sure, since neither of us had to carry it. Thanks." I stuck my pan under the spout.

"Hey, that means I got two women to cook my supper," Stryder laughed.

"I've owed you food ever since that jar of peanut butter I ate of yours on Big Bald. Slim pickings tonight. I pick up a maildrop tomorrow. How does lentil soup, humus, and pasta sound?"

"Great. All I have left is crackers, cheese, and candy bars." Delaware Water Gap was a milestone. Katahdin seemed just around the corner.

"Watch out for snakes." Bob warned as he buckled Sally's dog pack under her stomach the next morning. " There may be rattlers in these rocks."

"I will." I said rinsing out my pan. I'd seen a few black snakes. Minutes after getting on the Trail a snake moved as I picked up a foot. I touched it with the end of my walking stick. A series of rattles vibrated as the snake slipped into the underbrush. I grabbed my camera. On Wolf Mountain I found Bob and Grasshopper resting after nearly stepping on a rattlesnake. Grasshopper was a geologist from New York. Her parents lived in North Carolina and had helped her slack pack through the south. They'd kept her dog while she hiked the Smokies. "I'm getting off the Trail in June to go to London with my husband on business. I should reach New England before I leave. I'll be back to finish."

"What a great summer, hiking the Trail and going abroad. All we have to look forward to are rocks." The last twenty miles before Delaware Water Gap was the worst conglomeration of rock torture. The terrain ranged from loose, pebbly gravel that caused my boots to slide and my ankles to buckle, to sharp pointed rocks that jabbed my soles and punctured my feet, which felt like raw meat. With my head down and eyes riveted to the ground, my neck grew stiff and my eyes blurry. My walking sticks rhythmically clicked my feet and thoughts into focusing on each step. "New Jersey tomorrow," I repeated over and over like a deep ancient mantra calling me to some mysterious place I'd never been, but knew I must go. I lost my way twice for longer than I care to recall. Frustrated at walking over on the rocks twice, I gritted my teeth in pain as I retraced my steps back to white blazes. The approach Trail into the Gap followed beautiful streams that I would have enjoyed had I been in a better frame of mind. I didn't stop until I swung open the basement door of the hostel in the Presbyterian Church of the Mountain. Stryder was stretched out on a couch with his feet in the air reading a book.

"I don't think I could have taken one more hour of rocks. My feet are killing me. I am over it, absolutely over it! I've lost all my toenails except the two big ones. Maybe they won't hurt so much now that they're gone." Stryder listened to me rant and rave.

When I stopped to breathe he sweetly suggested. "There's plenty of hot water."

Without another word I left the room. Clean and relaxed, Bob, Grasshopper, Stryder, and I enjoyed a huge salad, pasta dinner, and coffee in Brownie's Restaurant. A phone call to Suellen was better than dessert. Our connection was deeper than my calling to do the Trail.

"How are your feet?" Suelen asked.

"Just fine," I said. They had to be fine. "Soon we'll both be in Maine. Katahdin is only eight hundred and ninety one miles away. I've walked an average of nineteen miles a day and spent twelve nights on Pennsylvania's two hundred and thirty-two miles of Trail. Roy, Buddha Jim, and Map Man have been respectful compatible companions. They are behind me now, as are Pilgrim, Broken Road, Grasshopper, Magot, and Chief. Lessons of how to walk my own walk are becoming clear. Leaving Pennsylvania makes me sad for only one reason. I feel sorry for local hikers who only know rocks as Trails!"

# Chapter 10

## *"Give me a call and I will come get you!"*

### New Jersey and New York

New Jersey's and New York's one hundred and sixty-two miles of Trail are routed through the most populous region of the United States. Weaving a Trail around highways, subdivisions, and industrial parks was nothing short of a miracle. Although Delaware Water Gap National Recreation Area hardly felt like wilderness, its tall hemlock trees and magnificent waterfalls were beautiful. Sunfish Pond, the first glacial pond encountered by north-bounders, shimmered on the summit. Under a brilliant blue sky, I followed a perfect reflection of trees as I circled the pond. Only songbirds broke the silence. Standing alone at the north end of the pond, I watched fish ripple the still water. The chaos and frenzy of Times Square, Madison Square Garden, and Washington D.C. were only a few hours drive away. Gratitude filled my soul for the peace and quiet.

Ten miles from Delaware Water Gap, dormitory style cabins with bunks, electricity, hot showers, and kitchen privileges were good reasons not to hike further than Mohican Outdoor Center, Deer greeted me as I approached the center. It was not officially open but the manager let me stay in support of my breast cancer campaign. After a hot shower and supper, I settled in a comfortable chair by an open door and wrote an article for the *Herald-Citizen* in Cookeville, Tennessee. I had promised to send an article once a month. So far two had been published. My work was interrupted by the same soft munching sound I'd heard in the Grayson Highlands State Park.

Three deer nibbled on grass barely five yards from the cabin. Safe within the Worthington State Forest, the sleek, mottled animals knew no danger. Neither did the scampering squirrels and beautiful birds that leaped in the branches above me. As dusk gathered, the deer retreated into the forest. I moved to the main house for a cup of cocoa. As I was headed for the door, a woman walked up the walkway.

"May I help you?" she asked.

"No thank you. I'm Wolf Woman, a thru-hiker staying in the cabin."

"Welcome, when'd you start? I'm Midnight, or Mel Blaney, thru-hiker last year."

"You finished last year? Did you hike alone?" I set my cocoa on the counter.

"No, Out of Africa hiked with me. We wrote a book together that just come out." Midnight picked up a copy of *A Journey of Friendship* from the display rack.

"Wingfoot told me about you in Hot Springs. Congratulations! I'll buy a book at the Conference office on my way home. I'm planning to write a book, too. Tell me how the trip was for you. What was it like when you finished?" I was full of questions.

"Returning to civilization was difficult. The adjustment was real hard. I sold my house and got rid of tons of stuff. Hiking simplified my life. I'm working here for a while. My partner has gone back to Africa for now, but we hope to start a hostel. Connecticut and Massachusetts really need one. The motels are so expensive up there. Who are you hiking with?

"No one. My daughter was with me for the first six days. I know a lot of hikers, but farther north I get, the more days people take off and the less I see them."

"Hikers get tired about this point in the trip. The Trail will slow you down. You won't be able to do more than ten or twelve mile days in the Whites. High mileage days are about over after Vermont. It's easy to get discouraged. Maine is tough but beautiful. The rocks you just went through are a piece of cake compared to the cliffs up ahead. I wouldn't have made it without Out of Africa's support. I can't imagine hiking alone.

"Here," Midnight handed me two bagels. "You must be tired of Trail food. We got so sick of ours we could hardly choke it down. It's great talking you."

"Thank you. I miss good bread almost as much as I do people. I can't wait to buy your book. It's been great talking to you, too. I don't realize how much I miss visiting with women until I meet one. Thanks for the encouragement."

Midnight's words scared and excited me. I wasn't sure they were exactly encouragement, but she spoke from experience. I'd made it this far alone; I would finish. Just because no one walked by my side didn't mean support wasn't with me. Tomorrow I'd meet Barbara. I didn't know what she had in mind or why she wanted to come, but my feet hurt, my toes were numb, and my spirits were low. Part of me wanted to get the trip over with while another part wanted to stay in the woods forever. So, the Trail would see to it that I slowed down, but could I adjust to the pace? I felt emotionally, mentally, and physically drained, and very tired of walking.

But I knew not to dwell on discouragement. Giving in to depression would send me off the Trail quicker than rocky terrain or days of rain. Foul weather moved out on its own accord. Dismissing debilitating thoughts was my responsibility. Picking up a pen, I took advantage of having electricity. *May 28: Finally, I'm in New Jersey. This state is easier than Pennsylvania. Stryder is a day ahead. Grasshopper and Bob are taking a day off. Soon Grasshopper will go to Europe. I won't see her again. I'll be sad not to see her messages in the journals.*

I'd heard Worthington's Bakery in Culvers Gap, eighteen miles up the Trail, was worth the stop. I wasn't much for sweets, but I loved muffins. The day was warm and the Trail much easier, but my swollen feet tingled constantly. I told myself the rocks were over and tried not to think about what lay ahead.

**143**

Culver's Gap was a quaint town built around Kittatinny Lake. Worthington's Bakery was closed. I was disappointed, but was relieved I didn't have to deal with getting compulsive about buying muffins. However, I was in town and hungry.

After a cheese and tomato sandwich in the Stag Horn Restaurant, I called Barbara. She knew where I was and would arrive in an hour. I walked to a beach behind the restaurant. Lying on my mat, I watched boats bob on the lake. Beach houses dotted the shore. Under the watchful eyes of two mothers, a menagerie of small children played in the sand. I felt far removed and disconnected. I pinched myself and touched my pack. I didn't feel connected to anything around me. A beach was not a new experience, but I felt lost and out of touch. I belonged on the Trail. I didn't have a clue where I was in relationship to anything familiar. I longed for the serene secure life I saw around me. The houses, stores, signs, and even the children's laughter were the same each time I got off the Trail. All the towns looked the same. But this town was not home. The forests were full of diversity and variety. Although I was safe from humanity in the wilderness, it was often unsettling. I felt comfortable with the element of risk. Nature couldn't leave me. It was I who walked through it. Staying in the woods meant I seldom dwelt with people, but this lack of connection caused my loss of reality. I remembered being in Europe with Kate after she graduated from eighth grade and I had graduated from college. We were on a train in Germany and feeling very disoriented and disconnected listening to everyone around us speaking German. Suddenly a baby cried. Our ears resonated to the familiar pitch and universal sound of the fussy baby. As the mother comforted the infant in her native tongue, we were comforted by the repetitious squalls.

Alone on the beach, I looked for a similar reality check. I felt like an alien in a foreign country. There were no white blazes. I concentrated on believing Barbara was making her way through the snarled city traffic to get me. More than needing a bath, I needed human company.

On the beach two children ran hand in hand. A third child flattened a sandcastle piled high by a fourth. Earlier all four children had been playing happily. Jolted from their conversation, the mothers jumped up to referee the squabble. One minute all was well, and the next minute someone's attitude disrupted the status quo. I understood how expectations result in dashed hopes. The result of mixed messages and the risks involved when letting people in personal space was played out before me like a rerun movie script from my own life. I'd not planned to deal with old baggage on the Trail. Neither did the child who'd built the sandcastle expect it to be smashed. When the sky pours rain or a mountains ascends without a warning, I accept the experiences as part of the process. Sunny days follow rainy ones and all mountains have summits. It seemed easier to take nature in stride than unpredictable human behaviors. Nature was teaching me to accept people the same way I accepted the environment. As to the children, one child's self-centered behavior ended everyone's beach experience.

"Hey, bathing beauty, you're not going to get to Katahdin that way." Barbara's New York accent jolted me back to reality. The sound of her voice was much more comforting than the fussy baby on the train or the pouting children shuffling homeward. "Let's get a motel room. You'll feel like a new woman after a shower."

"A motel room? We're staying here? You don't have to go home tonight?"

"I need a vacation, too. I'll pay for a motel room and tomorrow I'll visit with friends while you hike. I'll pick you up Liberty Corner Road in the afternoon. We'll go get something to eat and then I'll hike with you the half mile to Pochuck Mountain Shelter. Not carrying the pack will give your body a chance to rest." Barbara was a planner and had been studying the data book.

"Fantastic! That means two days of slack packing, hot showers, real food, and company. Barbara, I can't believe you're willing to take two days out of your life to come slack pack me. How come?"

"It's fun, just plain fun. You deserve it. So do I."

I didn't understand what was fun about spending money on motel rooms and having to hang out while I hiked, but I didn't ask any more questions. I didn't understand why she thought I deserved it either. But, I was glad she did.

Since entering Virginia I'd been fighting depression. As the Trail got easier, each day's progress had given me strength to keep going. By pushing myself, I'd managed to keep my body moving faster than my emotions. Now, well into the second half of my journey, I felt physically and emotionally exhausted. The rocks in Pennsylvania had taken a toll on more than my feet. My whole body ached and my once positive attitude was skeptical. I wanted to go home. I was afraid I couldn't make it over the Whites and Maine's wilderness. Barbara's entrance into my hiking experience was no accident. "How's this look?" Barbara pulled into a motel.

"Anything is fine with me. Remember, I've been sleeping on the ground."

After a shower Barbara took me to an up-scale restaurant. While I ate two helpings from the salad bar and a pasta dinner, Barbara's strong personality filled me with support. "Dot and I are worried about you. I know you've been a vegetarian a long time, but I don't think you get enough protein. Your body will break down if you don't get nourishment. I came so I could to feed you. I want you to finish. I don't want to see you get so weak that you get depressed and break down. You've lost a lot of weight since I met you in Virginia and look exhausted. You're a determined hiker and you have what it takes; just be good to yourself." Barbara was serious.

"I'd move fast even if I wasn't on a schedule. I get protein from nuts, dried beans and pasta. I need people, not food. My feet are the problem."

"Soak them in cold streams every chance you get. The numbness won't go away until months after the trip is over. You are going accomplish in one summer what I've been working on for twenty-five years. What pride you'll feel on top of Katahdin."

"Right now all I feel is numb and tired." Barbara paid the bill and we headed back to the motel. I was asleep as soon as my head hit the pillow.

After breakfast I loaded fruit, bagels, cheese, peanut butter, and apples in Barbara's daypack and headed for the High Point, New Jersey's highest elevation, at only 1,803 feet. After ten road crossings I came out at Liberty Corners Road, and there sat Barbara. I was as surprised as I was relieved. If nothing else, the trip was teaching me to trust people. "Hop in. We're going to a motel. I don't feel safe leaving the car on this road. I'm not in the mood to backpack anyway."

I climbed in and Barbara sped away. "Tomorrow I'll meet you at N.Y.17 with your pack and we'll eat before I put you on the Trail. You'd only have to hike two miles to Wild Cat Shelter. What Fun!" Barbara grinned as she pulled into another motel.

"But are you sure you can afford it? I mean hotels are expensive. Barbara, why are you doing this? What's in this for you?"

"I'm having fun. It's fun, just plain fun. I don't think you do fun very well. You need people to show you fun. Slack packing you is fun. Isn't hiking without the pack fun? Anyway, I like helping you. I don't think many people have stood behind you. What you are doing is important. Besides, I enjoy hanging out with you. You're an inspiration. This is my way of thanking you for the money you raised for breast cancer research."

I was stunned. Barbara's life hadn't been much fun for several years. She'd given up her full time teaching job in order to care for her ailing parents until they both passed away. But, I still didn't feel inspiring. I felt as though if I let myself burst into tears I'd drown in a salty sea of emotion. "I'm grateful to you and I'm glad you came. This has been fun. I hate to see it end," I blinked back tears.

After a nice Italian dinner we washed clothes before returning to the motel. I crawled into bed. Barbara surfed the television. Seeing flashes of familiar commercials reminded me of home. They touched a raw emotion, called homesickness. I stared at the screen. Huge tears rolled down my cheeks. Like a child I blurted, "I don't think I can keep doing this. Barbara I want to go home. I don't know why I'm out here. I wish I had never said I wanted to hike this stupid Trail!"

Barbara slid off her bed and sat beside me. Stroking my tangled hair, she said, "You are out here because you are supposed to be. You're where you need to be. You won't be out there much longer. You've almost made it. You can do it, one step at a time. You've made it this far, you'll finish. Let those tears fall. You need a good cry. Is this the first time you've cried?"

"Yes, I hate crying. It's too emotionally draining. I feel like I won't be able to stop," I blubbered into the pillow.

"Crying is supposed to be emotionally draining. You'll stop when you are ready." Barbara rubbed my back.

"What if I can't get over the Whites? I remember what Dot said in the shelter when I met you guys, about being a lightning rod during a thunderstorm on the Presidentials and about those struck dead on the ridge. What if I get struck by lightning or fall off a mountain? Moosilauke is supposed to be terrible. My feet will hurt worse by the time I get there. What If I get part way up and can't walk another step? I should have dehydrated my food. My food is too heavy. I hate carrying the pack." I blew my nose.

"If you fall down you'll get up. Remember how bad the rocks were in Pennsylvania? They were no picnic, but you got through them. I'm older than you and if I can get up Moosilauke, so can you. The next time you do the Trail you'll know to take dehydrated food." Barbara patiently addressed all my fears.

"There won't be a next time. What if I get lost in the White Mountains? I hear the Trails aren't well marked and I have to know Trail names. What if I can't find the white blazes?" I was clearly on a downward spiral.

"Tired woman, you will find the blazes. There'll be people in the Whites to help. Your goal is to hike the Appalachian Mountains end to end. New England is your home. Uncle George and Gloria will help you. Dot will help you in Vermont. You'll make it."

"Some thru-hikers say slack packing isn't the right way to do the Trail. They say if I don't carry my pack all the way to Katahdin I haven't officially thru-hiked." I sat up, clearly more worried about this issue than about not being able to finish.

Barbara patted my arm frantically as if I'd touched a raw nerve. "There are no rules on how to hike the Trail! I tell you there are no rules! This subject comes up every season. As long as you walk the Trail no one can tell you what to put on your back. Walking is the criteria to thru-hiking, not carrying. Hiking is walking not carrying and no one can tell you whether or not to carry a pack. The hikers who say it's wrong to slack pack are the ones who wish they had connections to do so. Walk your own walk and don't worry about how others hike it. Remember this is a hike, not a carrying contest. There are no rules. Rules limit the experience. You're in nature, not organizing a school board meeting! You're the freer from regulations and rules than you've ever been and probably ever will be. Take advantage of it. Individual opinions, independent goals, and instinctive plans should be respected. Now, try calling Suellen again. You'll feel better if you get a hold of her." Barbara handed me the phone and a box of Kleenex. When Suellen answered, Barbara slipped outside to have a cigarette.

"Ellen! I just walked in the door. I'm glad Barbara is with you. I bet it feels good to sleep in a bed and eat real food. In a few weeks I'll be up there. How are your feet?"

This time I didn't say "fine." "Suellen, I've been lonely, my feet hurt, and I don't know if I can make it." I moaned, bellyached, and groaned. Suellen's response was different from Barbara.

"You can come home if you want to. No one is twisting your arm to finish if you don't want to. You can quit any time you wish. I think you can do it and am looking forward to joining you, but if you want to come home, come on. It's your decision."

I didn't know what to say. "Are you still there?" Suellen asked.

"Yes. But I don't want to come home. I didn't say anything about quitting. I'm climbing Katahdin. I just miss everyone and my feet hurt. I'm getting back on the Trail tomorrow. This state is beautiful, the rocks are nearly all gone, and the weather is warm. Thanks for listening and putting things in perspective. See you in Maine."

Barbara walked in just as I said, "See you in Maine."

"So, you are going to Maine, eh? I knew talking to Suellen would not only put a sparkle in your eye but a spring in your step. If I'd thought you were a quitter I wouldn't have come. You just needed a good cry and now you need a good night's rest. I'm exhausted and I didn't even hike today." With that the lights were out and I was back on the Trail again, in my dreams.

In good spirits I crossed the New Jersey-New York line carrying Barbara's daypack loaded with peanut butter and jelly sandwiches, grapefruit juice, and water enroute for NY 17. During the twenty-five mile hike, the Trail led me over long sections of bog boards through some of the finest freshwater wetlands on the Trail. The birds, frogs, butterflies, and water plants distinctive sounds, colors, and patterns created an Appalachian Trail tapestry as I hiked the one hundred and twelve bog boards in Vernie Swamps. In the wooded areas, circular depressions in the ground marked charcoal pit sites where hemlock trees had been burned to melt iron. The elaborate mounds once held stacks of wood covered with ferns or wet leaves and topped with thick sod. The small mounds smoldered for two weeks and the thirty-feet ones for up to a month.

Much of the Trail in New Jersey and New York ran on rocks over exposed ridges. Watching sailboats tack back and forth in the wind on Greenwood Lake reminded me I was freer than the boats hemmed in by shorelines and schedules. Bound only by the Trail, I sailed along under my own power. The Trail followed the lake until it turned north, leaving the huge boats within the banks of the lake. I appreciated my freedom but was envious that the boat owners had homes to go to when the sun went down.

The sun was blazing hot. The faster I walked, the hotter I got, and the more thirsty and exhausted I felt. I didn't realize I had forgotten to bring my Polar Pure until I had finished off my water. At two in the afternoon, I still had eight miles to go. The humidity drained my energy and boulders slowed me down, but I kept going. Barbara was waiting. White blazes were everywhere and I wasn't sure where the New Jersey/New York State line was although I did see Prospect Rock, New York's highest elevation. Exhausted and drenched in sweat, I reached the parking lot a little after six.

"What happened? Are you all right? Your face is red as a beet. You look as though you're having a heat stroke. Hold your breath, while I pour water on your head."

Without giving me time to stop her, Barbara poured a jug of water over my head. Horrified at wasting precious water I gasped, "Barbara, how could you? What a waste!" Rescuing a second jug out of her grasp, I started chugging it down.

"Slow down, you'll make yourself sick. There's plenty more where that came from. You need to cool down slowly or you'll faint. You're shaking all over. I wondered how you'd do in the heat. Today was a record high. This heat spell won't last long. You'll adjust to summer gradually. Let's eat, I need to head for home soon."

I said little as we looked for a restaurant. After a salad, French fries, and ice cream we were back at the Trail. "Here's a new mag-flashlight and a mosquito net. You'll need the net more than the flashlight. The bugs will be bad in New England. Call me when you get to Connecticut and I'll try to come for one night. Remember there are no rules!" Barbara hugged me, jumped in her car, and drove away. I watched her go before following the dependable while blazes.

The sound of a guitar guided me into Wild Cat Shelter. In the dim light of dusk, I made out two figures. The musician was a young man from New York who had just gotten on the Trail and was headed for Katahdin. Section hiker Fairbairn, an Episcopal Priest from Cambridge, Massachusetts, also had settled in. She'd finished sections I was headed into. We were discussing our experiences when Stryder strode into camp.

"Stryder, bless your heart, I'm always so glad to see you! I thought you were ahead of me." I gave him a big hug. His long arms wrapped around me the same way my son's would have.

"I stopped for food in Vernon, but I'm on a roll now. Just think, we've knocked off another state. I can't wait to get to the zoo in Bear Mountain. On the other side of the Hudson Bridge, we'll be in Connecticut. Can ya believe it, Wolf Woman? Katahdin's right around the corner! And it's finally hot!" Stryder's positive attitude was contagious.

"The rocks are gone too. I'd rather worry about getting a heat stroke than hypothermia," My traumatic experience in the heat now seemed trivial. That evening we counted our blessings rather than our hardships.

"Only one hundred and sixty-one miles of Trail run though New York and New Jersey. Massachusetts with Connecticut have one hundred and forty-one. In three weeks, we'll be in the Whites. I can't wait!" Stryder was clearly excited. With Fairbairn on one side and my buddy Stryder on the other, my spirits were up, too.

Fairbairn left early the next morning. Leaving the guys asleep, I headed out just behind her. The day promised to be clear. When I caught up to Fairbairn, we sat down to enjoy a snack and conversation in the privacy of the forest. It was refreshing to visit with a spiritual woman who appreciated the glory of spider webs in the morning light and beading raindrops on strands of thin grass.

"I remember Jeff Hoch at Fontana saying that nearly everyone on the Trail is on a quest and looking for something as they travel," Fairbairn gazed through the trees. "A guide in Maine talked to me about how we find the Holy One as we hike. It doesn't matter how we name that One. The Holy One may manifest itself in hikers like wonderful people who help us, like your friend Barbara. The Holy One can touch us so deeply that few of us can spend much time, this close to nature, and not be touched by very powerful awesome moments." Fairbairn paused.

I knew what Fairbairn meant. "I think of the Holy One as a Higher Power. Nature in all its glory is the gracious provider of brilliant beauty as well as the scary storms."

"That's right, once when I was peak-bagging in New Hampshire, I was coming back down the Fishing Jimmy Trail heading to Lonesome Lake. It seemed as if the Trail went down and down to the very heart of the valley—to a place so deep it seemed saved up and held special, like a precious jewel. There at the bottom was a gorgeous brook, chattering its way down between little pools with rich moss on lush rocks. It was a sacred moment. I could feel the 'thinness' in the gap between the Holy One and myself. Against all I knew about ecological manners and social expectations, I wanted to take everything off and be soaked in the holy water. It's a good thing I didn't because immediately, half a dozen men came thumping down the Trail. But, if I had a family member to baptize, and could do it, I'd go get water from that brook to use."

"I can imagine the scene. The Holy One comes to me in the fog and morning mist. Thank you for sharing that special moment."

"Well, sister, I would love to sit and talk with you all day but we both need to travel if we are going to make progress today. You go ahead, I'm slower and will hold you back. You have twenty miles to go. I'm only going to the next road crossing. Then I'll get off the Trail and catch a bus for home. I have to work for a couple of days, but I'll be back next week. Maybe I will see you on the other side of the Hudson River. Be sure to let me know when you climb Katahdin. Go with God!" We exchanged addresses and hugged. I walked away wondering if I'd really see her again. The discipline and distinctive freedom of section hiking was intriguing. Depending on the weather or the time of year, section hikers complete sections in succession or skip around. For many it means years of returning to the Trail. Daily goals kept me moving. I'm not sure I'd finish a goal that took years to accomplish. Thru-hiking was stimulating, satisfying, and tapped every compulsive bone in my body. Katahdin was only eight hundred miles away.

Hikers claim Pappy's Deli off West Mombasha Road makes the best grinders on the Trail. Earlier in the trip I hadn't indulged in stopping because road crossings with stores were infrequent and I hadn't wanted to leave the Trail. Now, with stores easily accessible, I relieved the monotony of Trail food every chance I got.

"Hey brother, looks good. I'll join you as soon as I use the phone." Stryder sat on the curb munching down on chips, cookies, a pie, soda, and a huge grinder.

After ordering a vegetarian deluxe grinder, I found the phone and checked in with Suellen. We were still visiting when Stryder tapped me on the arm and waved goodbye. "There goes Stryder," I mentioned.

"Do you need to go?" she asked.

"No, I'll see him at the shelter. This hiking with people is a matter of putting in twenty miles before seeing each other again. We'll be on the other side of the New York State Thruway before we meet again. Everyone walks his or her own walk. There are no rules about how you walk, who you walk with, or what you carry; only that you walk." It felt good to hear myself say that. Support in this section came from women: Suellen, Barbara, and Fairbairn. In Pennsylvania, it had been men. Connections were important. Waiting for them to appear was the challenge.

Harriman State Park is the second largest park in New York. Covering 46,000 acres of beautiful woodlands, the park offers easy walking through fields with flora and fauna, and tough climbs up rigorous rock formations. Rain drizzled as I reached the famous Lemon Squeeze. I struggled sideways through the narrow passage. As I pressed my body through the long damp crevice, the moist rocks and cool air felt refreshing. The humid earth smelled like rich garden soil after a spring rain. Getting my loaded pack through the rocks was not easy.

After the Squeeze, the Trail led me over a grassy hilltop. The day had been long but my spirits were high as I approached Surebridge Mountain, the last mountain before William Brien Memorial Shelter seven miles away. Rain fell steadily. The climb started easy but quickly changed to boulders. Slippery rocks made walking difficult. Up ahead was a vertical rock wall. A few scrubby trees stuck out between the rocks. By feeling for toe holds and using the bushes, I slowly inched myself up the cliff. After an hour of hand-over-hand climbing, I reached up to pull myself over the top, when my boot slipped. Feet first, I headed for the bottom.

Desperately, I tried to catch hold of tree roots or bushes, but I was moving too fast to get a solid grasp. I grabbed at rocks and tried to lodge my feet between the rocks, but nothing stopped me. My adrenaline raced and my heart pounded, but neither moved as fast as my mind as I searched for ways to keep from twisting an ankle or breaking a leg when I reached the bottom. Foot or leg injuries could take me off the Trail. The water in my waist pack protected the front of my body from protruding rocks as I slid. My knees ricocheted painfully off the jagged rock wall. I concentrated on calculating how long it would be before I hit the bottom. When I sensed I was about to hit, I tucked my chin to my chest and lunged backwards. My padded backpack cushioned the fall. Stunned, but knowing I'd protected my feet, I got up slowly. My knees were scratched and bleeding, but I could walk. Not wanting to see how far I had slipped, and thoroughly disgusted at having to climb the rocks again, I started back up the slippery wet wall. Not until I reached the shelter did I realize what a close call the fall had been. The Holy One had been with me.

Several miles before reaching Fingerboard Shelter I stopped a group of backpackers and asked them if they'd seen Stryder. They hadn't seen any hikers. Fingerboard Shelter was empty, and there was no journal message from Stryder. Shortly after leaving, everything seemed strange. I couldn't make sense of my uneasiness. I hiked on, chalking up the disorienting feeling to my fall. The farther I walked the more confused I felt. Everything looked familiar, like I'd been here before. I felt like I was walking in a daze, a vacuum, or a tunnel. I came up over a hill and started over the other side. All of a sudden I came face to face with the same people I had talked to nearly two hours earlier. "Oh, no, I got turned around when I came out of the shelter! I'm walking south," I gasped, talking more to myself than to the man leading the group.

"Afraid, so. If you are headed to Katahdin, you'd better turn around."

Without another word, I made a sharp one hundred and eighty-degree turn. Now things really looked strange. I was seeing everything for the third time. Furious, I hiked as if there were no tomorrow. The rain had stopped by the time I got to William Brien Shelter. Stryder sat curled up on a bench reading a book. I was impressed at how much he read. He didn't carry a tent, mat, stove, few clothes, and only enough food to get him from one town to the next, but he always had a thick book. "You won't believe what happened to me," I flopped down in the shelter. "I fell down a mountain and then got turned around after I signed in at Fingerboard Shelter and walked south for two hours."

Stryder looked both amused and sorry. "I hope you didn't get hurt. That explains how your knees got chewed up. I have water when you get ready to clean them up and cook supper. I've gone backwards out of shelters before. It's easy to do. Every thru-hiker needs to go backwards once," He grinned. "You won't do it again." From that day on I always got my bearings when I left shelters. I never hiked south again.

"I fell so fast I didn't have time to get scared. All I could think of was cushioning my fall to keep from breaking an ankle when I landed. Thanks for the water. I'm too tired to cook. I'm just going to eat this deli sandwich. Three months ago today I left Springer. Falling down a mountain and making a wrong turn is no way to celebrate, but at least I'm alive and moving. There are no rules on how to hike, only that I keep going."

*May 1: What a long day! Seems like an eternity has passed since Fairbairn and I sat on the ledge over-looking the beautiful New York countryside discussing spirituality. Now twelve hours later, I am cold, exhausted; the world is wet, and I'm fortunate not to be lying at the bottom of Surebridge Mountain. One minute I'm in a motel with a new friend, the next instant I am barreling down a mountain, and now I'm in a stone shelter with my ole buddy, Stryder. Seems like yesterday I helped him doctor up his knees in North Carolina. Now mine are the ones that are bandaged. This trip will be over soon and I'm nowhere near ready for the diverse experiences to end. How fast my moods change. Yesterday I wanted to go home, now I want to stay. These shelters are familiar and home.*

Hikers are advised to cross the Palisades Interstate Parkway before six in the morning or wait until after rush hour. There is no bridge, crosswalk, or stop sign. Stryder and I decided to cross together for safety.

Shortly after six a.m. we stood in the rain on the edge of the highway and watched frenzied vehicles pour down the freeway. The scene was a culture shock. Rain spun out from under the whirling tires and bounced off swishing windshield wipers. It was a sight guaranteed to make every hardship on the Trail insignificant, every rock hiked over precious, and every hour spent alone worth cherishing. As urban North Americans sped to reach destinations and deadlines, we hurried to get across without getting killed. I looked up just in time to see a sign that read: "New York City: 23 miles." It was hard to believe the fourteen hundred miles I'd walked led me so close to New York City. It was sobering enough to realize how close the Trail is to civilization, now it was horrifying. In eight hundred miles I'd be deep in the Maine woods. Life would come full circle again.

Stryder picked up his pace as soon as we were across the highway. Watching him walk away reminded me of one of his journal entries in the Shenandoah National Park. It had read: "I'll miss seeing all the animals in the Park. The deer are so beautiful. I've love watching squirrels dash across the Trail. This is God's country because there are animals." Stryder was an ecology wildlife student at Appalachian State University in Boone, North Carolina. He was eager to get to the Trailside Museum and Zoo, seven miles up the Trail.

Before walking through the zoo, I needed to pick up my thirteenth maildrop at the Bear Mountain Post Office before it closed at noon so I could climb Bear Mountain. True to its name, Bear Mountain was a bear to climb. The rain and the rocks were obstreperous. By the time I reached the observation tower, I was ready for a break. Stryder was taking advantage of a dry place for a snack. I joined him. "Want to join me at Graymoor Monastery tonight?" Stryder asked as he packed up to leave.

"Yes, I hear they cook great breakfasts," I sat down and took a swig of water.

"Before you leave, the view is lousy but the historic pictures in the tower are great." Stryder looked at the rain.

"Thanks for telling me. See you later at the Monastery," I headed into the elevator as Stryder walked into the rain. Stryder was right, the view was terrible, but the pictures were interesting. The very first sections for the Appalachian Trail were blazed in this park in 1922 and 1923.

At quarter of twelve I walked in the Post Office. "Ma'am, I'm Ellen Wolfe a thru-hiker, here to pick up my mail. May I use the counter while you go to lunch?

"Lord, honey, I ain't going nowhere in this rain. I don't know how you hikers stand it in the rain, heat, and bugs. Lord, honey, you've got enough mail here to keep you busy until the sun shines again. You're mighty popular to somebody, quite a few folks, I'd say. Make yourself at home now."

"Thank you. I'll try not to make a mess." I carried the pile to the counter. Gloria's words touched my heart. "Go Girl! You'll make it. I've told everybody about you. No one can believe how fast you are moving. I'm behind you all the way. You're almost home!" I gained as much energy from her words as I did from the cashew butter, the fruit cookies, and Tic Tacs. The Trail was teaching me the meaning of support. Mail from Suellen, Katie, Judy, the Equity Center, Donna, the chair of the sociology department, my mother, the Knoxville American Cancer Society, Gloria, and Uncle George didn't just say they hoped I'd make it, they believed I would. Anyone coming in the Post Office could see that was true. I'd spread mail everywhere.

Back out in the pouring rain, I decided not to spend time or money at the Bear Mountain restaurant. The Monastery was still seven miles away.

I walked through the zoo gate and past the attendant. I looked more like a drowned animal in need of a cage than a thru-hiker with the privilege of getting in free. The animals in the zoo had been rescued and could survive in the wilderness, but seeing them caged up was not as enjoyable as I'd expected. Rather than delighting in the furry critters, I felt sorry they couldn't live in the woods. Seeing them increased my appreciation for the opportunity to live in a natural habitant. The bear cage was one hundred and twenty-four feet above sea level, the lowest elevation on the Trail. I remembered the bear I'd seen at nearly the highest elevation on the whole Trail back in Tennessee. I felt sorry for this bear. I remembered how strange and unsafe it had felt walking through sections of Pennsylvania and New Jersey during turkey hunting season. Twice in New Jersey I'd passed hunters wearing hunting attire and carrying guns through areas where the Appalachian Trail shares space with legal hunting zones. One hunter had suggested I tie orange in my hair. He said I was an easy target for trigger-happy hunters who might mistake my braided hair for a turkey comb. The warning made me nervous. I'd been called a turkey before, but I didn't think I looked like one. I was grateful hunters didn't either.

After following white blazes through the zoo and the tunnel, I hiked over the nearly half mile wide majestic Hudson River on Bear Mountain Bridge. I cautiously peered over the steel rails to the powerful energy below. Flowing beneath me was the same deep strength I'd seen when I'd crossed the French Broad, Nantahala, and the Little Tennessee Rivers in North Carolina; the James and New Rivers in Virginia; the Potomac and the Shenandoah Rivers between Maryland and West Virginia; the Lehigh and Susquehanna Rivers in Pennsylvania; and here in New York, the Schuylkill, Delaware, and the Hudson Rivers. Farther along, the same message of unity between land and water resonated as I looked down at New England's Housatonic, Androscoggin, Kennebec, and the Penobscot's West Branch Rivers. By the time I reached Katahdin, I had crossed nearly all the major rivers in the Eastern United States. As the earth cradles water flowing through the land symbolizes connection, the value of land and water bonding resonated in me like oxygen in blood.

Posted signs told hikers that the Monastery was not open for the season, but shelter was available under a pavilion. I'd looked forward to a hot shower but followed directions to a ball field. As I walked to the far side of the field, I fantasized transforming the concrete cover into a hot tub full of frothing foam. Such a fantasy disappeared as I ducked under the dripping, damp dome.

Connecting with Stryder, who was curled up in his sleeping bag reading a book, was the best it would get for comfort. Lorax, a thru-hiker I'd been following since March, joined us. We passed the evening by calculating the number of days until we'd reach New England, the Whites, and at last, Katahdin. The closer we got with our figuring, the more melancholy we became. Tired as we were of eating Trail food, walking in rain, sleeping on the ground, and walking on rocks, we were nowhere near ready to return to civilization. The wind blew driving rain onto our sleeping bags. We pulled our gear in a pile until we felt like poured, plastered peas in a pod on the pavement. After a long shivering night in wet bags, we welcomed the dawn.

Some days I tried to believe my sore feet felt better, but I knew I'd just learned to live with the pain. Facing reality is what thru-hiking is about. Although my body was Trail hardened and physically fit, mentally and emotionally I was exhausted. Whatever fantasies I had of carrying a pack for months had died. The drive to keep going rose from sheer guts. However, no matter how draining thru-hiking had become, I preferred being out here to anywhere else, and didn't want the journey to end.

That afternoon a pleasant surprise awaited me. As I came into a clearing on Shenandoah Mountain, I found Fairbairn resting on an outcropping of rocks. Firmly planted her straight posture and solid form looked like a regal Goddess radiating wisdom. "I knew you'd be coming. Your buddy Stryder just came by and said you were behind him," Fairbairn's smile warmed my soul.

"What a pleasant surprise." Her hug felt warm and strong.

"You were right; we meet again on the other side of the Hudson River. How weird to think you have been all the way to Boston, back at work, and have returned to the Trail. I've just been hiking."

"I wouldn't say, 'just.' This Trail is not easy. Stryder said the Monastery wasn't opened. I'm sorry about that. That's a great place to gather inspiration. Speaking of resting, when is your next day off? You look tired. How are your feet?"

"Terrible, they hurt all the time and stay swollen. I'll probably take a day off in Vermont. Two more nights and I'll be in Connecticut."

"Hiking from Georgia to Maine in one space of time is an incredible goal. I love backpacking, but two weeks is my limit. I don't know how you do it, but I know you will. If goals that are important enough to make they are important enough to finish.

"Being able to do it is not the point anymore. I wish I knew why it's so important. All those reasons I used to spout about wanting to do it since I was a child and raising money for breast cancer, now seem like Pollyanna excuses for escaping reality. There's more to this than just wanting to do it. What, is the question."

"You needed those reasons to get you out here and you have the strength to push those questions to a deeper level. The holy writings of my Jewish and Christian heritage are filled with metaphors of journeys people set out to do without knowing why. Often folks get fed up with the whole damn thing. Everyone, sooner or later, needs to regroup and figure out why they're doing it. Women and men ultimately say that the journey was home that what and whom they were seeking traveled with them. I can't know what you and the Holy One will find in the next seven hundred and fifty miles. But I trust that if this is in some way a holy journey for you to ponder your questions, the journey will wrap into the rest of your life in ways that don't, now even, occur to you. You may know when you stand on Katahdin's summit. Now, Sister, if either of us are going keep searching, we need to be at it. Be sure to email me after you climb Katahdin. Peace be with you." Fairbairn rose and hugged me goodbye. Like an obedient child, I put away my snacks, stood up, and put on my pack.

"You've got a place to stay when you come south. Thank you for your support," I said. Fairbairn was getting off at the next road. I was headed for a bunk and mattress at R.P.H. Shelter on Hortontown Road. The water was from a rusty hand-pump that definitely had to be purified. After a beans, pasta, and broccoli soup supper, I soaked my feet in an over flow puddle under the pump before joining the Stryder and Lorax.

*June 3: My feet throb and ache all the time. Putting my legs in the air or on the wall at night helps. The day was perfect for hiking. So far the bugs aren't out and the heat isn't bad. Fairbairn was such an inspiration. Seeing folks I've met on the Trail is phenomenal. This journey is more of an awareness experience than a wilderness one. I'm very much aware that I'm tried of being dirty all the time. The color and sound in the swamps were incredible and New York City is so close. I've taken lots of pictures. People say the best-kept secrets are in front of our face. I wonder if I'll think that's true when I get back to Tennessee, or will I pine for the Trail?*

The caretaker at RPH Shelter suggested we leave before the rush hour of the Taconic State Parkway began. Once again Stryder and I, joined by Lorax, stood watching traffic pour into New York City. After safely crossing the Parkway, the guys soon disappeared from sight. Alone again, I made my way over Mt. Egert, Interstate 84, and seven road crossings, enroute for Telephone Pioneers Shelter. During a quick stop at Mountain Top Store for a grinder and drink, I was on the phone with Suellen when Stryder tapped me on the arm as he'd done a few days before and waved goodbye. I watched him walk out the door, fully expecting to see him at the next shelter.

The last ten miles of New Jersey crossed roads six times. I couldn't wait to get back into the wilderness. Just before reaching NY 22, the Metro-bound Commuter Railroad offered hikers a train ride to New York City. For eight dollars one way on the weekends and holidays, hikers can catch a train bound for Grand Central Station. Seeing New York City is a high point in the experience for many. I couldn't imagine doing such a thing. Being on the beach in Culvers Gap was disorienting enough. Making a whirl wind trip to the Big Apple would be absolutely mind-boggling. I'd been there, done that, and was focused on a very different agenda.

Telephone Pioneers Shelter was empty. The peace and quiet felt good, but I missed Stryder. Having the same shelter family for a few days led me to expect his company to continue. Stryder's journal entry explained that he wanted to put in extra mileage while the good weather held. I expected to see him down the Trail. I poured boiled water into my bottles, used the privy, brushed my teeth, and crawled into my bag. Life was simple and uncomplicated. Lights flickered in the valley. Sounds from the highway reached my sacred space. Pulling out a deli sandwich, I ate slowly. I felt blessed, content, and ready for New England. I never saw Stryder again.

# Chapter 11
## "I Can't Stand the black flies."
### Connecticut-Massachusetts

Arriving in New England deserved a celebration. On my way to the Country Mart I hiked through a charming 1800's covered bridge. Long intricate shadows danced among the worn wood slats. Rhythically moving, the quivering designs shimmered like women's long skirts swishing across a barn floor. Suspended above the water, the bridge swayed from cables fastened to the shore. I felt like a gangly insect stalking my way through a woven wrapped web of rope. On the pay phone, Suellen shared her plans to meet me while I ate Moose Tracks ice cream. Yellow flowers dotted the sandy banks and sun sparkled through the trees as I walked back along the Ten-Mile River to the Trail. Not a sign of humidity hung in the still air. So far I only had two miserably hot days. One had been when I hiked out of Duncannon, Pennsylvania and the other was the day I crossed the New York / New Jersey State line. The Green Mountains in Vermont and the Whites in New Hampshire were only a few days away. The beauty boosted my spirits.

I spent my first night in Connecticut at Mt. Algo Lean-to. After calling the dear three-sided havens "shelters" for three months, it was hard to switch to the New England term, "lean-to." I suspect most north-bounders refer to the nightly stops as "shelters" all the way to Katahdin and south-bounders call them lean-tos. I was as accustomed to calling the dwellings, "shelters," as I was to being alone. Only thirteen hikers were ahead of me. None were women. Again, I began to wonder if I just might finish as the first woman for 1997. If I did, it would be because of innate drive, inner power, and dedicated support. Hiking was as much something I was, as something I did. I could competently move along the Trail, but finishing would still depend on attitude. I hadn't taken a day off since May the seventh. I wanted to hurry and finish so I could believe it was really possible for me to thru-hike the Trail alone, but I didn't want leave nature. I was tired of being dirty, but since culture sets the standards for personal hygiene, I accepted smelling like a human being. However, there was something in my psyche and repressed schema that recalled what it felt like to have clean hair, scrubbed feet, and an odorless body.

With my hair in a mass of knots, so tangled I could use it as a pillow, I lay in my sleeping bag sticky with the day's sweat and rehashed the question that had haunted me since March first. What was I doing out here? If I did not have to live this way, why was I? There was something basic, primal, and just plain endearing about living in the wilderness and not caring whether I was clean, wore different clothes, ate out of the same pan every meal, or even ate the same food. I was healthy, strong, and no worse off for the repetition. Trail life felt as normal as normal had ever felt. It was comforting to be in control and not subject to human judgments. I didn't have to set a good example, be professional, put on a good front, or walk to someone else's drummer. While the society I had exchanged for solitude provided security, it wasted a ridiculous amount of time and energy on pompous actions, game playing and trivial concerns.

Living on the Trail provided a new slant on productivity. Being productive meant dealing with sweat, thirst, aches, and bugs, not making money or acquiring a vita. Mileage was all I wanted to accomplish. I only needed my food to be edible, my water purified, and my shelter to be dry, all of which I acquired by walking. The longer I stayed away from culturally construed routines, the more I dreaded returning to them. Amidst my simple lifestyle, the need for communal energy gnawed at my bones. In a valley a train's long, low whistle reached my corner of the world. People moved collectively to their destinations. The passengers and I were confined to tracks in order to reach our goals. I moved through my solitary journey in the open at my own pace. The people on the train sped through nature in steel boxcars, but with each other. I sighed knowing I would never again have so many hours of solitude. The thought was paradoxically sobering and relieving.

After an oatmeal and dried fruit breakfast, I headed for the Cornwell Bridge. Uncle George and his wife Lorraine were to be at Gloria's. I'd call them from Baird's General Store. After a long walk and two rides into a community of only two hundred people, I was disappointed to reach only the answering machine. Baird's Store, however, had incredibly good grinders and salads. With a big lunch, I settled on the creaky wood porch at a round iron table to watch the distinctive folks from this exclusive New York town come and go. After lunch I asked a young fellow for a ride back to the Trail.

Typical of Connecticut's fifty-one miles, my June sixth hike to Pine Swamp Brook Shelter wound through pine forests, wild flowers, and tall luscious ferns. The elevation was low and the trails well maintained. The rain seemed to be gone forever. An incredible beaver dam created a large swamp behind the empty shelter. I watched for beavers but only saw gnawed-off tree stumps and broken limbs. Deep-throated bullfrogs and high-pitched spring peepers welcomed me. The water was full of wriggling jumping creatures that had to be purified well before using it. With the abundance of water came hoards of insects. The mosquitoes and black flies were terrible. With a net over my head I cooked pasta with cheese. The buzzing swamp melodies were here to stay.

At the first hint of daylight I was on my way to pick up my sixteenth maildrop at the Falls Village Post Office before it closed at ten o'clock. A handful of Trail mix and the anticipation of a hearty meal in town would keep me going. The eight miles would take four hours, if the terrain stayed easy. Driven by the challenge, I fully intended to make it. I crossed the iron bridge that spans the Housatonic River and sped into the quiet town of only five hundred and fifty two people. I didn't stop until I stood at the Post Office window at quarter of ten. Sorting mail was a routine. In four days I would connect with Uncle George in Dalton and Barbara would come back for a night's stay in two days. The more I could slack pack, the more likely I was to make it. My feet were constantly in pain and stayed swollen. I didn't know how much weight I had lost, but the belt on my backpack was pulled in as far as it would go. When I'd left from Springer, the belt had been snug, now over a foot of slack dangled from my waist.

I felt safe in the land of my heritage. The cards and letters from Uncle George, Gloria, and my mother were full of support. "You are in New England now." "You won't have any trouble now that you are up north." "You are almost home." "It won't be long now, let the spirit of New England move you home."

I felt intimately connected to New England's Appalachian soil that I'd been pursuing for weeks. I remembered Daddy pulling bright red beets and brilliant orange carrots out of rich loam and wiping the moist soil off on his white tee-shirt that was full of holes. "Here, take a bite. The best way to eat vegetables is straight out of the garden. Your mother wouldn't agree with me, but I say a little dirt won't hurt you. There's a difference between soil and dirt. Growing vegetables is growing miracles." The experience became so engrained that cultivating my own gardens became a piece of my legacy.

This far northeastern corner of the United States had provided my childhood with the four distinct seasons of variety and balance. Hot summers ripened wild strawberries. Brilliant autumns produced luscious fruit baskets. Freezing winters allowed the soil a dormant time. Balmy springs brought apple blossoms and sweet peas. These seasonal experiences left me with delicious memories. Living in New England had meant a strong connection between weather patterns and food production. Now, as I stepped through southern New England in early June, I watched for wild blueberries along the ridge tops, fruit trees in the fields, fiddle heads along creek banks, and Indian cucumber leaves in the moist woods. New England trees produced some of the best maple syrup in the world and some of flakiest orange toned birch. These New England symbols represented the beginning of the end of a process that had begun over twenty-five years before in the North Georgia Mountains. Reaching the northernmost terminus of the Trail would end a two-decade struggle to return home. Suellen's presence in Maine would symbolize the closure of my journey north. Returning to Tennessee with her on the highway would signify a future of contentment, comfort, and companionship.

The Post Office window closed, but customers continued to collect their mail from boxes. One man, curious about my box of almond butter, Tic-Tacs, raisins, mole skin, and pictures of Daddy, stopped to chat. "You going all the way?"

"Yes sir, I left March first," I answered.

"Really! You're traveling fast. Where're you from? Anyone hiking with you?"

"No I'm from Cookeville, Tennessee." Not wanting to get into a discussion about hiking alone, I changed the subject. "This is an adorable little town! I hear the population's only a hundred?"

The man gave me a brief summary of the town's history and resumed his questions. "Do you see other people? Is it hard coming to town? What's it like being out there alone for so long?" Surprisingly, he wasn't shocked that I hiked alone and was genuinely interested in my feat. After packing up, he suggested a restaurant for lunch.

"The Trail has a definite community although there is nothing dependable about the experience except the white blazes. I never know when I'll see people. Coming into town is necessary to get supplies, but I resent leaving the Trail. This journey is the most freeing, obsessive compulsive, soul driven experience I have ever had. Living on the Trail has stripped me of everything inconsequential and meaningless. It is life in its rawest, simplest, most basic form." Bob was impressed and wanted to help.

"I'd be happy to take your pack to LaBonne's Epicure Market in Salisbury and you back to the Trail." Salisburg was only eight miles away, but every mile I didn't have to carry the pack helped my feet. Gratefully, I climbed in his car. Instead of taking me back to where I had gotten off the Trail, Bob took me to the other side of town. "This will save you about four miles, including the road walk. You'll come out by the Limestone Spring Lean-to. Just follow the blue blaze to the AT."

"Thank you for your help and for taking the pack. My feet appreciate it!" I was on the Trail again, free from the weight of the pack, but not feeling real good about the short cut. Purists would call this yellow blazing. This section had at one time been part of the Trail, but it was not part of this year's 2,160.3-mile route. I could tell the blue blazes had once been white, but I was clearly missing four miles of the 1997 Trail. Making it to Katahdin only entitled me to a 2,000-mile patch. The other hundred and sixty miles could theoretically be yellow blazed or skipped altogether. Where and how to skip the miles is a favorite topic of conversation among thru-hikers. However there was something wrong about missing any part of the Trail. I remember how guilty I'd felt when Stanley gave me a ride from the Post Office in Bland, Virginia to the Trail. I'd missed the half-mile road walk from where I had gotten off the Trail to where the Trail led back into the woods. I justified that skip because it was raining. This time it wasn't raining and I didn't have the pack. The half mile blue blaze from the shelter to the main Trail added back mileage, but I'd miss hiking over Prospect Mountain. Walking in and out of towns, backtracking in Harrison State Park, and following blue blazes to and from shelters added mileage, but this was an intentional skip. Seeing white blazes again brought tears to my eyes. Like a naughty child making heartfelt amends to a parent, I vowed I'd never take a short cut again, and I never did.

Billy and Rand's Views offered spectacular scenery of the New England countryside. Big white churches and Holstein cows dotted the rolling hillsides. Salisburg, with a population of two thousand people, was no ordinary town. It was home to many wealthy and famous people, including movie stars, movie producers, and politicians. Neither was La Bonne an ordinary grocery store. A clerk in the deli department informed me that Meryl Steep had passed me in the doorway. She suggested I watch for celebrities. I thanked her for the advice but added, "I look so out of place here. Nobody famous is going pay me the time of day."

"Oh, I don't know," smiled the clerk. "When you climb Katahdin, you'll be famous. I couldn't do what you're doing. Not many north-bounders make it up this far. Good luck to you. Hiking alone from Georgia to Maine is quite a feat."

Heading behind the store with my grinder and grapefruit juice, I pondered the idea of being famous for finishing the Trail. Fame is not an objective for the two hundred hikers that finish each year. My thoughts were interrupted by the sound of fiddles, bagpipes, bongo drums, and clicking heels. I followed the sound and was delighted to find a group of male dancers in kilts entertaining the townsfolk on a cobblestone patio. People sat on store stoops and park benches. I joined the elite. No one asked me to leave, but no one spoke to me. It was actually quite refreshing not to have to answer questions and to be able to sit quietly. Watching the men's feet fly to the lively music was a refreshing change from watching mine plod through the forest. When the men stopped for a break, I started to leave. "Hiker woman, come back." I turned around. One of dancers motioned to me. I made my way back through the crowd.

"Are you a thru-hiker? Which way are you headed?

"Yes, I'm a north-bounder. I started March first from Springer Mountain. I enjoyed your music and dancing. Where are ya'll from?" I'd detected a southern accent.

The man didn't want to talk about dancing. "We're from South Carolina. I own land in north Tennessee and the Trail passes behind the back of my property. My wife and I feed the hikers coming through. I've always wondered how many of them finish. I'm thrilled to know you've made it this far north. How many are in your group?"

"I'm alone. I meet hikers in the shelters, but this is a solo journey." I told the man about raising money for breast cancer. A crowd gathered around us. People began to ask me questions. My connection with the performers erased the stigma of my appearance. We talked until the men were summoned to board a waiting bus.

"Good luck, I'm proud of you! What do you know! I've actually met a thru-hiker, way up here in Connecticut, and a lone woman hiker at that! How incredible." The dancer waved as he climbed on the bus. Walking away, I thought it odd that someone in line for fame had no place to spend the night. I stopped at a phone and made plans with Barbara to meet me on U.S. 7 near Sheffield, Massachusetts, at 6:00 p.m. the next day. She would pick up the pack at La Bonne's on her way. Trail Magic again!

I hung up feeling I could dance my way to Katahdin, and to a place to sleep. The next shelter was four miles off the Trail, but I needed to be in town to leave my pack. The town didn't offer a hostel, and no churches took in hikers. The cemetery was too close to the road. About dusk I spotted a flower shop in front of a house with an empty garage attached. "Perfect," I thought to myself. I dropped my pack on the porch, and walked in. A woman looked up from arranging flowers. "May I help you?" she asked pleasantly.

"Yes, Ma'am. I'm a thru-hiker and wonder if I could spread my sleeping bag in your garage for the night. I'll be gone by daylight and only need water. I'd appreciate it."

"I only work here, but if you don't tell anyone you spoke to me and don't settle down until after dark I don't see why not. You can get water from the garden hose."

"Thank you. You're very kind. I'll be quiet and will stay gone until dark." I hurried out before she had a chance to change her mind. After putting my pack in a corner of the garage, I wandered back to the patio to watch the people. It felt good knowing I had somewhere to go at dark, even if I did have to go to bed without a bath and sleep on the garage floor. I called Barbara again and told her the pack would be in the garage at the flower shop.

*June 7: A flower shop called Sweet Haven Farm was one of the dearest places I'd stayed. Seeing cultivated plants was odd after being in the forest where plants grow without special care. Knowing what a job it is to contain flowers to pots and vegetables to plots, I've enjoyed watching plants grow in the wild. Controlling plants is like hiking on a schedule. Being in town made me feel like a big pumpkin sitting in the middle of neatly manicured lawn attached to a long, thick vine trailing to a garden. Like the pumpkin, I too, had wandered away from a wild home to a cultured environment. In the forest my appearance blended with the environment. Both pumpkins and I are rooted deep in the soil. Mine was a 2,160 Appalachian route over roots.*

At the crack of dawn with my fanny pack and raincoat tied around my waist, I left a note for the shop owner explaining that Barbara would pick up my pack and headed back to the Trail. Connecticut's highest summit, Bear Mountain, is a treacherous climb up 2,316 feet of rock. A small wooden sign at the bottom of Sages Ravine welcomed me into Massachusetts. Wide waterfalls splashed and beautiful brooks gurgled, but the gnats, mosquitoes, and black flies were too thick to stop and enjoy them as I climbed Race and Mt. Everett Mountains. Crossing another state line, another highest point, and looking forward to meeting Barbara again signified more full circles in my journey.

On the south side of Mt. Everett an exhausted young couple asked me how far it was to the parking lot. I hadn't passed a parking lot. With my maps we discovered they'd taken a wrong turn and were miles from their group. I shared my water and told them if I saw their friends I'd let them know they were coming. At the top of the mountain, an anxious group of New York City teenagers were so relieved to know their friends were all right that they invited me to share their lunch. We were enjoying carrots, chips, soda, salsa, and peanuts at Guider Pond Picnic Area when the hungry, thirsty, lost couple joined us. The teen-agers asked me all the usual questions. They couldn't imagine what it was like not to have to deal with traffic, noise, and schedules, or to experience total quiet. Black flies swarmed us as we ate. Having not had a bath for seven days didn't help matters. They swarmed and buzzed in and out of our ears, eyes, nose, and down our necks. When the food was gone and we'd dealt with the flies as long as possible, the young people crammed into their cars and headed back to the city. I walked off thinking how truly fortunate I was to experience this peaceful space of life in spite of the flies.

A hiker on Mt. Everett warned me that Jug End had been rerouted and was poorly marked. Barbara was to meet me on South Egremont Road, however roads are seldom marked at Trail crossings and I had no way to know where I was when I came to a highway. I flagged down a car. A woman stopped and told me South Egremont was down the road a mile and up the next highway another mile and offered to give me a ride to where Barbara was waiting. Staying on the Trail would have meant several more miles.

"Where have you been? I've been worried to death. Did you get the roads mixed up? I left you a note on the post at the end of the field." Barbara was clearly upset. "Our first stop is a motel so you can shower before supper."

"I didn't have a clue which road I was on and didn't see the note. All I saw were black flies!"

"I'll get you some DEET before I leave."

"How will I get it?"

"Mt. Wilcox North Lean-to is about a mile and a half from Beartown Mountain Road. I'll carry your pack to the shelter and stay until you get there. I'll bring sandwiches and have supper with you before I head for home."

"You'd do that for me? Barbara you're too good for words."

"So are you," Barbara gave me a knowing look. "Think of all those miles you drove and contacts you made raising $10,000! This is the least I can do. This is the last visit though. Is your Uncle George coming to Dalton? You need to take a day off."

"Yes, but I won't take a day off until I get to Vermont." We pulled into a motel. "Get in there and take a shower. I'll bet you haven't had one since I saw you last."

"You're so right," I grinned as I headed for the bathroom. It felt good to be with Barbara again. She was such a saint. After eating and washing clothes, we stretched out on our beds and talked until two in the morning. When the lights finally went out I tossed and turned. Sleep hadn't come easy for weeks, maybe months. Being in a bed didn't stop my feet from tingling and twitching. My muscles jumped and my legs ached. I took more Ibuprofen. At least my toenails weren't infected and didn't hurt since I had lost eight in Pennsylvania. If I stopped walking my feet would get better, but that was not an option.

Sunshine streaming through the blinds woke us early the next morning. "Today's section won't be as rough as yesterday. You've hiked Massachusetts' worse section today." Barbara and I made small talk as we sipped coffee and ate bagels in the Bagel Shop. We both hated good byes. "I'll be there this afternoon with supper and repellent."

As I soon as I headed across the field at Mass 41 the black flies started swarming. The weather was beautiful and the humidity was low. Thinking of Barbara and knowing tonight could well be the last time I'd ever see her brought up old tapes about mixed messages. I wondered about the difference between commitment and letting go. Barbara had moved into my life in such a powerful way and now her purpose in my experience was over. Time moved people. The reality made me sad. Distance, circumstances, and timing impact relationships. I still wondered why Barbara had taken such an interest in helping me. But I was glad she had. Meeting women hikers was especially meaningful.

Barbara was right, the seventeen-mile hike between Mass 41 and Mt. North Wilcox Lean-to was easy, but the bugs were worse. I tried walking with the bug net over my head, but I couldn't breathe. I rolled the net over my face, walked faster, and chanted: "keep going, keep walking, just keep moving," Hiking in my gaiters protected most of my legs and my long-sleeved shirt kept them off my arms. I waved a short branch, my children had called "bug sticks," in front of my face. The few horse flies and mosquitoes we'd tried to distract in the Smokies were nothing compared to this. "You will do what you have to do when you have to do it." Words Judy Madonia had taught me became my mantra. I concentrated on not panicking as I hiked around Benedict Pond and over the Ledges. The pond was beautiful. I could have enjoyed it if the black flies hadn't been so bad. Barbara would be at the second lean-to on Mt. Wilcox.

Knowing she was waiting with supper kept me going. When I reached the blue blaze Trail, I grabbed a handful of flowers and threw myself into over-drive. All I could think of was covering myself with DEET and Barbara's nur-turing spirit. Over a rise I could see the back of the shelter two hundred yards down the Trail. I let out a war-whoop and expected to see Barbara's tall form come around the corner.

"Barbara, I have something for you." No Barbara appeared. Assuming she was napping or engrossed in a book I yelled again. "Barbara!" She'd always met me and she had the pack. I knew she was there. "Barbara, wake up." Expecting to find her napping, I rounded the corner and screeched to a halt. The shelter was empty. The backpack sat propped up against the shelter. A crumpled piece of paper and a bottle of DEET were attached to the front. Tossing the flowers on the ground, I clamped my teeth together to keep from crying and reached for the note. It read: "After I left you this morning I drove up to Beartown Mountain Road. The road was full of potholes and ruts. I don't want to risk taking this old car down the road again so I am leaving the pack now. I hate like hell not to see you again but I don't dare come back. I'm sorry there will be no sandwiches, but here is some DEET I had in the car. The bugs are TERRIBLE. Call me if you need me. Remember there are no rules. You'll make it to Katahdin. Love, Barbara." Blinking back tears, I read the note several times, stuffed it in my pocket, and covered myself with DEET. I felt abandoned. The poison stopped the insects from biting but not from landing or swarming. The air was as black as my spirits. I'd trusted Barbara to be there and in so doing, had set myself up for discouragement. The bugs were so terrible we couldn't have eaten without swallowing mouthfuls of flies anyway.

Pacing back and forth I arrived at two conclusions. One, Barbara was gone. Dwelling on the pain of not seeing her again would not make the flies leave. And two, I was not sleeping with bugs. Three hours of daylight remained. The data book indicated a road three and a half miles down the Trail. I didn't know what I'd do when I got there, but I'd walk until something changed. Soaked in sweat, covered with fly remains, and smelling like a chemical plant, I retraced my steps back to the main Trail. The pack felt heavy and the sky looked cloudy. If a storm was coming, I didn't care.

I reached Fernside Road at sundown. The white blazes continued to the right, but I felt riveted to the spot. Scanning the field that ran parallel to the Trail, I saw no houses, people, or signs of civilization. To my left cows mooed. The long, deep, mournful sound echoed across the valley. I stood still and listened. They were calling me. The mooing continued. Without thinking, I turned away from the Trail and headed left, toward the mooing. Rounding a bend in the road I looked up and saw a huge house. The cows stopped mooing. Men were building an elaborate stone wall, and landscaping work was in progress around a newly completed swimming pool. The owner of the house obviously was wealthy. A man in the driveway looked up. "You lost?" he asked as I approached.

"No sir. I'm a thru-hiker. I just got off the Trail. I was going to stay at Mt. Wilcox shelter but the black flies are just a bit too much. I wonder if you might have a spot in a barn or a shed where I could lay out my sleeping bag for the night?"

"Do you have a tent?"

"No, Sir, I don't. I usually stay in shelters."

"I have one in my airplane." The man motioned to a huge field across the road. "I was on my way down there. Toss your pack in the back of that truck and you can ride down with me. I'll be with you as soon as I tell my wife. We have dinner plans this evening but I've got one last thing to do. I might get you to help me if you don't mind."

"Not at all, I'd be glad to," I said as I put the pack in the truck. The man opened the screen door and hollered,

"Honey, I'll be back in ten minutes. I'm going to the field. Oh, there's a hiker here. I'm going to let her use the tent for the night." There was a pause. The man glanced at me and asked, "You hiking alone?"

"Yes sir."

Turning back to his wife the man added, "Yes she's hiking alone." There was another pause as he listened, "Yes, the hiker is a woman."

The man let the screen door slam. He hurried around the back, pushed up the tailgate, and I climbed in. As we pulled out of the driveway I looked up to see a beautiful woman with a lovely shawl wrapped around her shoulders. Her silver hair was tastefully swirled in a bun on top of her head.

"I'm Player Crosby," the man extended a hand.

I returned his handshake. "I'm Wolf Woman, my name is Ellen Wolfe. It's nice to meet you. I appreciate your help. The bugs have gotten bad. I had a tent in the beginning. I sent it home to cut down on the weight."

"Smart plan, but the bugs are going to stay terrible in the deep woods. When did you leave and where are you from?" Player wanted to know.

"Cookeville, Tennessee. I left March first."

"Really! You're making excellent time. And you've done it all alone?"

"Yes, I know lots of hikers, but I'm ahead of most of them. I don't take a lot of days off. I need to get back to teach college in the fall."

"What do you teach?"

"I start a new anthropology teaching job. I used to teach elementary school."

Player stopped the truck and got out to open a gate. Back in the truck, we drove past a large barn, farm machinery, and a herd of cows. The cows stood silent as we drove by. I smiled and silently thanked them. A small airplane sat in the middle of the field. I was spellbound and couldn't help but ask, "You own all this land and everything?"

"Yes. I retired early. I've made good investments in Costa Rica. I still fly down to help out with an environmental project in the winter when they need me." I didn't know who "they" were and I didn't ask. "The tent needs airing out. I haven't set it up since my last trip. You may take a shower in the house after we leave. You are welcome to take the truck to town to get something to eat. The keys are in the ignition and the tank is full. Just park the truck at the house when you leave in the morning." Player pulled a tent and poles out from under

167

the plane. "Here's a lantern and a therma-rest."

"Thank you so much. You'd really let me take your truck to town?"

"Yes, of course. Anytime I travel I'm given a car to drive when I arrive in a city."

I was in shock. Minutes earlier I'd been lamenting the fact Barbara that had left me alone with the black flies. Now a perfect stranger was offering me not only his tent, but also his truck and a hot shower in his house. I wasn't sure a wealthy businessman expecting to rent a car when he arrived in an airport was quite the same as a thru-hiker wandering up to a private home and asking for a place to spread out a sleeping bag. However, I wasn't going to analyze the analogy. Restaurant food and a hot shower are pure Trail Magic.

"It's so beautiful here. You're very kind."

"I'm glad to help. I've been stranded away from home without a place to stay many times before. People have to help each other out in this world."

After setting up the tent I helped Player load poles in the truck. Back at the house he invited me in. "Want something to drink?" Player swung open a walk-in refrigerator.

"A diet Coke, please." After showing me the bathroom, Player excused himself and went outside. I was dragging clothes out of my backpack when Player stuck his head out the door.

"My wife reminded me of our guest house. See that green house over there?" Across the road stood a house nearly as large as my house in Tennessee. "We've had workmen in there all last week but they're gone now. The beds are clean, there are plenty of towels, and there's a phone you can use. My wife thought perhaps you'd be more comfortable in the house, unless of course you can't stand the thought of not camping for a night." Player grinned.

"I believe I'll stay in the house. Thank you so much. Have a good evening."

"Go ahead and drive the truck down there so you'll have it when you get ready to go to town. I'll leave a map to Tryingham on the front seat of the truck when we go out. Let us know if you need anything." The door slammed.

Stunned, I gazed up the road. I thought of the black fly infested shelter I'd been standing in less than an hour ago. How could a place so uninviting be so close to this comfort? Is this how it feels for the poor to live among the rich or is this an example of how close and yet distinctly diverse people's lives are? Changes occur depending on resources, awareness, and what people are willing to deal with. My life had been transformed from the possibility of sleeping on a hard platform, breathing fly-filled air, and eating cold trail food to staying in a comfortable house, free from insects and eating hot restaurant food. All because I refused to have black flies as bedmates. Being willing to take risks and move gave me choices. The shelters had been safe havens but when the circumstances changed, I changed.

I tossed my pack back in the truck and drove to the adorable wood-framed house. The front room had a wood stove, couch, chairs, a large wooden table, and a spacious fully equipped kitchen. Braided rugs and New England furniture created an appealing space. Upstairs I found two bedrooms with a full bath, a washing machine and a dryer. I peeled off my clothes, started them chugging, and climbed in the bathtub. "Unbelievable, absolutely, unbelievable," I thought over and over as I soaked my black fly bites. After my bath I followed the directions Player had left in the truck, just as he had promised. It felt good to trust and be trusted. I'd made a decision, been aware, and listened. Incredible Trail Magic happened, thanks to the mooing cows.

In Friendly's Restaurant I ordered a vegetarian taco sandwich, a big salad, decaf-coffee, and ice cream. Eating ice cream was a habit that would have to stop when I got home. A wave of deja vu swept through me. I didn't know where I was. I felt overwhelmed and confused. Nothing looked familiar. I had picked Friendly's because there was one near my mother's home in New Hampshire. But New Hampshire felt millions of miles away. Even the New England accents sounded strange. I didn't recognize the food. I longed for the Trail. Only after retracing my steps back to the little green house and climbing in my sleeping bag did I feel connected.

I touched base with Suellen and Kate before calling Uncle George. He'd meet me in Dalton, Massachusetts, on June the 11th. The bedrooms felt crowded even though they were bigger than my bedroom in Cookeville. I was used to space and air, so I settled on the couch. A full moon spilled long yellow streaks through the window. Burrowed deep in the soft couch cushions, I was grateful to be safe from insects and still have nature.

By seven the next morning the truck was back in the yard and I headed back to the Trail. I snapped pictures. Last evening felt like a dream. The morning was chilly for early June, but a clear sky promised a good hike to October Mountain Lean-to nineteen miles away. Hiking over stone wall fences reminded me I was in New England. So did black flies and mosquitoes that attacked as soon as I entered the woods. I covered myself with DEET, got a bug stick, and concentrated on last night's Trail Magic.

Upper Goose Pond was one of the most serene lakes I'd seen. No homes, tourists, or construction marred the tranquil blue beauty. Only the fish jumping and singing birds broke the silence. It had been days since north-bounders had zoomed by me. Seldom did I see day-hikers. I hardly missed the presence of people anymore. Birds and squirrels were delightful company. As I walked through the pristine wilderness and over the marshlands on bog boards, my thoughts spiraled. The landscape and scenery were beautiful, but after nearly two thousand miles, a view is a view and a flower is a flower. Nature is deeper than beauty. The black flies and mosquitoes weren't bad on the summits where the air stirred, but in lower elevations and thick woods they were atrocious.

One and a half miles beyond October Branch Lean-to, on Washington

Mountain Road, lived Marilyn Wiley, known as the "Cookie Lady." She and her husband let hikers fill water bottles and gave them homemade cookies at their blueberry farm. I hurried along the Trail that paralleled the highway and up the one tenth of a mile to their house. I hoped they had a screened in porch. "This year's first hiker! How many are with you?" greeted Mrs. Wiley from her garden as I walked up the driveway.

"None."

"Alone, really? Where did you start?"

"Springer Mountain. I left March first. Might you have a place I could spread out my mat? I don't have a tent, and the black flies are terrible."

"The bugs are awful, aren't they? Going all the way, wonderful! You may sleep on the couch. We have two exchange students from Mexico with us staying in the guest room."

"You are brave to hike alone." The man said. "We haven't had many women stop, and few north-bounders. Where are you from?"

"Cookeville, Tennessee. I grew up in Vermont and New Hampshire."

"I hear a bit of Dixie coming through, but you've not lost the Yankee. Come on in and get out of the flies. They've been eating us alive in the garden all evening. Leave your pack on the porch." The comfortable house had a glassed-in porch that ran the length of the house. A large spacious kitchen-dining area opened into the living room. I brought in my sleeping bag and clothes. After a shower I visited with the Mexican students. Marilyn baked muffins that I enjoyed more than cookies. She gave me clean towels for a shower and let me use the stove to cook supper. Marilyn and her husband showed the journals they'd kept since opening their home to hikers. "We considered opening a hostel. Occasionally a hiker will stay, but not often."

I took advantage of having electricity and got out my journal and pen. *June 10: Today the black flies led me to homemade muffins. Snuggled here on a couch, with the third muffin still in my mouth, I'm amazed at how miraculous connections with people make this journey so fantastic. When I need a bed, the Trail gives me one. When I need comfort, someone shows up. This wild and solo journey teaches me to trust the spirit of risk, adventure, and people.*

After a bowl of cereal, the next day I headed into the crisp morning air for Dalton, only ten miles away. I practiced pacing. Every day I'd set significant mileage goals and always managed to meet them. Hiking without a tent and limited food helps. My aching feet would have appreciated rests more often, but the pesky flies kept me moving. Hunger, thirst, weather, and insects keep hikers focused.

I visited with section hikers on the ridge, but still reached Dalton by noon. Stretching out in a grassy area near the road, I promptly fell asleep. "Taking siestas in the sunshine is no way to get to Katahdin." Uncle George's booming voice woke me. I scrambled to my feet as he added, "You deserve it after walking so far."

"Uncle George! You found me."

"Did you doubt old Uncle George? How are those feet? Here, drink this milk."

"Thanks, I haven't had chocolate milk since I was a kid. My feet are not so good. Did you bring boo boo pencils to fix them?"

"No, for crying out loud, you've out-grown boo boo pencils! Anyone who can walk alone from Georgia to here doesn't need boo boo pencils."

"But Uncle George, look at these knees!" I wailed, slipping back to being a little girl in the presence of this strong adult figure from my past. Seeing Uncle George was like seeing Daddy, and Daddy always made everything better. Besides, I wasn't going to let Uncle George get away with not living up to his claim to fame by making my bruises and scratches go away and rejuvenating my swollen aching feet.

"Let's get that pack loaded up and find a place to get you presentable enough to go to a nice restaurant." Uncle George picked up the pack. "For crying out loud, no wonder your feet hurt! This thing weighs a ton. What have you got in here, a rock from every state?

"No, but that's a good idea. I'll start picking up some for Christmas presents. Some of the weight is the pack. That's the largest men's pack Lowe makes. Depending on how much food and water, about thirty-five pounds."

Uncle George flashed a grin I recognized from years ago. I was amazed how much he looked like Daddy. He was a smaller man than Daddy had been, but both men combed their white hair back and had the same strong, square, New England jaw. Both had bossy, jovial personalities, and were full of themselves. When the two of them had gotten together, their ridiculous silly jokes and spontaneous humor were endless. After hunting trips they would tell such big tales that we knew they could not have happened, except of course to George and Pete. Both men were sensitive, caring, and gentle. Being with Uncle George was the next best thing to being with Daddy.

Uncle George broke into my thoughts "I had a terrible time finding you. If it hadn't been for those hikers over there I might still be driving around this darn town looking for you." Uncle George pointed to the section hikers I'd met on the mountain.

"That's called Trail Magic. Like the stories you and Daddy told about hunting. Of course my stories are true. All you guys ever brought home were tall tales."

"Ah, come on now. Here's the Post Office."

Inside, the postal clerk wanted identification. I hadn't been asked to show identification since Damascus. Uncle George had left a note for me at the front desk that read: "Ellen Priest, stay here! Your Uncle Geo is looking for you."

It had been twenty-five years since I'd used my maiden name. Using it felt very appropriate, but it confused the clerk. The name on my driver's license didn't match the note. After a bit of explaining, I got my mail.

Uncle George paid for two rooms. I suggested we share a room to save money but he said that wouldn't be appropriate and I deserved a good night's rest without listening to an old fellow snore. If he snored anything like Daddy used to, I wasn't going to argue. I showered and then Uncle George helped me go through the maildrop. "You've got to eat more protein and calories. This last section is really going to take a toll on you. Gloria and I will help you slack pack in Vermont and the Whites but you must have the strength to do the walking. You don't look as emaciated as I thought you would, but you can't afford to get any thinner."

"I get plenty of protein. I eat every couple of hours. It's my feet I'm worried about. See how swollen they are." I held up two, puffy, red, nailless feet.

"Those are still Pete's feet! Your mother tells the story of me coming to see you when you were first born. The first thing I said when I saw you was "My God, she's got Pete's feet!" They're swollen, but you've got your father's foundation and there's not a doubt in my mind you'll climb Katahdin." Uncle George swallowed hard at the mention of his best friend. "Those feet need ice water. While you look at the mail, you're going to soak those feet in ice water before supper. We will soak again before bed. I'll be right back with ice." There was no use arguing. In five minutes I was lowering my feet in a bucket of ice water.

"I can't stand it. Now my legs ache! I want boo boo pencils, not ice cubes! Where's the old-fashioned treatment you used to use?" I wailed, but to no avail.

"This is an old-fashioned remedy. Now read your mail and leave those toes in there for twenty minutes." Uncle George was sterner than Daddy would have been.

Among my mail was a large envelope from Earl Nash from Cookeville. He had donated money to the cause and wanted to keep up with me. He had sent letters to several maildrops but I'd always come through before they arrived. Each time Mr. Nash got the letters back, he added a new one in a larger envelope and mailed it to the next maildrop. Here in Massachusetts the greetings had caught up with me. By comparing the postmarks, I was amazed at how far I'd walked. His persistence encouraged me.

"Okay, time's up. Put on clean sock liners and wool socks and we'll get supper."

"Sounds like a winner. I'm starved." Soaking my feet did help, but I wasn't about to let Uncle George know that.

In a nice Italian restaurant, Uncle George and I caught up on the years of graduations, marriages, divorces, births, and deaths that had passed. Daddy's funeral in 1986, was the most painful to recall. "He was the only brother I ever had," Uncle George said, tears forming in his big blue eyes. "He had so many good years left. He would have been so proud of you and would have hiked parts of the Trail with you." Uncle George spoke slowly and painfully. All his jovial silliness was put aside.

"Why did you come get me, Uncle George?" I needed to know.

"You know your old Uncle Geo is a big hiker. I've hiked all over the Whites and at one time even thought about doing the Trail. Hiking is as dear to my heart as that ole scrounge of a father of yours was. Helping you is helping my best friend. Your father would have done the same for me. Best friends are there for each other. We were so close we'd make up stories and not remember who started them. We promised each other that who ever died first had to give one hundred dollars to the other man's wife. If I made up the story, I owe Gloria a hundred dollars. But if he made it up, he owes Lorraine a hundred dollars. Trouble is, Pete's gone and I can't remember who made up the story."

Our laughter eased the sadness. The silly story was so typical of George and Daddy. I could see them sitting on a verandah on a hot summer's night talking nonsense.

"Ask your mother about hunting pheasants in the cemetery. She'll remember. Pete would take her out for a date to the Winchester cemetery. I'd go along in the backseat covered up with a blanket. In the cemetery Pete would get her to drive, even though she didn't have a license. He'd join me in the back seat and we'd shoot at wild pheasants out the windows. We never did kill one. I'm surprised your mother kept dating him. She was a good sport when it came to our shenanigans. Ann's a good woman. How's she doing?"

"Just fine, she's popping around like she was twenty." It'd been six years since her ovarian cancer surgery.

I'd never met Uncle George's four children and six grandchildren, and he'd never met my children. We had a lot of catching up to do. He asked about my brother Peter and sisters Jane and Susan. A valuable piece of my heritage had been rekindled because of my decision to hike the Trail. By daring to accomplish a dream, I'd heard priceless stories of my heritage and revisited an unfinished chapter.

"Finish your milk. We both need to get some sleep." Uncle George yawned. I did as I was told. The night air seemed chilly for early June. On the Trail I adjusted and accepted weather changes but in civilization I expected protection. Life on the Trail had developed tolerance for adversity. Back in the motel room I talked Uncle George into postponing the ice soak.

Banging on the motel wall woke me at six in the morning. It was to Uncle George's wake-up call.

"I'm up!" I banged back, as my feet gingerly touch the floor. Walking for the first half-hour of each day was excruciatingly difficult. The bottoms of my feet were so tender they hurt when they touched the ground. The tops of my toes were numb. I dressed quickly and opened the door so Uncle George could bring in fruit, bagels, peanut butter, candies, peanuts, pistachios, and a daypack. I filled the pack as I drank milk and ate breakfast. "I'll be waiting for you at Mass 2 in North Adams at six tonight. Think you can do twenty-three miles?"

"I don't know why not. I did twenty-eight in the Shenandoah National Park."

"Okay! The sooner we get you on the Trail the better. The weather looks like it's going to hold for a while. We'll ice those feet again tonight."

By seven I was ready to hike my last full day in Massachusetts. Every two days I turned a page in my data book. I'd covered the one hundred and forty-one miles in Connecticut and Massachusetts in eight days and only spent two nights in shelters. Sleeping with black flies was not a prerequisite for climbing Katahdin. I missed the open space, but not the buzzing.

Climbing Massachusetts's highest point, a 3,500 feet summit to Mt. Greylock was not easy. The summit was socked in with fog but Bascom Lodge offered a snack bar, meals, and a lounge. As I approached the lodge, I assumed the two backpacks leaning against the building belonged to south-bounders. I hadn't seen north-bounders for days. "Lorax, I can't believe it! I haven't seen you since Pennsylvania," Lorax stood up hugged me. "And," I turned to the other hiker, "I'm Wolf Woman. Have we met?"

"I met you in Georgia when Kate was with you. I'm Snake Eyes."

"Oh yes, I remember! You shared the skunk and beautiful sky adventure with us on Blood Mountain. Seems like a hundred years ago. I see you have new tents."

"We ordered them from Campor when the bugs started getting bad and had them sent here. They're made of bug proof no-see-um netting. You just put them over the sleeping bag. How are you dealing with the insects without a tent?"

"Tonight my Uncle George is meeting me at Mass 2 and last night I stayed in Dalton. Night before that I was at the Cookie Lady's house and before that I was in a guest house on a wealthy guy's land." I shared my experience in the Tryingham valley.

"What luck! Sounds like Trail Magic big time. I'm ready for this hiking experience to be over, how about you? I just hope the weather holds. I'm so sick of rain."

"I know how you feel. We're so close and yet so far. We still have eight hundred and seventy miles to go after we reach the Vermont State line. My feet hurt all the time and I'm exhausted, but my spirits are okay. It's been a long journey. Actually I hate to see it end. The trip has been one big risk, but I've got massive doses of Trail Magic to depend on until I touch that sign. When are you getting back on the Trail?" I sighed.

"We're hanging out here until they serve supper. Then we'll hike to the shelter."

"See you down the Trail. Be careful." The wind swirled thick fog on and off the mountain. I began to have a deja-vu experience. I'd been in fog and wind so many times everything looked familiar. I felt as dazed, confused, and disorientated as I had when I hiked backwards in Harrison State Park. I checked the data book to get my bearings. Even beautiful, extraordinary, phenomenal experiences have a saturation point. Everything is replaced and nothing remains the same. A rock or a tree in Georgia is a rock or tree in Pennsylvania, New Jersey, or Massachusetts. Weather and terrain change, but wet is wet, hot is hot, and rocky is rocky. Tomorrow's adventure would be different, but the same. The Trail was teaching me to appreciate diversity and repetition. I was ready to know that it was really possible for me to hike 2,160 miles, alone.

As I hiked down Mt. Greylock, the wind raised havoc with the trees. Black clouds threatened a storm that never materialized. I focused on reconnecting with the spunky, sixty-seven year old spirit from my past. Around a bend, sat Uncle George. "You did it! Here's milk and an apple. You covered that twenty-three miles at 2.5 miles per hour. That's darn good! I'm proud of you. How was Mt. Greylock?"

"Rough, but no harder than some I've climbed."

"How are those feet?"

"Tired and sore, but no worse. Thanks for the snack. Are we far from the car?"

"No, compared to the distance you've hiked. Do you know edible plants?"

"I know edible wild plants in the Smokies, but I don't recognize much up here. I know May Apples are edible. I've been watching them grow ever since I left Georgia."

"You never know when you might need to make a meal out of nature," Uncle George identified plants all the way to the road. I was honored to have instruction from such a wise woodsman. "Is it strange to hike in town?"

"Yes, very weird. Road walks in Damascus, Virginia, Duncannon, Pennsylvania, and parts of New Jersey are the longest." Uncle George had already picked out a motel. After a shower and supper, we went for ice cream. Uncle George insisted I get plenty of dairy products. In the motel room I soaked my feet in ice water as we studied maps.

"You'll see white blazes, but not as many as you're used to. The Trail names change often. Some of the Trails you will hike are the Crawford Path, Madison Gulf Trail, Webster Cliff Path, and the Wildcat Ridge Trail. I'll try to get my sister's chalet in the Whites for a few nights. Promise me you'll soak those feet for twenty minutes every night at Gloria's."

"I will," I promised. "Daddy would have only made me soak them for ten."

Gloria would pick me up on Vermont Route 9 near Bennington. I couldn't wait to stay at Daddy's house. I hugged Uncle George real big. He took pictures of me on the Hoosic River footbridge. "You can do it. Keep walking.

You're almost home," he called. I turned and waved from the woods, barely able to see through my tears.

# Chapter 12

## *"Keep those magic feet going!"*

### Vermont - New Hampshire

Crossing the Vermont line near Eph's Lookout signified a milestone. I had returned to my roots. Seeing the rambling farmhouses nestled in the gentle curves of rolling green hills filled my with soul pride to be in the Green Mountain State. Smooth slabs of granite, embedded with mica chips, invited me to sit a spell in the warm June sunshine. Bubbling over smooth stones, a brook was the first landmark in the Data book. Bog boards stretched for miles through lively marshes. Occasionally bridges crossed the brooks, but usually I had to tie my boots to my pack, stuffed with my socks, and waded across in my sandals. Goose bumps rippled down my spine as currents swirled about my legs in my pursuit of white blazes.

Maneuvering in the water took me back to the hours I'd spent building houses out of twigs and pebbles along the brook banks behind my childhood home. I didn't need doll houses. Creating rooms from the soft mud and furniture from nature had brought me hours of joy. Once again mud, pine cones, rocks, and leaves brought me pleasure. Flower-filled fields blazed with every color of the rainbow as this twelfth state of my journey welcomed me with clusters of purple geranium, red columbine, yellow ragwort, orange Indian paintbrush, and blue or yellow stargrass. Pink lady slippers, purple crested dwarf iris, blue delicate violets, and green Indian cucumber leaves adorned the shaded woods. The ground was alive with squirrels and chipmunks. They seemed as thankful as I that the short cold days were now long and warm.

After climbing Harmon Hill, the Trail descended steeply over a vertical stair-step embankment of rock. When walking became too dangerous, I sat down and eased off the sharp jagged steps. One slip could easily have sent me tumbling over the bank. To make matters worse, the sun disappeared. Black clouds rolled in. Lightning bolted across the sky. A deluge of rain fell. The ten-minute storm soaked me to the bone and transformed the already treacherous Trail into a slippery waterfall. After painstakingly scooting over the rocks for an hour, I crossed the road looking like a waterlogged beaver. "You made it!" Gloria screamed as she pulled into the parking lot. We hugged, jumping up and down like schoolgirls. My pack bounced in rhythm to our joy.

"Oh Gloria, I've gotten you all wet. I got caught in a storm coming off the ridge."

"I'll dry. The important thing is that you made it. I saw the storm coming before I left the house and brought you a change of clothes in case it hit. I have apples, muffins, crackers and cheese too." Gloria opened the back of the car.

"Gloria, you're such a dear. I didn't mind getting soaked, knowing I'd be going to Daddy's house. It feels so good to be in Vermont." I pulled off drenched clothes and changed into a pair of Gloria's shorts and shirt. It felt odd to have different clothes on. My hiking clothes were part of my body, like fur is to animals, I only needed clothes for protection. Being free from the hoop-la of styles and fashion was very liberating.

"Uncle George brought the Bennington maildrop to the house. We'll be home in an hour." I didn't care how long it took. I'd been looking forward to the drive for weeks. I soaked in Vermont's beauty and nostalgia as I entertained Gloria with Trail stories.

"I still can't believe Player thought I deserved transportation just because whenever he travels he expects to be given a car. That kind of thinking is an example of how people project their experiences into daily living. Player treats people the way he expects to be treated. If people followed Player's example, our society would be a heck of a lot more balanced with a lot less prejudice and discrimination."

"You're right. That's also a lesson about not accepting circumstances even though you've learned to feel comfortable in a particular environment and," Gloria added, "about reaching out to people."

Putney, Vermont is a cozy, comfortable New England town with a population of about 25,000. Gloria had grown up in Putney and Daddy had made it his home after his divorce in 1964. Keene, New Hampshire, where my mother lives and where I lived during high school, is only a half an hour away, but Mom was in Maine for the summer and not available for a visit.

Complete with cattails and a sandy beach, the pond Daddy had built welcomed me as we drove up the gravel driveway lined with raspberry bushes. Stone steps led from the driveway to a backyard full of flowers. Tall hollyhocks and dahlias grew against a wall constructed to block out the noise from I-91 behind the house. Daddy had sent hollyhock seeds, which had originally come from a friend in Montana, to my first home in Georgia. I'd planted the seeds in every home I'd ever lived in, including Cookeville. Daddy's hollyhocks were a piece of my legacy.

A neatly cultivated vegetable garden thrived near a beautiful New England stone wall. Angel statues were tucked among wild flowers in a sculpted rock garden. "You see the expression on this one?" Gloria pointed to an angel with his chin in his hands. "This statue is saying, 'It's my turn.' The angels keep your father's spirit alive. In this garden is a rock from every place your father and I traveled together."

"I have special rocks at my house, too. Must be a tradition we both picked up from Daddy," I was amazed at how much the yard resembled my own. "As many times as I've been here, I never noticed the similarities between this yard and mine."

"Maybe you needed to distance yourself from the familiar in order to see your legacy. Getting away often helps us recognize the value of our roots. Now how about some fresh asparagus and milk? You know how much pride your father took in his asparagus bed, and your Uncle George has instructed me to be sure you drink milk."

"Bless his heart, I ate so many bagels and drank so much milk that I ought to be able to float all the way to Katahdin in the hole of a bagel on a milk filled stream."

"Your father was a big bread eater and milk drinker, too." Gloria glanced back at her angel garden as she open the door. "You have time for a shower before dinner."

"That was delicious," I announced when I was so full I couldn't hold another bite of Vermont cheddar cheese, fresh asparagus, Boston baked beans, and home-grown vegetables. "It was the kind of meal a vegetarian and a Yankee would walk over fifteen hundred miles for."

"I'm glad you liked it. Now let's put a load of clothes in before it gets any later."

"I only have one load," I said, following Gloria to the basement.

"That's it?" asked Gloria as I dropped two pair of shorts, two shirts, a fleece jacket, underwear, socks, and the Duncannon sleeve-less shirt beside the machine.

"That's it," I repeated.

"What do you wear when you're in a laundromat?"
"I wear my rain coat or I wash a shirt out by hand in a creek and wear it wet the next day." Gloria stared in amazement.

"I know you're a survivor, but you need at least two cotton shirts now that the weather's warm. Follow me." I followed Gloria to her loft bedroom.
"See how this fits." She handed me a new red sleeveless cotton shirt.

"Just fine, but it's brand new. I'll ruin it."

"There are plenty more where that one came from. I want you to have it."

"I'll climb Katahdin in it," I said, giving her a hug.

After putting my clothes in to wash, I called Barbara's sister Dot, who lived a few miles away in Brattleboro. Within minutes she was in the living room orchestrating a slack pack plan. By putting Gloria's Yankee ingenuity, Dot's native New York City drive, and my determination into action, we figured out to how to get me slack packed all the way to Killington. Dot would take me and Gloria would pick me up after I reached Manchester. The next accessible road was nearly twenty-four miles from Vt. Route 9.

After a hardy breakfast the next morning, Gloria and I headed back to Bennington. The sun was just coming up as Gloria and her dog Jake walked me over the bridge at the Trailhead. "Have a good day," she called as she snapped pictures of me disappearing into the woods.

Knowing Mt. Greylock was thirty-five miles behind me was worth the anxiety of climbing the rickety steps of the abandoned fire tower on the summit of

Glastonbury Mountain to see it. Looking out over the soft landscape gave me a sense of where I'd been, even though I didn't have a clue which mountains the Trail had wound through. This sense of mystery gave me reason to trust the process.

Unmarked roads had caused me the most anxiety of any part of the hike. On the afternoon of June 14, they caused a major panic attack. Gloria was to meet me at 5 o'clock on Arlington-West Wardsboro Road. After passing Story Spring Shelter at four that afternoon, I figured I had three and a half miles left. After passing the shelter, I came to a dirt road. Gloria was not there. The data book didn't mention any roads between the shelter and Arlington-West Wardsboro Road. I thought I'd gone too far. I stood in the middle of the rutted road and stared at the wilderness around me. Gone were the days of busy road crossings and frequent stores. I walked down the road but saw no white blazes. I turned around and walked back a few bends in the other direction. This didn't feel right either. I'd trusted white blazes for hundreds of miles, but suddenly I felt horribly confused. Why was this road here if Gloria wasn't? My mind raced.

After aimlessly wandering around, I finally found a blaze. It was nearly five o'clock. I ran. Running exacerbated my anxiety, but I sped on. Rocks and mud made the going difficult, but I couldn't stop. Running kept the black flies off and channeled my panic. I had to keep going.

Long after six o'clock, I heard cars. "Gloria, are you down there?" I kept running, listening, and watching for Jake. "Gloria, I'm coming!" I called over and over. I didn't think the Trail would ever end. After what seemed like the thousandth bend in the Trail I saw Gloria, Jake padding behind her. "Gloria!" I ran faster.

"Ellen, are you all right? I've been worried. What happened?"

"I don't know," I blurted out hysterically. "I got lost, not really lost, but I came out on a road that wasn't marked in the Data book and I got confused. I got scared. I didn't have a clue which way to go. I didn't know whether to keep going, go back, or to walk down the road. So I ran. I didn't think I was ever going to get out of the woods."

"Now, now, let the tears flow. You are exhausted. Hiking without a pack helps your feet but twenty miles every day is too much."

"I've got to keep going! I'm not going to quit." I was scared Gloria would want me to quit. I simply had to keep going.

"I didn't say anything about not finishing, you just need a break, a day to let your body relax."

I sniffled all the way to the car. That evening I started my menstrual period, which I often did when I was around women. I had started when I got to Fontana Dam with Judy. I got another period in Hot Springs when Judy and Suellen were with me. I didn't get another period until I was at Auntie Sue's and then not again until one of my visits with Barbara. Female energy prompted my body into its natural cycle. The periods never lasted more than two or three days and weren't a problem, except for anxiety. I chalked the panic attack up to PMS, and wouldn't hear of taking a day off.

Safe in the car, it felt wonderful to turn the responsibilities over to Gloria while I ate fruit and drank water that didn't have to be purified. I would never take clean water for granted again. During the long beautiful ride, I began to relate to Gloria as a friend, not just as my stepmother, and she viewed me as a grown woman not just as Pete's daughter. Gloria's desire to be part of my hiking experience had opened the door to establish a new definition to the extended or alternative family.

That evening I checked with Suellen, my sister Susan in Spofford, New Hampshire, and I called my friend Patricia in Tennessee to wish her a happy 50th birthday. I was sorry I'd miss her gathering; but I was where I needed to be, doing what I needed to do.

The next day I headed for the crossing at VT 11 & 30 near Manchester, seventeen miles away. The weather was beautiful and the flies weren't as bad since leaving the swampy lowlands of Massachusetts. Stratton Mountain was a tough climb but offered incredible views. The woods were a delightful blend of huge hemlocks dripping with pinecones, and shaggy white birch fluttering with pinkish orange hues. The forest entertained me with its variety of colors and designs.

Down the Trail I found Lorax and Snake Eyes taking a break in a swampy low area. Watching them stealthily slip handfuls of Trail mix under their head nets was too funny. They looked like kids who thought covering their heads would disguise them as they ate stolen cookies, or even monsters from outer space trying to prevent a symbiotic relationship from happening with the million tiny black invaders. It was good to see them, but not wanting to deal with the black flies, I hiked on. Thirty minutes later the fellows zoomed by me on their way to the Manchester hostel.

Spruce Peak Shelter is over a slight ridge on a blue blaze Trail. Dot wanted me to see her club's shelter. I was surprised to find a little boy playing with toy trucks outside it. His mother sat in a rocking chair on the porch. "What a great shelter." I said.

"Sure is. You thru-hiking?" the woman asked.

"I'm on the home stretch," I said as I checked out the cabin-like shelter with its windows, wood stove, inside picnic table, bunk beds, and a covered porch.

"When did you leave?"

"March first from Springer Mountain. My daughter was with me then."

"Early March, eh? You haven't seen Tippy Canoe or Chief have you?"

"I haven't seen Tippy Canoe since North Carolina and I left Chief back in Montebello, Virginia. I'm surprised he hasn't passed me. How do you know them?"

"My sister was on the Trail in March, but it was too cold for her so she came home."

"Was your sister's name Boone? Did she go by Featherspirit?" I asked excitedly.

"YES! How did you know? Did you meet her? What's your Trail name?"

"Wolf Woman."

"I can't believe it!" The woman jumped up and hugged me. "Boone told me if I saw you, Tippy Canoe, or Chief to say hi. She asked me to leave a message in the journal, which is what I was doing when you came up." The woman held up the journal. "Boone won't believe you walked in here. She said you and your daughter were carrying heavy packs and were moving slow."

"We were, but I've gotten rid of a lot of stuff. Kate only hiked with me for six days. I really enjoyed hiking with Boone. She and Kate hit it off real well. Did she tell you about the skunk in the Blood Mountain shelter?"

"Yes, she was scared to death and said you told her it wouldn't spray if everyone stayed quiet. She said she didn't believe you but you sounded like you knew what you were talking about, so she quit talking. She thought Georgia would be warm in the spring but her sleeping bag wasn't heavy enough and she nearly froze to death. I still can't believe I'm meeting you. You're the first woman I've seen, and I don't think there are many guys ahead of you."

I was glad to hear that. "There are a dozen or so guys, but I don't think there are any women. It's sort of weird thinking I might be the first woman thru-hiker since I'm so slow. The secret to finishing is to keep moving. I haven't had a day off since the middle of Virginia. Tell Boone I think it was the smoke from her pipe that saved us."

"Well whatever, it's amazing to see you. I can't wait to tell Boone."

"If I write her a note will you see that she gets it?"

"Sure." I took a sheet of paper out of the journal and wrote a long note. I, too, was amazed at the serendipitous meeting. Boone was such a strong hiker. She always got to the shelters before Kate and I did. She just wasn't prepared. I remember listening to her teeth chatter above the howling wind. Meeting her sister and nephew this far up the Trail filled me with an awesome sense of pride. After leaving Dot a note in the journal and handing Boone's sister the letter, I headed over Spruce Peak Mountain.

After a shower and foot soaking, Gloria rubbed my feet with native-made eucalyptus ointment. Uncle George called every night, so we didn't dare miss a night. We didn't tell him we didn't add ice cubes to the water.

I was ready the next morning when Dot and her son Michael came to take me back to the Trail. She only lacked a few sections of completing a thru-hike after twenty-five years of hiking. My whirlwind way of doing the Trail was incomprehensible her. "You're about to enter into one of the most beautiful sections of the whole Trail. It's also one of the roughest. You can do it, but not with the kind of kind of mileage you've been doing. The views are incredible, the forests are superb, but the climbs will slow you down." Listening to Dot made me feel guilty for moving so fast, but the sooner finished, the more time I'd have to relax before school started.

Hiking twenty-six miles my third day in Vermont brought me to Wallingford. It felt odd to hike up Bromley Mountain Ski Trail with no snow to trudge through. From Baker and Style I had incredible views of mountains packed thick with trees, not snow. Further along, no boats, beaches, or tourism marred the pristine stillness of Griffith Lake. Even the tenting area had a sacred aura. Two people sat on rocks enjoying the quiet. On the far side of the lake a fisherman cast his line into the clear water. I couldn't take my eyes off the transparent stillness as I encircled the deep body of blue. The only sound came from splashing fish and singing birds. Passing the caretaker's tent reminded me that volunteers are scarce in this sparsely populated state and a four-dollar camping fee is required to help with maintenance. I breathed deeply of the pure wilderness, unspoiled charm, and natural beauty. New England offered the ultimate hiking experience. I had left freezing winter temperatures devoid of vegetation for flourishing summer warmth.

I came around a bend and found Michael standing on the bridge. "You headed for the top? I joked. The teenager mumbled something about not wanting to get his sneakers muddy. Smiling, I decided someone could make a fortune writing a book of teen-ager's excuses. "Sorry I'm late. That was quite a hike," I said scrambling up the bank.

"I'm surprised to see you so soon," Dot said as I climbed in the car. "That was the hardest section in Vermont. People usually need two or three days to hike it. You crossed Baker, Bromley, Styles, Peru and passed eight shelters and two tenting areas."

"My grandmother used to say, 'ignorance is bliss, and what you don't know won't hurt you.' I've done this whole hike in a rather blind fashion. I was too busy raising money to read up on terrain conditions. Since day one the journey has been full of surprises, risks, and fears as well as phenomenal variety, wonder, and beauty."

While enjoying another hot meal and suffering through another foot soaking, Gloria told me that Marianne Ogden, a free-lance writer for the *Keene Sentinel* newspaper, was coming to interview me on Wednesday, June 18. My mother had informed the *Sentinel* that I was in Putney and had asked them to do an article on me since I was a Keene High School graduate. I decided the interview signified a day off.

Dot came early the next morning to take me for another ride through the quiet, elegant Vermont towns. The rural state was not impoverished or destitute. Big white churches sit at the head of the squares. Fine wood homes with big barns, solid enough to withstand northeastern tempests, line the village streets.

Holstein and Jersey cows munch in pastures and tall corn grows in straight rows. The growing season is short, but the New Englander's pride themselves on dairy farming, delicious gardens, and quality orchards.

Six miles into the hike I fearfully crossed the Mill River suspension bridge that swung far above natural tubs carved out by years of water pressure on the rocky sides of Clarendon Gorge. I would have stopped to enjoy the water, but I had miles to go; and I knew it wouldn't be safe to swim in the deep pools alone.

After climbing Killington's 4,241 summit, the highest summit since rounding Mt. Rogers 5,729 foot summit in southern Virginia, the Trail wound around the mountain on a ledge of boulders between tall hemlocks and sweet smelling balsam trees. The Trail had been cut in a circuitous route to avoid erosion and prevent damage to the forests but was very tedious.

Thick fog socked the mountain under a blanket of damp grayness, and rain drizzled from low clouds. I marveled at how quickly the terrain and the weather changed, and how the changes impacted my spirits. Exhausted and anxious, I carefully calculated each step. I remembered how warm the morning had been only a few hours before. Just as nasty weather and rough terrain reappear, pine needle paths and sunny skies would return. Believing was the difficult part.

Dot was nowhere to be seen when I came out on the highway an hour later. "Are you Wolf Woman?" A woman called from the porch of a motel on the hill.

"Yes I am."

"Your friend, Dot, called and said she's had car trouble. Someone in a Volkswagen will be here in an hour. You may wait up here if you like."

I hurried up the hill, glad for a chance to use a bathroom and to get out of the chilly wind. The sun was nearly down and the temperature had dropped considerably. An hour later a Volkswagen pulled into the parking lot with a friend of Dot's at the wheel. On the way to get Dot, who was waiting between Killington and Brattleboro, we stopped at a Deli to get a sandwich and let Gloria know where I was. Finally at Gloria's home, I flopped in bed without taking a shower, grateful tomorrow was a day off.

Like a hen, I was awake with the sun the next morning. I rested until Gloria left for work and then got ready for my interview. Sitting with my feet in a pan of cold water, I talked candidly to Marianne about the trip. Weeks later, while reading the June 29 article my mother sent to my Gorham maildrop, I was shocked to read a line Marianne quoted me as saying. "I'm over this and I want to go home." I was tired, but to admit I was finished striving for a goal I had waited so long to fulfill was disturbing. The sentence made me realize the importance of focus. No matter how emotionally or physically tired I was of climbing, I would not give up. Katahdin was a long way away, but climbing her symbolized the drive of a spirit that rain, rocks, loneliness, and even black flies could not break. It represented a commitment.

After climbing hundreds of mountains and getting into excellent shape, the White's inert pile of rock presented horrible anxiety. I'd heard of people getting struck by lightning, falling off the cliffs, breaking limbs, and getting lost. I imagined the worst, but I knew nothing could stop me. After the interview, I settled on the couch for a nap. Barbara called from New York to remind me, "There are no rules, just keep moving."

After dinner at the Putney House Inn, I remembered to call Mr. Hawks, whom I'd met in the Shenandoah National Park. If I could stay at his house the following night, Gloria could bring the pack to Dartmouth College in Hanover, New Hampshire on Saturday. There was a chance he wouldn't be home, wouldn't remember his offer, or would say no, but I wouldn't know if I didn't ask. I dialed. A child answered the phone. "Hello, is your dad there please?"

"Just a minute, please."

"At least he's home," I whispered to Gloria.

"Hello."

"Hello, Mr. Hawks, this is Ellen Wolfe, I met you back in May in the Shenandoah National Park."

"Oh yes, how are you getting along?"

"Very well thank you. I'm in Putney. I was wondering if I could stay at your house tomorrow night? I won't arrive until early evening and will leave first thing in the morning. I'm not carrying a tent and the black flies are too terrible to stay in the shelters," I tried to sound desperate.

"Sounds fine with me, but let me ask my wife." After a long pause, Mr. Hawks returned to the phone to say that his wife usually wasn't in favor of taking in hikers, but this one time would be all right. "I'll be home that afternoon. Here are directions from the Trail." I carefully wrote down everything he said, thanked him, and hung up the phone.

"YES! Trail Magic again! Gloria, I can't believe it. I've been saying that for months. I wonder if by the time I climb Katahdin I will believe incredible things happen."

"I hope so," answered Gloria, "because you deserve to."

The five nights I'd spent with Gloria had given my body a chance to refuel, rejuvenate, and renew my spirit with Daddy. It was especially significant to be there on Father's Day.

Dot came the next morning in a van she had borrowed from her school. Gloria loaded me with enough food to make it for the two days on the Trail without the pack. Uncle George promised to pick up the maildrop in Killington on his way to the White Mountains. After good-byes and promises to write, I headed back to Sherburn Pass.

The Appalachian Trail and the Long Trail share the same one hundred and three miles from the state line to Sherburne Pass at Killington. There the Appalachian Trail abruptly angles right toward Katahdin and the Long Trail continues north into Canada. The Trail was easier after it headed east but the elevation was lower and the bugs were terrible. Hiking logging roads between boundary lines made of stone walls felt nostalgic as I followed the directions to the Hawks from Winttui Shelter. Mr. Hawks and his wife Karen graciously shared cookies and iced tea with me on the deck of their lovely log cabin. Karen and I discovered she had graduated from Keene High School five years earlier than I. We had even had some of the same teachers.

As we talked, the family cat basked in the sunshine. Mr. Hawks said they always brought the cat in at night so the coyotes wouldn't get it. I hoped to see a coyote. I had only seen two bears, one skunk, one porcupine, two groundhogs, one rabbit, deer, salamanders, frogs, squirrels, and birds.

I gratefully accepted Karen's offer to cook scrambled eggs and toast for a late supper, and take a shower. I was invited to join the family for pancakes and real maple syrup for breakfast. Being in a New England home where the people appreciate the value of real maple syrup brought back memories of the woodsy flavor Daddy used to achieve by boiling sap from the maple trees around our Vermont home.

The next day I'd not hiked more than a few miles of my last twenty-five mile day in Vermont, when I saw a peculiar animal not more than ten yards to the right of the Trail. The small animal looked frightened as it kept up an awkward gait north. I walked quickly to keep up with it as the small animal scrambled parallel with the Trail.

Hesitating at brush and downed trees, the animal was too low to the ground to climb over objects. Its body was covered with bright white spots that were more evenly formed than that of a fawn. The animal had a long pointed face and a long thin tail. It was burnt-tan in color and had high pointed ears that flopped back and forth as it ran. It never made a sound. The animal and I travel around several corners together. Then it abruptly turned left and ran down the Trail in front of me before disappearing into the forest. Uncle George later confirmed my suspicious that the animal had been a young coyote, and that I should have been glad the mother had not been around.

The environment gave me a sense of being a part of renewal and rebirth. Wild blueberries and summer flowers flourished. Sunshine filtered through the forest's thin new growth. Dusty log roads, stone wall fences, and babbling brooks were mine to enjoy. North of Hanover the Trail came out on a paved road and led me into a neighborhood. Out of a yard raced a small black dog intent on biting. I was using both walking sticks to keep the dog at bay when a woman came out of the house and called her pet. The dog stopped barking and trotted obediently into the house. After shutting it in the house, the woman returned. "I'm sorry," she began. "My dog is afraid of hiking sticks. He always barks at hikers who carry them. You a thru-hiker?"

"Yes. Do you know how far the Foley House is on the Dartmouth campus?"

"No, but we can find it. I'll give you a ride."

"Thanks, I have map," I offered. After a few wrong turns, the black terror's owner deposited me at the Foley House. It felt good being in a college town, across the Connecticut River, and in my thirteenth state with only four hundred and forty-two miles to go! I was the only hiker, so I had several sofas to choose from. After a shower and a short visit with students, I walked to town and discovered the Hanover Consumer Co-op to be the best grocery store on the Trail. Loaded up with Trail mix, bread, cheese, fruit, and a sandwich, I headed back at the Foley House to call Suellen and Gloria, before borrowing a blanket from a student.

Letting my feet get used to touching the ground when I got up each morning was as much a habit as enjoying bagels and cream cheese had been back home. As I sipped almondine decaf-coffee, and munched oat bran bagels with walnut cream cheese, a wave of deja vu passed over me. I was in the Java Coffee Shop in Knoxville sitting next to Suellen, until I looked down at my green shirt, worn tan shorts, and scuffed-up hiking boots with Uncle George's purple wool socks sticking out the tops. Feelings of nostalgia happened frequently. Coffee, clothes, bagels, restaurants, and even sections of the Trail looked the same. People create the difference.

After breakfast I borrowed a tee shirt from a female student so I could wash my shirt and underwear in the sink. The sun was already warm. My clothes would dry on the porch rail by the end of the day. I journaled on the front steps until Gloria and her friend Shirley arrived. After enjoying a restaurant lunch, they headed back to Putney. Tears filled my eyes as I hugged Gloria. I would not see her until after the hike.

Snake Eyes had arrived and joined me for supper. Back at the Foley house I filled my raincoat pockets with food, water, and my camera for my last twenty-mile hike before reaching the Whites. Uncle George would come pick up the pack before meeting me at Dartmouth-Skiway Road. As the sun peeked over the rooftops, I slipped out of the Foley House, leaving Snake Eyes to enjoy his day off. Stone fences, wild flowers, and babbling brooks welcomed me to New Hampshire.

Late in the afternoon I arrived at Lyme-Dorchester Road. I paced in the gnats and black flies before flagging down the second car that had come down the road. The driver confirmed my suspicions that the road connected to Dartmouth Skiway Road and offered to leave a note if Uncle George's car was parked on the highway. Another hour passed. Finally a van came along. A woman stuck her head out the window and called, "I'll bet you are Wolf Woman."

"Yes, how did you know?"

"We passed your Uncle George going up the Trail as we were coming down to where the Trail intersects with the Dartmouth Skiway Road. He asked us if we'd passed a woman thru-hiker. At the road we saw a note attached to a car. He took the liberty of reading it and figured you'd be at this junction. Hop in, we'll take you to his car. Wait until you see the pink banner he's tied across the Trail with a message telling you there's milk in the cooler. He signed it, Uncle George; that's how we knew his name."

"How kind of you to come. He hikes a lot, but apparently didn't know the Trail comes out here," I said as I climbed in the back seat. Uncle George's car sat at the edge of the highway, but he was nowhere in sight. The man volunteered to hike up the Trail and look for him. Thirty minutes later, down they came. Uncle George was exhausted, sorry for the mix-up, and as ready as I was for a cold drink. I was glad to be safe and heading to a chalet for the next four nights. "You'll like the chalet. I have food so we can cook. I picked up your pack and the Killington maildrop, so we're all set."

"Sounds great. The mountains are beautiful. They look like I remember them."

"Tomorrow you'll hike the ones in front of us," said Uncle George with a sweep of his hand.

The chalet had a great view of the roaring Pemigewasset River. Uncle George planned to fish while I hiked. After showering, I cooked spaghetti and made a salad. We spent the evening studying the Trail maps and, of course, soaking my feet. At six, the next morning I woke to marching music blaring up the stairs. "Smarts and Cube are waiting for you. Time to be on the Trail if you are going to do nineteen miles today." Uncle George was toasting bagels when I came down. I ate a bowl of granola and downed a glass of juice while packing up bagels, apples, peanuts, and plenty of water. A clear sky promised a good day.

On top of Smart's Mountain, I rested and ate. The climb up Mt. Cube was not difficult, but coming down an old knee injury flared up again. Switchbacks were a thing of the past. My sore knees and swollen feet were glad to find Uncle George waiting at NH 25 C with milk and a bagel. Back at the chalet, we fell into a routine. I showered and cooked supper. We studied the maps while we ate and I soaked my swollen feet.

I'd heard so many horror stories about Moosilauke that I dreaded the climb. Rising to an elevation of 4,802 feet, Moosilauke ascends straight up 3,700 feet in the first four miles. It is the first northern mountain that soars above the tree line. The rocky terrain was by far a bigger challenge then the steep climb to the boulder summit. At the top, I watched for the Benton Trail and followed it only three tenths of a mile before turning a sharp right onto the Beaver Brook Trail. Watching the beautiful Beaver Brook cascade into huge pools, plunge over waterfalls, and splash over rapids took my mind off the steep knee crunching descent.

After Moosilaukee came Wolf Mountain and North and South Kinsman. Mt. Wolf was not only vertical, it was one sheer cliff. The hike was so slow, tedious, and dangerous. I couldn't imagine carrying a full pack. Time and again I thought I had reached the top, only to discover I had yet another peak to climb. Clinging to shrubby bushes, I pulled myself hand-over-hand over the rocks. I crawled over the ledges and slid on my bottom down cliffs too steep to walk upright. A cold howling gale had blown up. I fully expected to be blown off the cliffs any minute.

In a 50 mile-an-hour gale, I finally reached the top of North Kinsman and headed down the other side. My knees trembled and my whole body felt weak. It was difficult to appreciate the stands of balsam fir until I was safely off the ledges.

Uncle George had invited his hiking friends up to meet me at Lonesome Lake Hut at five o'clock. All day I'd been anxious about making it. I watched 5 o'clock come and go and tried to hurry. I didn't want to disappoint Uncle George, but I was powerless over the rough terrain. I pushed on. At nearly six, I saw Uncle George. "Where have you been?" he hollered.

"What do you mean, 'where have I been'? I've had a terrible day. I thought I was going to get blown off the top of Kinsman." I burst into tears as I recounted the rocks, cliffs, and boulders I'd climbed and how badly my feet hurt. Uncle George let me cry. "I just couldn't get here any faster. The woods are beautiful and it hasn't rained, but the wind was ferocious and the terrain was just rough."

"Now now, I'm not upset with you. It's been a while since I've done this section and never in one day. It usually takes me two or three days to do what you have done in one. This was probably not a good day to have the fellows come meet you. Drink this milk and rest. We're almost at the hut and then we've only got three miles before we'll be down to Franconia Notch and the car. Cheer up, the best of Beaver Brook is yet to come."

Uncle George led the way. It was good not to have to hurry and have Uncle George with me. Lonesome Hut, the smallest of the huts in the Whites has water, food, and an attendant on duty. After a rest we continued on. The cliffs weren't as scary with Uncle George beside me. Hanging to the rail handles mounted in the rock was fun with Uncle George along to share the experience. We took pictures at Beaver Brook. The water was soothing and fascinating. I was exhausted, but my attitude had definitely changed, even though the terrain had changed little. Again, people made the difference. The last three miles were sheer joy, even though my feet and knees knew all too well we were going over rocks downhill.

Ten miles a day is an average day in the White's, but my next goal was Franconia Notch on U.S. 3, sixteen miles away. At the chalet I washed clothes for the last time. My slack-packing days ended because there were no more convenient roads and plenty of huts in the Whites for me to stay in. If space is available, thru- hikers can stay free in exchange for work. Reservations are recommended, but I didn't want the pressure of having to be at a particular hut on a specific day. I would take my chances. Uncle George agreed to take the stove, sleeping bag, mat, and extra food to the Barn, a hostel in Gorham, where I'd be in four days. Hiking without a tent and a sleeping bag was a risk, but the whole trip had been a risk. As I headed for bed the phone rang. My mother had tracked me down by calling Gloria. "You're so close, I wanted see if I could help."

"I'm through slack-packing for now and am counting the days until I can rest at the beach." I hung up wishing she'd called sooner.

After my last chalet breakfast, I packed snack food in Uncle George's daypack with my rain gear, camera film, toilet paper, and warm clothes. I would be really winging it. The harder the Trail got, the bigger risks I took. Maybe the rougher the terrain the more I trusted the process.

Gale Head Hut was thirteen miles away. Low mileage was a must, no matter how emotionally difficult it was to adjust to. I'd been accustomed to turning pages in the Data Book every day or two. I hadn't turned a page for three days. It would take me eight days to travel the one hundred and twenty-five miles between Lyme-Dorchester Road and Gorham. I wanted to make good time while the weather held. But the rocks and cliffs would slow me down. The White Mountains were teaching me to accept the things I could not change.

Uncle George tried desperately to keep the gathering tears in his blue eyes from spilling down his cheeks as he gave me a quick hug at the Liberty Springs Trailhead. "I couldn't have made it this far without you," I blubbered. I was used to crying.

"Ah, come on now you're tough. You would've found a way. I'm proud to have been part of your experience. You're doing something I've always wanted to do." Lowering his usually booming voice, he added, "Your father would have been proud of you. He would have supported you all the way," Uncle George's words faltered, "He was my best friend, and best friends are there for each other."

"You've been as good to me as Daddy would have been, although Daddy wouldn't have put as many ice cubes in the water." Laughter eased the sadness.

"Get going now, be careful, and keep those magic feet going. I know you'll make it. You've got what it takes. Pete's feet will get you up Katahdin."

"Thank you, Uncle George, I love you." Focusing on a white blaze through tears, I walked away, leaving another support person at the edge of the Trail. My part of this experience was to walk. I would miss his company, but was looking forward to staying in the huts and not hiking under the pressure to reach road crossings.

I was now in the middle of the challenging Whites. Although Little Hay-stack Mountain at 4,760 feet, was by no means little, it not as difficult a climb as the Kinsman. Shrilling tiny birds amazingly lived above the tree line. The view from Lincoln's lofty 5,089 feet summit was breathtaking. A perfectly clear sky granted me superb visibility for hundreds of miles. Mt. Garfield was a continuous climb up 4,488 feet of rock. I considered staying at Garfield Ridge Campsite, until I remembered I didn't have my gear.

Friendly people and supper greeted me as I entered Galehead Hut. Bunkrooms and a compost toilet were built on each side of the dining room. Only six people had reservations for the night, so the crew assured me there was plenty of room. Luvtuhike, Crash, Trail Trooper, Snake Eyes, Lorax, Chisel, Mobius, Let it Be, Sausage Man, Gripper Man, Uncle Leo, Alex, and Dragon Tail had come through, no women. I would climb Katahdin before claiming the honor as 1997's first woman thru-hiker.

My New England hut mates couldn't imagine thru-hiking. "There's no way to understand until you commit to doing it, put a pack on your back, and take to the Trail. Thru-hiking is the riskiest, most challenging, and most rewarding experience of my life." I told them as I filled up on salad, soup, bread, and companionship.

Snuggling under a stack of wool blankets on a bottom bunk with wind whistling around the windows felt wonderful. I felt millions miles away from civilization, even though I crossed a highway nearly every day. After a hardy breakfast of hot cereal, fruit, tea, and a baked fruit dish, I swept the floors in exchange for my stay. Zealand Hut was only seven miles away and Mizpah Hut was eighteen, so I headed for the Crawford Notch hostel.

For the second time in four months I climbed Mt. Guyot. The first Mt. Guyot was two thousand miles away in the Smoky Mountains. Named after Arnold Guyot, the famous Swiss geographer of the mid-nineteenth century, the White Mountain 4,500 feet climb was no match for weak knees. I seriously wondered if the peak had a summit. The Trail wound over Zealand on a circuitous route along dangerous precipices and near sharp drop offs. I felt exposed and vulnerable so far above the tree line. One slip on the loose gravel could send me tumbling down the mountain. I recalled my days of climbing with a loaded pack in the pouring rain and in ferocious winds to dispel my fears. The black flies were nearly non-existent at the high elevations. At Zealand Hut I headed straight for the  pan of leftover fruit cobbler and banana bread. Larger than Galehead, the hut had several bunkrooms and a wide porch. Cold, clear water tumbled over a beautiful waterfall into an area designated for swimming.

From marshy summits spread with bog boards to flower-filled banks along lower elevations, changes in the vegetation were delightful. The warm June days brought hopping green frogs and wriggling orange salamanders into the Trail. Thick, lush vegetation and leafy deciduous trees were a change from the barren summits where only scrubby pines and bushes survive. Leaving the hardwoods forests, papery white birch trees fluttering with pinkish orange bark greeted me.

Crawford Hostel was 3.7 miles off the Trail so I caught a ride from the highway. Three brightly painted cabins were located in the yard. The main house provided guests with a fully equipped kitchen, reading room, and bathrooms. The hostel attendant assigned me the task of tidying up the outhouse in exchange for my stay. After finishing my job, I showered and settled in while visiting with hikers. One man was particularly interested in my experience and offered to drive another hiker and myself to a restaurant. While enjoying pasta and salad, I entertained the fellows with stories. In honor of my forthcoming accomplishment, the man, a stockbroker from Boston, paid for my supper.

Back in the cabin I met a cousin of Bob Peoples, who ran Kincora Hostel back in Hampton, Tennessee. After breakfast my new friend drove me to the Trail. Today's goal would take me to Lake of the Clouds Hut on Mt Washington, eleven miles away. Fragile alpine flowers and plumb lichen grew along the Trail as I hiked over Mt. Webster at 3,910 feet, Mt. Jackson at 4,052, Mt. Pierce at 4,310, and the Webster Cliffs. The breathtaking scenery was worth every step. I kept an eye on the fast moving clouds in case of the ever-possible change in weather as I hiked exposed above the treeline for the next twenty-five miles. Mt. Washington shone like a beacon of hope as I approached its lofty 6,245 feet summit. I stopped at Mizpah Hut for the left over food and to put moleskin on my heels. Harvey and Cindy Winslow were ecstatic to meet me. Tracking thru-hikers was a pastime of theirs. They confirmed I was the first woman thru-hiker for the season. I knew if I took a day off a woman might get ahead of me.

Joining ninety hikers under one roof at Lake of the Clouds was a culture shock. People scurried about in clean, stylish hiking clothes. Meals were served in a long dining room adjacent to rooms packed with rows of bunk beds. I was assigned to the last bunk in the overflow room and allowed all the free food I wanted after scrubbing down the bathrooms. Stuffed, over-stimulated, and exhausted, I crawled into the bunk in a room with eight other people, propped my feet up on the wall, and fell asleep.

Breakfast was served at seven. After doing my chores I ate and loaded up on leftover bread and fruit before hiking over the ridge to Madison Hut where more free food waited. The views were so breathtaking I couldn't stop taking pictures. The Whites, more spectacular than the scary stories, provided powerful reasons to trust.

At my twentieth maildrop I'd received a letter from Lum indicating he wanted to fly from his home in Minnesota, pick up the Trail in Gorham, and hike to Katahdin with me. He'd kept up with my progress by calling Suellen. I'd called him from the chalet. I would hike to Pinkham Notch, hitch hike to Gorham, stay at the Barn, and rest a day while I waited for him to fly in. He suggested we hike Pinkham Notch to Gorham north to south because it would be easier. I checked in with him the night before he boarded a plane, and with Suellen who was counting the days until she, too, could head for Maine.

At the Barn the owners, Maggie and her husband Paul, proudly showed off their week-old baby girl before showing me the barn loft full of beds. They accepted my offer to pull weeds in the yard the next day in exchange for my stay.

After breakfast I picked up my maildrop, and sorted the equipment Uncle George had left. Then started my chores. Digging in soil was spiritually therapeutic. I analyzed my feelings about Lum finishing the hike with me. I'd struggled with loneliness and enjoyed my few days with hiking companions, but I'd managed just fine alone. Merging my tempo with someone else's for the final month would add anxiety as well as camaraderie to the experience. In four days, Suellen's arrival in Andover, Maine would allow me to slack pack much of the rest of the remaining days. It seemed too late to need a hiking partner.

Late that night Lum's boots coming up the stairs woke me. I was suddenly glad to see him. We tried not to wake up the four hikers who had joined me, including a woman, Katahdin-bound Down Under from Australia. I was relieved to learn she was a section hiker and had gotten on the Trail in Vermont.

After we filled up on muffins the next morning, Paul gave us a ride to the US 2 Trailhead to slack pack twenty-one miles to Pinkham Notch. Hiking south felt strange. The only north-bounder we passed was Snake Eyes who was two days ahead of Lorax. Boulders filled the Trail as we climbed Carter-Moriah Mountain range rising 4,000 feet in steep sided notches. Using bushes and feeling for toeholds in the sheer rock, we scaled Mt. Moriah. Nestled on the edge of the tranquil lake at Carter Notch Hut, we rested. Lum took a nap while I soaked my feet. Tucked among massive 4,000 feet mountains, the lake sparkled with the serenity of sacred space as towering firs swayed in the crystal clear air.

The sinking sun moved us to pull on our packs. Scaling Wildcat was extremely tedious. Having Lum scrambling beside me was comforting, but his presence didn't take the knee-popping pain out of descending Wildcat at 2,000 feet in two miles. Using him as a sounding board, I expressed my utter disgust at the rough terrain. We reached the road as the sun reached the horizon.

The next morning we again stood at US 2 Trailhead, this time to hike north. The terrain was easier after crossing the Androscoggin River. Behind the pristine Gentian Pond and campsite, the majestic Mt. Success invited me to climb New Hampshire's last mountain and enter my fourteenth and last state. At the border, steady rain didn't stop Lum from snapping my picture under the small wooden sign that read, "Welcome to Maine."

# Chapter 13

## "I did it!"

### Mt. Katahdin, Maine

The further I hiked, the greater my faith grew. I knew I would make it through the remaining risks that stood as high as the goal of walking my dream. In two hundred and eighty-one miles I could relax. Summit after summit the vast regions of sacred space shortened between Katahdin's sign and peace to my soul. Mt. Carlo, Maine's first summit, rose 3,562 feet. Laced with bog boards through muddy swamps at 3,794 feet, Goose Eye Mountain is Mahoosuc's most impressive mountain. A weaving juxtaposition between steep elevation and difficult terrain, the Trail kept the experience in perspective.

A wilderness club of teens and leaders had claimed all but two of the campsite platforms at Full Goose Shelter and Campground. Camping on the ground was not only not allowed due to rocks and roots, it was virtually impossible. In high elevations the black flies had not been bad, but near water they were atrocious. We quickly cooked rice and pasta before climbing into Lum's two-person tent.

Sharing tent space with the retired sixty-seven year old Minnesota hiker reminded me of how close I'd come to sharing a motel room with Luvtuhike in Virginia, and to bunking in with seventeen guys in the Smokies. From the first weeks to these closing miles, opportunities to learn to trust men continued. I'd spent every night in a different shelter, usually with only males, and none of them had posed any threatening, inappropriate, or disrespectful behavior. I had a tiny Swiss army knife, a whistle, and a can of mace, but I'd not once threatened to use them. From the very beginning I believed I'd be safe. Fully dressed, I lay in my sleeping bag listening to Lum sleep and realized it had taken a 2,160-mile journey to learn that some men can be trusted. I relaxed, knowing the tent protected me from the bugs, the platform protected me from the ground, and trust protected us from each other.

At the crack of dawn Lum and I ate pop tarts and Trail mix as we broke camp. We headed for Mahoosuc Notch. Listed on the National Register of Natural Landmarks, it is the roughest mile on the whole Appalachian Trail. Glacially carved, the steep walled notch is filled with huge boulders. Climbing through the notch can take two to three hours. Accounts ranged from dangerous and scary to beautiful and exciting.

Filled with apprehension, I listened to Lum's description. "It's like climbing up, over, down and through boulders as big as houses. Don't toss your walking sticks or pack down because they could disappear between the rocks and into the water below the boulders. The climb up the arm of the notch is even tougher. You've made it this far. You can do it. "

"If I have to go through the notch in order to get to Grafton 26, I'm ready!" I declared. Suellen had left Tennessee several days ago. Lum and I had called her car phone from Gorham and told her we'd be at the Grafton Notch parking lot on July 4th. Although it was only eight miles away, it would take us two days. After months of absence, I would have walked to the moon to reconnect. Drizzling rain would make the already dangerous climb even more treacherous. As we pulled each other over icy slick patches and deep ravines, we came to spaces too small to get our bodies and packs through. After establishing solid footing, we took turns crawling through the rock cracks and handing the packs and walking sticks to each other. Occasionally we could see the water below, but always the gurgling sound reminded us that one careless move would send us through a rocky cave and into flowing icy water below us. Red blazes marking a high water route would add time and confusion to the climb. Following white blazes was critical. I was grateful Lum had come. The journey had taught me I deserved kindness. After adjusting to the danger, the jungle gym adventure felt like a child's playground.

Two tedious but exhilarating hours later, we stood gazing back at the incredible tunnel of massive tightly lodged rocks between the perpendicular walls. The 3,777 feet arm of the notch was next. Hand over hand in biting wind, steady rain, and thick fog we lodged the toes of our boots in rock crevasses and pulled ourselves up Old Speck, Maine's third largest mountain. Exhausted and soaked, we welcomed the sight of Speck Pond Shelter where two south-bounders greeted us. One of the hikers I'd passed on the bridge just before Snowbird Mountain back in March. At the time he was practicing for a thru-hike. We'd discussed the smoke billowing out of the Smokies. Now months later in Maine, we met again. He was nervous and green, but full of enthusiasm. Although seasoned, I was fearful to claim my accomplishment until I touched the sign on Katahdin's summit. Two hundred and seventy-one miles remained before I'd close this chapter on balancing movement with process.

The hike from Old Speck Shelter to Maine 26 seemed like the longest hike of the whole journey. Lum tried to assure me we would hike the 4.6 miles by noon, but I felt trapped by the terrain. After what seemed like hours of stepping over rocks and roots, I spotted cars through the trees. It was only eleven-thirty. Lum sensed my excitement and lingered back. Suellen's van faced the woods across the parking lot. I could see her reading a book. Tapping on the window, I asked, "You waiting for someone?"

"Ellen! You made it! They told me at the Bed and Breakfast there was no way you two could make it from Gorham in two days." Suellen was beside herself with joy as she hugged me, even though I was soaked, musty, and smelly.

"I had a special reason for meeting today's goal," I said. Turning to Lum who had joined us, I introduced him to Suellen. "I'd still be back there stuck in the notch if it wasn't for Lum. He literally pulled me across the crevices and gullies."

"I don't know how you did it. Get in and tell me all about it while I take both of you back for a shower." I climbed in the front and Lum fit himself in around camping gear in the back. As soon as the doors were shut, Suellen buzzed down the windows. The draft was cold on my skin so I buzzed mine back up. Suellen instantly buzzed it back down and asked, "Don't y'all need a little air?"

"No, I'm a bit chilly. How 'bout you, Lum?"

"No, it's a little breezy."

Suellen, however, thought fresh air was definitely a necessity. "I think y'all smell like human beings!" she said, buzzing down my window as I proceeded to take my boots off and add to the fragrance.

I breathed a sigh of relief. My days alone were over. The months of having people hike in and out of the process were over. Even Lum, whose presence had been so valuable these past four days, had decided to fly back to Minnesota and not continue on to Katahdin. I would climb Katahdin alone, but my aching body and throbbing feet told me slack packing these last days were necessary to meet my goal. By monitoring and adjusting I would complete the journey; only then would believe I could do it.

Irene, who ran the B & B with her husband, reminded me of my mother. She hurried out of the house with her arms open wide. "Oh honey you look so exhausted and you can hardly walk, but you made it." She looked at Lum, who except for some soreness was none the worse for the wear and added, "And Lum, bless your heart for coming to help this woman through the notch. I hear it's just plain ghastly."

In the presence of nurturing women I let myself be pampered. Irene handed me a glass of ice tea. "It was rough in places, but I like physical challenges," Lum grinned. "Wolf Woman is no ordinary hiker."

"I'll agree with the, 'no ordinary' part, but hiking through dangerous places scares me. It seems you guys thrive on them," I took a sip of tea.

"That may be, but I've never seen such drive and determination in a woman before," Lum shook his head.

"Drive and determination, that's what my daughter said about me. If only determination would drive away fear."

"You two hungry?" Suellen asked. The homey Bed and Breakfast felt comfortable, but foreign and strange. Everything seemed out of character. From lathering a wash cloth, combing my hair, putting on Suellen's clean shirt, to slipping into my Birkinstock sandals, I hardly knew who I was.

Sitting in Addie's Place with a grilled sandwich, salad, and French fries in front of me felt even more confusing. My stories came slowly, as if I were talking about an experience that belonged to someone else from another time

**196**

period. I couldn't find words to describe the experience of moving through the incredible land. I tried to tell stories, but depended on Lum to fill in the details when my mind went blank. Suellen knew there'd be plenty of time to hear everything. Back at the Bed and Breakfast I packed food for the next day's ten-mile hike to East B. Hill Road.

After enjoying Paul's famous breakfast with Whippoorwill a female section hiker, and with a south-bounder and his parents, Lum and Suellen took me back to the parking lot before Suellen drove Lum back to Gorham's bus terminal. With mixed emotions, I watched Lum disappear down the road. Lum had tried to reassure me I'd climbed the most dangerous and difficult sections. It was fitting I would finish alone, but the fear returned. Hiking with Lum had shown me how differently women and men view physical challenges. Alone, I was free to be frustrated without feeling I should enjoy the treacherous sections.

I remembered the day Lum had been way ahead of me on Goose Eye Mountain. Driving rain made the rocky climb very slippery. I was sick of it. Suddenly I faced a perpendicular rock ledge. At eye level a white blaze marked the next step. Trembling from fear and chilling rain, I unsuccessfully made several attempts to pull myself up over the ledge. I simply could not. Suddenly out of thin air, a crew of south-bound volunteers appeared at top of the ledge. Like a pack of angels emerging from a cloud burst, they formed a human chain and pulled me over the ledge. "

"Happy hiking," one young woman called over her shoulder as they departed as quickly as they'd appeared.

Trembling now more from the power of Trail Magic than from cold, I started crawling up the vertical rock. I was halfway up when a gust of wind blew my pack cover off the pack and over my head. At the same instant I started slipping back down the mountain. Trying not to panic, I grabbed a short scrubby tree and held on with one hand, while frantically peeling the clinging cover off my face with the other. I gripped the bush with two hands and took a deep breath before resuming my snail's pace.

Glancing up, I saw Lum sitting on the summit laughing. Seeing nothing funny about any part of the experience, I moved into high gear. I crawled frantically for Lum's extended hand and exploded. "I could have fallen down the cliff. Nearly dying is not funny," I sobbed. Lum put an arm around my shoulders.

"I'm sorry. You just looked so funny crawling up the rocks with the pack cover over your head. Climbs like this energize me. I guess women don't experience physical challenges quite the same."

"I may have looked comical, but this is not a sexist issue. Maybe women are more intuitive when it comes to safety than men."

Farther on, as I scrambled up the rungs of a ladder fastened to the cliffs of Baldpate Mountain, it occurred to me that one way or another I'd made it so far.

There was no reason I couldn't continue to do so. A clear blue sky granted superb mountain views and a gentle breeze kept the gnats away. The beautiful sight and sound of Dunn Notch Falls tumbled beside me all the way to the parking lot where I found Suellen reading. "I just got here. Today's hike must have been easier."

"My feet don't think so, but yes it was. Thank you for the snacks. You'll spoil me like Uncle George did bringing treats."

"You deserve it!" Suellen smiled as she handed me a quart of grapefruit juice. Studying the maps and data book each night became a routine. By the next afternoon I'd be at South Arm Road, ten miles closer to Mt. Katahdin. Hiking low mileage made be feel like I'd never finish. I also feared a woman would hike pass me. Lum said that wasn't likely because the Whites slowed everyone down. Still, I anxiously checked all the shelter journals. Finishing as the first woman was a realistic possibility. To do so became important, especially since it had not been a goal at the start.

After putting me on the Trail the next morning, Suellen drove to Paul and Irene's campground on the Ellis River where we had planned to sleep in a small trailer. By evening the trailer was like an oven so we set up our six-person tent.

July sixth was another beautiful day. Maine's volunteers believe in keeping the Trail rugged. Rivers and brooks seldom have bridges. Just before climbing up the slippery side of Moody Mountain, I had to ford Black Brook. The fast flowing knee-high water looked scary, but above the bank I spotted the white van. Help was there if I fell in.

"Be careful." Suellen called from the bank above the swirling water.

I pulled off my boots and stuck my socks inside before starting across. The water rose to the bottom of my shorts, but no higher. By leaning on my walking sticks, I made it safely across.

On the way back we picked up a sandwich in Andover and stopped to take pictures of a covered bridge over the Ellis River. Nostalgia swept through me as I tried to imagine my mom as a child fishing in this very river with her father. I thought of my own childhood camping trips and wondered about the difference between a life journey and that of a river. Is a river a vessel that holds water or does water pass through the river? As I move along on the Trail, am I the journey moving over the land or is the Trail the journey and I the vehicle receiving the experience? The water flowing under the bridge had traveled further than the White Mountains, but it was not the same water that my mom and her dad, nor even I had watched years ago. Neither would I be the same at the end of this circuitous route. As clearly as the pebbles glistened in the sunlight, my authenticity would become clear as the journey's purpose unfolded. A vessel is cleansed as water flows though it. Mesmerized by the movement below the bridge, I watched the land and waters balancing dance. Standing by my side, Suellen also felt the dance.

By eight the next morning, I was headed for Old Blue's 3,600 foot summit and the Bemis Mountain Range. My aching feet nearly convinced me to take a day off, but a clear horizon promised a good day to hike. "I must keep going while the weather holds. The climbs are dangerous when they're wet. When I lose the sunshine to rain, I will rest. See you at Maine 17 about three." I told Suellen. I could only guess how long thirteen miles would take me.

The Bemis Range was a series of rocky knobs between four peaks. Blueberries were just appearing, black flies were all but gone, and white blazes were under my feet. On the other side of Bemis Stream the Trail proceeded straight up a slippery bank of wet leaves and loose gravel. Early in the trip the terrain changes intrigued me, now they frustrated me. By the time I reached the van, I was covered with mud and sweat, exhausted, and in need of a good cry. "This is ridiculous. I was doing fine until I climbed that bank. Look at me," I wailed. "That's no place to put a Trail."

"Go ahead and cry. You are totally exhausted. How are the feet?"

"I don't know. They are too numb to feel."

"I wish you would take a day off."

"I will when it rains. I'm glad I didn't know how rough some of these sections were going to be. The Trail is way down in that valley somewhere." I reached for a bottle of grapefruit juice.

The owners of the Farmhouse Inn in Rangeley were so were so excited to have a woman thru-hiker as guest that they kindly gave us two nights lodging for the price of one. In our suite we cooked soup and made grilled cheese sandwiches. Suellen had me back to Maine 17 by eight. "I'll be at the head on Maine 4 by four this afternoon," I said as I climbed out of the van with a daypack full of crackers, cheese, fruit, and water.

"I'll be there," she said. "I'll go to the laundromat while you hike."

The climbs were not difficult and the swampy land was lined with bog boards. I loved balancing on the narrow boards among bright birds, slippery salamanders, fat frogs, and water plants. Each pristine pond was more beautiful than the last. The Trail was so easy I made it to the parking lot by mid afternoon. After an hour of waiting I'd had enough of the gnats buzzing around my head and flagged down a car.

"Sir, which way is Rangeley?"

"Straight ahead, need a ride?"

"Yes please." I climbed in. We'd gone only a few miles when I shrieked, "There's the Farm House Inn."

As I climbed out, I noticed the Suellen's van was gone. I checked our room, left my pack, and decided Suellen was still at the laundromat.

On the road again, I hitched a second ride back to the parking lot. I waited a half-hour and caught a third ride back to the Inn. A very worried Suellen was folding clothes in our suite.

"I'm so sorry, I lay down to take a short nap and slept longer then I intended. I saw your pack and knew you'd been here." Suellen feared she had let me down.

"I suspected that's what happened when I got back here and the van was gone. I thought you might go to the Trail from the laundromat so I went back. Fear not, everything worked out the way it was suppose to."

"I'm just glad you're safe. You're so resourceful. Let's eat out after you shower."

"Sounds good."

After dinner in the Red Onion Restaurant I went straight to bed. I was asleep as soon as my head hit the pillow, but not for long. In the middle of the night thunder boomed, lightening flashed, and rain poured. I woke only long enough to utter one sentence; "I am not hiking tomorrow!" All the next day, we wrote letters, cooked soup, and slept while the rain fell.

I was thoroughly refreshed on the morning of the 9th, Suellen took me back to Maine 4 to hike to Maine 27, thirty-two miles away. Suellen would stay at the Farmhouse Inn for another night before going to Stratton. I headed for Spaulding Mountain lean-to.

A teen-age boy with a daypack climbed out of a car as Suellen pulled off the road at the trail. Not far down the Trail I caught up to him. "You going far?" I asked.

"As far as I can until noon. My parents are picking me up at five. First time they've let me hike alone. I'm Jesse from Lewiston, Maine."

"Nice to meet you. I'm Wolf Woman, a thru-hiker from Tennessee."

"You've hiked the whole thing? How long is the Trail?" Jesse led the way.

"The Trail is 2,160 miles long and starts at Springer Mountain, Georgia. Think you'd like to do it someday?" Jesse was already getting a lead on me.

"Yes, after I'm through school. I love hiking. You doing it alone?"

"Yes, except for the first six days when my daughter was with me. What year in school are you?"

"I'll be a sophomore next year," Jesse had stopped to let me to catch up.

"You'll know when the time is right to do the Trail. I waited thirty-five years."

"Really? Wow, that's amazing! My mom will never let me."

"My mom wasn't too thrilled about idea either, but she got used to it after I got out here. If doing the Trail is a goal, you'll find a way to make it happen. You go ahead, I don't want to hold you back. You're a stronger hiker than I am."

"I wish my mom thought so. I'd like to get out here more often than she's willing to bring me," Jesse bounded down the Trail.

How amazing, I thought after he left, a teen-ager who loves to hike. Perhaps when I get back, I'll talk to teen-agers about setting goals and accomplishing dreams. That is, if I manage to reach my own goal.

Around every bend Jesse waited for me. His presence was comforting. The Saddlebacks are among the roughest in Maine. Reminding me of the White Mountains, their exposed three miles of bare granite and alpine ridges spread from the east of the Horn to west of the fourth highest peak on the AT.

Just before heading up a steep open climb, Jesse stopped and pulled on a fleece jacket. Bright boy, I thought as I stopped to do the same. Fifty mile an hour winds whipped at our bodies, causing our eyes to smart and tears to run down our faces. Huddled against the wind, Jesse waited near the top.

"It's cold. You staying out in this tonight?" Jesse sounded concerned.

"Yes, but I'll be off the summit. I've slept in worse weather back in March. Descending is the hard part. My legs get shaky and my feet are sore. You going farther?"

"Yes, I think I can get to the Horn," Jesse stood up. I followed. The wind was so fierce we had to lower our bodies and secure each foot before picking up the other. Often Jesse offered me a hand. After thirty minutes of struggling, we finally reached the top. I looked north but wasn't sure which peak was Katahdin.

Back below the tree line, we stopped to rest. I told Jesse I was a teacher and about my breast cancer research campaign.

"I can't wait to tell Mom about you."

I laughed, "If we sit here and tell stories much longer, you won't make it to the Horn and back to the parking lot by five. Your mom might not believe a teacher and a mother detained you. I could write a note like parents write excuses for their children."

Laughing, we headed down the Trail. At the Horn Jesse and I exchanged addresses. I missed his shy, strong presence as I climbed Saddleback Junior, forded Orbeton Stream, and moved over Lone Mountain. Following white blazes etched on stones beside a babbling brook ended my eighteen-mile day at Spaulding Mountain Lean-to. A south-bound male and a female college student taking pictures for a project had already settled in. We enjoyed an evening of story swapping. Of the few journal names I recognized, none were women.

During the evening an overly friendly raccoon kept pulling our equipment off the edge of the shelter. At first the huge raccoon was amusing, but after nearly snagging down a food sack and pulling my data book on the ground from a mere foot in front of my face, we were forced to stuff everything loose in our sleeping bag and hoist the food sacks higher. The precautions saved our possessions, but did not stop his pestering attempts to get into the shelter. Thanks to the pesky raccoon and my tingling feet, I welcomed the dawn.

The climbs up Spaulding, Sugarloaf, and both North and South Crocker were steep, rocky, and hard, but beautiful. The rougher the terrain and harder the climbs, the more beautiful the scenery. I was surprised to find a footbridge across the Carrabasett River. Thru-hikers are expected to ford deep water as often as slide down rock cliffs. I managed the challenges by naming people I'd met, listing foods, and reminiscing about the incredible experiences. The white blazes led me dangerously close to the ledges. The loose gravel on the Crocker Mountain was particularly hazardous. I had to pick my way around the precarious twists and turns. Descending to Stratton meant a five and a half-mile climb from the second highest point in Maine, the 3,000-foot summit of North Crocker. Finally I spotted the van, glistening like a white blaze in the afternoon sun.

Suellen had booked a motel room next to Whippoorwill, the section hiker we'd met at Pine Ellis. While enjoying dinner with us at the White Wolf Inn, she told us that climbing Katahdin would complete her childhood dream to do the Trail. As a child growing up in the mid-west, she'd seen pictures about natural wonders in the East. Now, as a nurse in her fifties, she'd been returning to the trail for five summers.

After breakfast at the Northland Cash Supply Store, I headed into the woods wondering what compells women to do the Trail. As I crossed the Bigelows, my last range, I wondered if women's reasons for coming to the Trail are more emotional then men's. Perhaps they come with sentimental goals to feel the earth, touch the natural wonders, and experience the sensation of being in nature, while male hikers come seeking the physical challenges of the steep climbs, precarious precipices, and deep water. Whippoorwill hiked only a few miles a day. Pat, Grasshopper, Phoenix, Dot, Barbara, Sylvia, Down Under, and Fairbairn also allowed plenty of pondering time. Tricky climbs and perilous maneuvers were endured, but not the highlights of their experiences. I, too, felt anxiety for the dangers. My pace balanced my needs. Smooth terrain was definitely more delightful than climbing rock ledges. Balancing soggy bog boards and splashing through cold brooks were enough of a physical challenge.

The Bigelow Mountain Range's brutal ups and downs offered spectacular views. The fragile ecosystems with rare plant and animal life on the alpine summits of West Peak at 4,150 feet and Avery at 4,088 feet made the steep rocky climbs worth the effort. Only by moving through the challenges could I see the landscape. Passing East Bigelow Shelter meant that East Flagstaff Road, my sixteen-mile day's destination, was only 1.4 miles away. Stopping on the right logging road would be as tricky for me as finding the crossing would be for Suellen.

Just as I was getting anxious I'd never find the road, I saw a tent in the middle of the Trail. When I got closer I recognized lawn chairs, a portable table, and camp stove. I heard voices down the Trail and saw the van. Suellen looked up,

"Ellen, you made it." Suellen hurried to meet me. "You won't believe what happened! In town they told me there were several road crossings and none of them were marked. I was afraid I wouldn't find the right one, so I drove up here early, found this road, and decided to walk one mile and see if another road crossed it. I'd been walking thirty minutes when Down Under came along."

Down Under, who I'd hadn't seen since Gorham, swallowed her last bite of a peanut butter sandwich and jumped up from the lawn chair to hug me.

"I'd run out of food and was praying someone would come along when I came around a bend and there stood Suellen with a pack full of food and water." Down Under's Australian accent twitted as she declared Suellen an angel of mercy.

"Down Under was the angel with the maps," Suellen handed me a sandwich and continued her version of the story. "She came along just as I was about to turn back and find another road. Trail Magic happens to people who drive vans too!"

"It sure does," I said as we headed back to the camp. "How do beans, mashed potatoes, and vegetable soup sound?" I lit the stove and filled a pan with water from the milk jugs Suellen had filled in town.

"Anything sounds good." Suellen rested while I cooked supper and Down Under set up her tent. We relaxed until the sun slipped behind the hills. Down Under crawld in to her trip tent, and we settled into our spacious one. On a foam pad under a pile of quilts, Suellen and I were snug in the tent until thunder crashed, lightening flashed, and the sky opened up, dumping a deluge of water on our camp. We had a piece of plastic under the tent but had forgotten to spread one under the foam pad. Water started seeping through.

"Suellen, hand me everything on your side. I'll spread plastic out on your side then we'll rise up, I'll spread it underneath and then we'll move everything back." We worked as a team by the light of my mag-light, Suellen's headlight, and flashes from the sky. Soon we were dry.

A wet world greeted us next morning. We stuffed wet gear in plastic bags and shoved them into the van. After breakfast Down Under and I headed out for a twenty-mile slack pack day to Caratunk. Suellen would meet us at the other side of the Kennebec River. She would call Steve, the ferryman, and ask him meet us with his canoe.

July 13, one week before I climbed Katahdin, was the only day I hiked with a woman. Down Under was close to my age, barely five feet tall and probably didn't weigh a hundred pounds. She, like Roy, hiked in sandals. She was hiking during her summer break from a Christian college in the Midwest.

As we hiked around Flagstaff Lake and Pierce Pond, we swapped stories of our respective country and culture. At the end of West Carry Pond we rested and took pictures of incredible driftwood. Tiny soft raindrops, so slight we could not see them or feel them on our skin, bounced delicately on the still wide pond. Miniscule circles rippled in all directions. Having someone to share the natural Trail Magic was especially nice.

I was amazed at Down Under's skill. She moved with ease over floating or sinking bog boards and scrambled effortlessly up the steep rocky mountains. Being light and small was an advantage. I'd never been light or small, and climbing had been a struggle since the beginning. I'd entered the world as a nearly nine pound baby and had accumulated an over abundance of fat cells as a child. I used food to deal with my parents' divorce and later to deal with subsequent crises. For years, food had been the subject of conversation in therapy sessions, self-help groups, and with friends.

From the time I realized I was head and shoulders taller and weighed more than everyone else in seventh-grade, I felt doomed to a life of bigness. I could hide daddy's wide feet under school desks and in crowds, but my body loomed in all directions. I'd watched my mother battle her weight, to no avail.

On May 20th, 1974, at age twenty-four in a size sixteen, I consumed most of David's first birthday cake and took up most of the photo. I vowed not give in to a life of fatness. At 5 a.m., before my wife and mother duties began, I started running. It took four months to be able to run a mile. By the fall I was running four miles a day. I spent an hour a day with Jane Fonda's first exercise video. The pounds began to disappear. By the time David was four, my 5' 8", large-framed body was down to 124 pounds. I was swimming a mile three times a week in a near-by lake, running six miles a day (eleven on Sunday) doing the workout tape five days a week, and doing farm work. I knew nothing about addiction and didn't know I'd exchanged an obsession with food for compulsive exercise. I only knew I was thin.

I took weight off and put it back on for the next eighteen years. Finally in 1992, at age forty, I learned about addiction, eating disorders, and discovered recovery. Tough as family issues were to face, I learned I had a choice and did not have to be a victim to any aspect of my past. The idea of developing a healthy living was an incredible revelation. By being aware of what I ate, drank, and how I used my body, I learned about the connection between the emotional, mental, physical, and spiritual aspects of my life. Developing a healthy balance became my goal. Now years later, after accepting progress, not perfection, I watched Down Under move with ease. I struggled to keep up.

I reflected that my lack of interest in finding a hiking partner may have resulted from fear of not being able to keep up with someone else's stride. I didn't want to repeat an experience I had during my first semester back in college in 1983. I'd expected to make an A in a track and field course because I'd been jogging around the neighborhood for nearly ten years. I painfully learned there's more to running than moving around the block. The course required jumping hurdles. Even after learning the steps, I could not get my legs over the hurdles. At the University of Tennessee in Knoxville, I went to the Tom Black Track at the crack of dawn morning after morning and practiced until my knees were bloody from falling and my arms were sore from lifting the hurdles. Never once did I clear a hurdle. I had more stamina than the considerably younger students in the class, but always was the last one to finish running laps. After running past Dr. Jones more times than I care to remember and hearing him yell, "lift your knees, get those knees up," I finally decided he was asking the impossible.

One of the most critical moments in my life came the day I burst into tears and said, "Dr. Jones, I can't lift my knees any higher. I had braces on my legs as an infant because my feet turned in. Apparently my legs don't have the flexibility to bend high. I've been running for years, but didn't know I compared so badly to other runners."

Dr. Jones put one hand on my shoulder and looked me straight in the eyes, "Don't give up on running or on exercise. You have an incredible amount of stamina, strength and endurance, but you have no skill, coordination, or background. What do you really want to do?"

"I have always wanted to teach. I decided to major in physical education when I starting running," I continued to sniffle.

"Change your major to education and keep running for well-being and health. You haven't lost any time in your course of study." I took his advice, as well as a C in the class. The experience taught me to be honest about my limitations, as well as strengths. I learned to focus on my abilities, not my disabilities and to be positive about making allowances. The same stamina and courage it took to admit I couldn't keep up with other runners rose from the same place that admitted I could not keep up with other hikers. Not being able to stretch my legs high was an annoyance, not a deterrent to thru-hiking.

As the day wore on, so did Down Under's energy. She was more nimble; I was more durable. It became my job to boost her morale each time I caught up to her resting in the Trail. Our nineteen-mile day ended with me reaching the Kennebec River thirty minutes ahead of her. While Steve, the ferryman, and I waited for her, I talked of my breast cancer research campaign. Steve supported me by waiving my ferry fee.

As the sun sank behind the trees, Down Under wearily took the middle canoe seat. Steve and I rowed the sleek craft up the river's edge before heading into the strong current and angling toward the shore. Down Under and I helped him dock the canoe before meeting Suellen on the highway. We drove to one of Steve's cabins. Each rustic cabin had a bathroom, gas stove, three beds, and a refrigerator for $10.00 a night per hiker. Suellen had spread the tent out to dry, moved in our supplies, and scrubbed down the bathroom. Down Under and I showered then I cooked pasta, soup, and pesto sauce to eat with bread and peanut butter. Like teen-agers at a sleep over, we sprawled on our sleeping bags and snacked as we planned the next day. Moxie Pond Road was our next thirteen-mile destination.

At the crack of dawn I roused my sleeping cabin mates with the aroma of tea, hot cereal, and bagels. After eating and packing up we drove to Caratrunk's general store and Post Office, so Down Under could pick up a maildrop. Then, under a beautiful sky, Down Under and I headed out to hike around more ponds, over more bridges, and across more logging roads. Maine's deep forests were wild and primitive.

This northern-most state is neither tame nor docile. We had to pick up our feet up high so as not to catch our socks on the exposed tree roots. Rotted bog boards, mud filled Trails, and washed out banks made hiking slow. Downed trees, thick overgrowth, and tall grass are common in this state of long severe winters and limited volunteers. Tired and muddy, we rejoiced to see Suellen's van at the other end of the day.

Suellen gave us hugs and helped us off with our packs. Down Under sank in the back seat. "Today was hotter and that made it harder."

"I'm exhausted, too, and my feet don't feel like we only did thirteen miles."

"How about a swim? I spotted a deserted cabin with a dock on Moxie Pond," asked Suellen as she slowly steered the van around potholes in the road.

"Sounds great," I said stretching my feet up across the dashboard.

"Here it is. No one's around." Down Under and I eased into the water, clothes and all. The cold water felt good on our sore, tired bodies. Suellen handed us soap. After peeling off our soggy layers and hanging them on the dock, we swam and played until lengthening shadows chilled the air. Suellen helped us into dry clothes. After a hot shower at the cabin I cooked supper and we planned the next day. I planned to make it to Monson, eighteen miles away. Down Under wanted to break the trip up into two days.

The following morning Down Under and I had only hiked ten minutes when she was ready for a rest. I rested long enough to exchange addresses with her and give her a hug. I never saw Down Under again. The same deep sadness swept over me that I felt every time hiking paces and agendas separated connections. I accepted the fact that people moved in and out of my experience, but I never got used to the pain. I missed Down Under as I forded the Piscataquis River, straddled bog boards, and hiked around the ponds. The loss registered as fear. The fear did not rise from a sense getting lost or falling off mountains. I'd survived those fears alone. I feared aloneness. I enjoyed being without interruptions, but I feared the emptiness that the presence of another human being filled. Trail Magic had come from strangers and friends more than from my biological family. I hiked faster. Suellen was waiting. She waited not only to take me to a place for the night, she waited to take me back to Tennessee, a place I now called home.

After crossing the Piscataquis River, I passed a sign that pointed three miles ahead to Shaw's boarding house. I decided to walk up the road and ask directions to Monson by way of the road. Men working on the roof of a house on the corner told me to walk to the four way crossing and wait at a church because the left fork led to Monson. They assured me Suellen would come down the road because there was no other way. I walked to the church porch and waited. To sit on church steps under a gray sky in a remote village, and assume Suellen would drive by was a bit absurd, but I knew she would. Taking risks taught me to trust people and process. Only one car drove by in thirty minutes. I didn't see any people except the workmen. Ten minutes before the time we'd agreed to meet, her van rounded the corner. I bounded off the porch and into the street. "I can't believe I found you. I had no idea where the road where we were to meet was and I couldn't find anyone to ask." Suellen was clearly distressed.

"I had enough faith for both of us. I asked the men working on the roof of that—uh, there was a house on the corner near that tree. Suellen, when I walked down that road there were two men working on the roof of a house. The house and the men are gone." An eerie feeling swept through me. I climbed in the van and we headed to Shaw's in sacred silence. Risks and Trail Magic were connected.

Picking up my Monson maildrop was another closure. Keith Shaw and his wife ran the last hostel for north-bounders and the first for south-bounders. Keith had lost a wife to breast cancer and waived the cost of our stay as his support in my cause. Joining south-bounders and section hikers around the dinner table, as I stuffed myself on corn, boiled potatoes, salad, beets, bread, baked beans, and milk, gave me a deep sense of pride and satisfaction. Making it to the wilderness earned admiration from fellow hikers. All I'd done was walk. The spirit of people had always been with me.

After one of Keith's made-to-order breakfasts, I was back on Shirley Blanchard Road. Crossed only by logging roads, the hundred-mile wilderness is the most remote section of the whole Appalachian Trail. Because of the distance without road crossings, I covered thirty-six miles in two days and stayed in Long Pond Stream Lean-to. Suellen spent a second night at Shaw's. Guards at the shacks on the logging roads had maps, but the likelihood of us connecting felt as remote as expecting water in tributaries to reach the ocean. Yet they do and so would we.

A sign at the beginning of the wilderness suggested hikers have enough food to last ten days and not to underestimate the difficulty of the section. With only 112 miles to go, ecstasy not fear raced through me. Thick evergreen trees streaked with early morning sunlight cast glorious shadows across the Trail. I felt as though I was walking a labryinth created by the radiant spirit that sustains all life. As the Trail led me around Spectacle Pond, Bell Pond, Lily Pond, North Pond, and dramatic Little Wilson Falls plunging sixty feet into a slate gorge, the lush land rolled with thick green moss. The wilderness was alive with wildlife. Careening fish, chirping birds, and croaking frogs created a symphony as I hiked through the moist jungle-like environment. At Big Wilson Stream and Long Pond Stream I pulled off my boots to ford the knee-deep water. Just after the stream I felt both sadness and joy to read the sign, "99 miles to Katahdin." My body was ready for the hike to end, but mentally I was not. I still was not clear about the purpose of my journey. Safely I'd been led every step of the way. Perhaps the purpose was as simple as having the experience of balancing risk with routine and solitude with companionship.

No one joined me at Long Pond Stream Lean-to. The solitude allowed night sounds to fill the shelter. By placing incense in the shelter boards beside my sleeping bag, I discouraged the lingering black flies from swarming. I treated some water, hoisted my food in the rafters, and snuggled into my sleeping bag. I wanted to savor the night sounds, but the sooner I fell asleep the sooner morning would come. I hoped to climb Katahdin in seven days.

The precarious ledges and straight climbs of Barren and Chairback Mountains reminded me of the Whites. The cliffs on Chairback were so steep that I took my polar pure and camera out of the pack and dropped the pack off the cliffs before scooting over the boulders on my bottom. After the long descent, the seat of my pants were in shreds. I patched them with duct tape that I'd kept wrapped on the top of my walking stick. Few trees grew so I had nothing to grasp. I inched my way down the boulders, rolling the pack one section at a time. When earth reappeared under my feet, I hurried until I reached the van shining like a long white blaze.

"Waiting for someone?" I asked, tapping on the window and rousing Suellen from a nap.

"You made it. We did it again," Suellen was beside herself with joy as she hugged me real big. "How are your feet?"

"Numb, sore, and tired, but no worse. They'll make it eighty-four more miles. Where are we staying?" It felt comforting to leave lodging decisions to Suellen.

"A guard told me that the Paper Company allows camping on the Pleasant River for only $7.00. The river flows right beside our spot."

I gasped as we pulled into a cozy camp spot. "This is perfect." After a good suds up and a soak down in the river, I felt like a new woman. Seated around a campfire, we enjoyed instant mashed potatoes, beans, bread, and carrots, while studying the data book. The next accessible crossing was nearly twenty-eight miles away at Jo Mary Road. I'd hiked that far in one day in Virginia, but knew I couldn't in the Wilderness. A thirteen-mile hike would get me to Logan Brook Lean-to and then Jo Mary Road on July 19. After nearly a week of roughing it, Suellen was ready for a motel room in Millinocket.

After hot oatmeal, apricots, and nuts we packed up and drove back to Katahdin Iron Works Road. The weather held as I hiked to Gulf Hagas, West Peak, and Hay Mountain. The closer I got to Katahdin, the more I believed the clear skies would last. I didn't want just to climb Katahdin. I wanted to see where I'd been, at least a few hundred miles. The Trail followed a series of short dips and climbs along the gorged out Gulf Hagas before climbing Hay Mountain at 3,244 feet. With each mile I became more melancholy, and more ecstatic.

I simply couldn't relax until I was safely off Katahdin's summit.

Facing a creek, Logan Brook Lean-to was perched on the back of White Cap Mountain in thick woods. I was surprised to find two women settled in. One of the women would finish her five-year goal as a section hiker the following day. She had climbed Katahdin earlier in the week and was being picked up at Gulf Hagas the next day. Her friend, also a section hiker, prepared a Whisperlite cooked cake to celebrate. Spending the night with only two women, after sharing shelter space with mostly men for nearly five months, was a serendipitously special way a celebrate my last night in a shelter.

*July 18: I remember Joseph Campbell discussing whether human beings represent a light bulb or are the vehicle through which light shines. If bulbs or Trails are vehicles through which people experience life, it was nearly time for me to watch for my next vehicle. If I finish this five-month journey I'll prove I'm capable of accomplishing what I set out to do, but only with support. From total strangers, reconnected acquaintances, close friends, and relatives this solo journey has been about allowing people into my life while accepting my needs and wants as significant and worthy of pursuing. Each mile becomes more precious than the last.*

At daybreak, after hugs from the women, I was on the Trail again. I'd admitted I was tired of backpacking and would be glad when the trip was over, but in the broad light of day, with Suellen waiting fourteen miles closer to Katahdin, my adrenaline raced. The first three miles were down hill. Around every corner I looked for moose as I climbed Mountain View Pond and Little Boardman. The Trail was full of moose droppings but I had yet to see a moose. Blue herons fished in shallow water, orange salamanders wiggled in the moist land, and frogs of all size hopped out from under my boots. An aura permeated the land. The longer I was in the wilderness, the greater my reverence grew for the sacred, unspoiled beauty. I felt privileged to hike such exquisite land.

Suellen and I were both nervous about finding Jo Mary Road. Finding the right logging road would be a miracle. Believing we would connect took a monumental leap of faith. The data book indicated three and a half miles between Copper Falls Lean-to and the road. I passed many ponds. I didn't know the names of any of them. Rocks, mud, and overgrowth covered the ground. Without the blazes I wouldn't have known I was on a Trail. After what seemed like hours, I rounded a corner and there sat the van.

"We did it! We were both led to the right road. I can't believe it."

"We are really in the boon docks. I've never been so far out in the wilderness before in my life. Wait until you see this campground I found. It belongs to the lumber company. I have the tent set up right on Jo Mary Lake and," Suellen lowered her voice, "our tent faces Katahdin."

"Really! You mean you've seen her?" I had yet to see The Great Mountain.

"If the clouds aren't covering her face, you'll see her in just a few minutes." Suellen pulled the van into a campground. "There she is." Beyond our blue tent, green Coleman stove, red and white checkered tablecloth, and the silver lake was the most incredible mountain I'd ever seen. I sat, unable to move. She rose up out of earth like a magnificent backdrop against the wide still lake. Her long flat summit descended gradually to the earth. She looked welcoming, wise, stoic, sacred, and nowhere near as overwhelming as other mountains.

"She's your last challenge. How does it feel to see her so close?" Suellen asked, as we walked to the water's edge. Gentle waves lapped the shore. The sand felt soft under my sore feet.

"I'm anxious to meet her." I said, barely able to take my eyes off the towering pile of rock. "I'm ready, more than ready." I stood for a long time letting Katahdin's gentle nurturing spirit flow across the lake and into my soul. It wasn't until chilly breezes caused me to shiver, that I walked slowly back into camp. "I'm also ready to eat and take a shower," I grinned. Suellen got the stove going and I cooked spaghetti. After supper I took a shower and got packed up for a day of slack packing to the road six-tenths of a mile north of Crescent Pond.

The Maine Trail guides indicated a gravel logging road at the base of Nesuntabunt Mountain, three miles north of Wadleigh Stream Lean-to. Because the road was not marked in my data book I was very nervous about finding it, but I was willing to take the risk in order to keep from carrying the pack and staying with bugs. Here at a lower elevation, the mosquitoes were almost as bad as the black flies. For the first time, fifty-nine miles and three days from the end, I would look for a road that didn't exist in my data book and hope both of us could find it. The road split the distance between Jo Mary Lake and Abol Bridge in two twenty-mile days. But that would be tomorrow.

As the powerful energy of a full moon rose up over Katahdin, Suellen and I focused our attention inward. Spilling across the lake and up the beach, the moon cast yellow beams into our tent filling us with the awesome sense that Mother Nature was sending us a spiritual message. From the sky to the mountain to our spot on the shore, the moon let us know we were where we needed to be and that I was about to climb Katahdin. Clouds faded the brilliant light. Breezes gently moved the clouds and the moon reappeared. There was more to my cyclical journey than walking home to New England, hiking for a cause, or meeting my childhood dream. There would be more moons, more shorelines, more camping adventures, and more walks, but never again would I be at this spot, at this time, having this experience. Life repeats patterns, but never exactly the same. The moon's message was to cherish every moment. Even after our weary eyes closed out the brightness, the moonbeams continued to wrap us in warmth and wonder. The thirty-five years of waiting to walk 2,160 miles had taught me to trust.

After eating pop tarts with peanut butter for breakfast, Suellen took me back to Jo Mary Road. We would spend the next two nights at the campground. Suellen would spend all day finding the gravel road. The profile map promised me a flat day, which meant I would be splashing through water and swatting mosquitoes in low-lying bogs. Sandy beaches and interesting driftwood laced the shoreline of the many lakes.

Because my family had enjoyed L. L. Bean products for years and I'd seen the shelter in the catalogs, I followed the blue blaze Trail to L. L. Bean's Potaywadjo Spring Lean-to. It looked new and had a lovely privy complete with curtains in the windows! I was relieved to see no women's names in the journal. Some of the thirteen fellows ahead of me had probably finished. I wondered how many people who had quit regretted leaving the Trail. Early in a project enthusiasm is high, support is abundant and people band together. As time continues interest lags, help dwindles, and people move in different directions. Those with value and resilience equal to the task stay motivated, have dedicated supporters, and remain steadfast to reaching closure. I needed to stay focused if I hoped to meet my goal.

Fear waxed and waned that I wouldn't find the road, but I need not have worried. Long before I needed to start looking, I saw the van. The horizontal blaze assured me that white blazes would always be a part of my life. I ran. "We did it!"

"It wasn't easy and I wasn't sure this was it, but I found Abol Bridge. Dropping you off in this dense, desolate wilderness and believing that the Trail would bring you to where I am waiting has been nothing short of a miracle. I'm glad I didn't know how extensive this challenge was going to be," Suellen gathered up her chair. "Now, let's get out of these bugs."

I grinned as I climbed in the van. I knew about getting through experiences and the hindsight wondering how on earth I'd managed it. But those days were nearly over, at least for this particular process. Never again would I have to carry the heavy pack and walk twenty miles in search of a home. Trusting the data book and the blazes had been sources of strength. Pitting my ability against each day's destination was the biggest challenge. The insecurity of never knowing for sure when the shelters would appear or whether I would arrive before dark had been a far greater challenge than the rough terrain or being alone out in the middle of nowhere. If I ever hiked the Trail again, knowing what to expect would take much of the challenge out of the hike and minimize the need to be resilient. I remember telling a newspaper reporter that pitting myself against the elements was one reason that I wanted to hike the Trail. After nearly five months, I was ready for stability.

Back at the campground we cooked rice and drank hot tea. A strong wind had blown up. I lined the tent with big rocks. We listened to the wind howl in the tall pines and the waves boom against the shore. We waited for the rain, but not a drop fell. My desire to finish the hike in clear weather had spared us the brunt of the storm. The wild windy night tested my faith, but I held fast to my convictions and believed sunlight would welcome in the day. It did.

"I'll see you at Abol Bridge. Enjoy your last full day," Suellen said as she watched me disappear into the woods before driving to Baxter State Park. The days of having friends drop me off in the woods and return to a safe, secure environment were nearly over. Soon, I too, would be returning to familiar surroundings. The thought made me both sad and pleased. Thru-hiking brought up strange yet valuable juxtapositions of emotions. Twenty more miles would put me at Abol Bridge, the next ten miles would put me at the base of Katahdin, and on July 23 I planned to climb the five miles to the summit. It didn't matter whether I didn't want the journey to end or couldn't wait to be finished, time would move on and I would move with it. One step at a time, this thirty-five year goal was about to end.

It was appropriate that I should pass Rainbow Stream, Rainbow Lake, Rainbow Spring, and Rainbow Ledges at the end of my journey. I'd carried a rainbow bandana from Springer to Katahdin. Rainbows, like storms, are transitions that signal change. I'd seen both. I'd learned to walk through transitions. The multicultural awareness I'd experienced gave me peace.

If ferns grow under tall trees, May Apples adjust to temperature changes, and tributaries provide water for vegetation, I believed our multi-cultural world could be just as unprejudiced and receptive to changes. As I made my way past the rainbow landscapes, I smiled with pride to have found a place of comfort in the world.

Walking over Abol Bridge and signing the journal at the country store signaled another closure. "There she is, even closer. She is waiting for you," Suellen stood with me on the bridge. We gazed past the marshland and beyond the trees. Late afternoon rays shimmered on Katahdin's rocky form.
"It's overwhelming to think I've finally made it. She looks gentle and powerful, like a good strong woman."

"Speaking of a woman, I met a darling ranger at Baxter State Park today. The campgrounds are all full, but Jen this ranger I met, told me about The Big Moose Inn Bed and Breakfast in Millinocket. I have reservations for three nights. You'll love it. Shall we go now? You look exhausted." We'd barely started down the road when I got hysterical.

"Moose! There's a moose!" All of a sudden I wasn't tired. Suellen pulled to the side. I jumped out with my camera before the van had come to a full stop. Suellen had seen one moose on a logging road and another in a field, but I'd about given up thinking I would. Zooming in with the camera, I got several good shots. His huge body lumbered slowly across the swamp before disappearing into the woods.

Jen worked at the Big Moose Inn as a receptionist. She told us to help ourselves in the kitchen. She and a friend joined us as we ate soup and sandwiches. "You are fortunate, the weather is supposed to be perfect for the next couple of days," she said. The mountain is usually socked in with fog. I'm so excited you're here! I don't know when we have had a woman thru-hiker stay with us. My mom and her friend Carol, who works with Encore, a breast cancer support group, want to meet you." Jen was a gracious host, but my feelings were numb. With only two days and fifteen miles to go, I simply couldn't relax.

Sleep had not come easy for weeks. The pain in my feet never stopped. I had taken more ibuprofen in the last couple of months than I'd taken in my whole life. As I lay staring at the ceiling in the dark room, the soft bed felt foreign and being closed up in a room felt claustrophobic. My legs twitched more than usual and my mind raced. I wanted to go back to the open shelters and the wide spaces. I used every form of self-talk I could think of but my mind raced until I remembered black flies, mosquitoes, and the freezing temperatures. Next thing I knew sunlight streamed through the window.

Only ten miles remained and I shouldn't have been in a rush, but suddenly I wanted to hurry. Today's hike would take me to the base of the mountain. Then I would hitch hike a ride out of the park and back to the gate where Suellen would be waiting. I couldn't wait. By nine o'clock I was following Katahdin Stream around swamps, past the boundary marker of Baxter State Park, through Daicey Pond Campground, and into Katahdin Stream Campground. Mt. Katahdin loomed even closer.

We enjoyed another meal with Jen and her family and retired early. July 23 dawned with more sunshine, muffins, and pleasantries around the breakfast table. I had on the same clothes I'd worn for four months and twenty-three days. The day began much like everyday had for weeks. Yet, there would never be another day like this one, the end of my journey. I couldn't believe it was nearly over. Matt and Orion, two local college students whom I had met on the Trail the day before, were just arriving as I laced up my boots. They took pictures of Suellen and me in front of the plaque at beginning of the Trail. They promised Suellen they'd keep an eye on me, and take pictures at the top. I waved to Suellen for the last time. "I'll be waiting. Take your time and enjoy," Suellen called as I began the five mile, 5,267 foot climb, to Katahdin's summit.

The first hour of climbing was gradual and well graded. Katahdin Stream Falls, at 1,650 feet, was breathtaking. As the grade became steeper, the vegetation became scrubby and the rocks reappeared. Halfway up the mountain the one-mile-long rock climb began. Jutting toward the sky the size of vehicles or houses, the boulders reminded me of Mahoosuc Notch, except these rocks were hanging over my head on a vertical slant, not side by side in a horizontal ravine. Handles drilled into the rocks provided support. Matt or Orion kindly pulled me over ledges when my legs couldn't reach. After pushing, pulling, and crawling on our hands and knee, we reached the one and a half mile treeless tableland where delicate alpine flowers and scrubby brushes grew.

My teen-age idol, Henry David Thoreau, hiked Katahdin in the 1830's. One mile from the top we reached a spring named in his honor. Matt and Orion stopped to purify water. I needed water, but could see the sign wedged in the rocks on the summit. I kept going. I needed to finish alone. Rising into a clear sky, the weather-beaten sign symbolizing the balance between faith and focus called me. I walked, never taking my eyes off the sign. On the summit of Mt. Katahdin, I stretched out my hand. As I touched the sign, I whispered, **"I did it."**

# Chapter 14
## *"Goals are dreams with a deadline."*

### Returning South

Scattered clouds parted. A sky, as blue as Daddy's eyes spread warmth over the summit, the sign, and myself. The visibility was perfect. For hundreds of miles in all directions exclusively water and trees balanced the landscape. No houses, farms, towns, cows, or roads - only blue lakes and green trees met my gaze. Silent strength and ecstatic power flowed through me. The realization that I had walked hundreds of miles farther than I could see gripped me with an awesome sense of connection. I had reached the summit because I'd connected the universe, nature, and the goodness of humanity. Walking 2,160 between Georgia and Maine was a testimony to the powerful interdependence between humanity and the environment.

The day-hikers were oblivious to my accomplishment. I was alone with the moment, alone with the spirit of purpose, process, and pride. Sitting down under the sign, I pulled out a package of crackers and cheese. I had eaten at least one package every day for the last one hundred and forty-five days. Just as I finished, Matt and Orion crowned the summit.

"I don't know how you got here so fast." Matt called out. I can't wait to tell my mom about you. I'm sure she couldn't climb this mountain. I'm proud of you. It must feel great to be standing here!" Want me to take your picture?" I handed Matt the camera.

"Thru-hiking is not for everyone. Take a couple in case some don't turn out," I grinned between sentences. "Thru-hiking was something I had to do." I sat in front of the sign, stood behind it, and walked to a cairn. Matt handed the camera back to me.

"Wolf Woman hiked the whole Trail," Orion announced to some teenagers.

"The whole thing? You're kidding," one of them challenged.

"No way!" said another.

An adult even countered me. "Are you really a thru-hiker?"

"Yes, I left March first and hiked alone except for the first six days. Of course the spirit of my friends and family have been with me." Suddenly, like black flies in a swamp, a dozen New York teen-agers swarmed me. I felt like a robot, a movie star, or an alien who had just returned from a planet that didn't exist. Some of the kids were in awe, some thought I was nuts, and most didn't believe me; but they wanted to know my story. Among their arrogant or dubious comments was genuine interest. As clear as the blazes had been, my reason for hiking the Trail became obvious. By sharing my story I would help others recognize and follow their dreams. Suddenly I knew why I had arrived in

Damascus on Daddy's birthday, April 11, 1997 and why today, a year later on April 11, 1998, I've finished putting the account of my journey on paper. By staying in touch with my dream, the answer had come.

Below an azure sky, shimmering lakes connected mountain peaks. This five-month odyssey, a very short space of time in context with a lifetime, proved that every mountain had a summit, every storm and end, and every stream an opposite bank. By visualizing closure and using mental perception to blaze the way, spiritual awareness to focus, physical ability to move my body, and emotional discernment to sense the next right thing to do, I stood on Katahdin.

Climbing down the 3.8-foot Abol Trail, at a 5,250-foot descent, was shorter but exceedingly difficult on my knees. Barely off the summit my left knee collapsed. By leaning on my walking sticks, I inched my way back into the forest with Matt and Orion. By the time I reached the road, I wasn't sure my knees would ever be the same. They had held up until the very end. I was grateful my body had stayed strong. I had walked the whole way without serious injury or sickness.

After reaching the road and exchanging addresses, I caught a ride to the gate and the fellows caught one back to their car. I was glad to have pictures of the last examples of fine male Trail Magic. Suellen was waiting, as I knew she would be, on the other side of the gate. I limped painfully across the dusty roadway, collapsed into her arms, and gasped, "I never could have done this without you. I did not walk alone."

Suellen held me and softly said, "You won't have to celebrate alone either. Jen, her mom Jody, and Carol want to treat you to dinner at the Big Moose Inn." I climbed in the van and sat still. A wave of peace moved through me. It was over. The long walk was over. I had fulfilled my dream and met my goal. I felt numb. I'd finished as the fourteenth person and the first woman thru-hiker in 1997 to walk through the fourteen states of the Appalachian Trail. I'd walked all day every day for four months and twenty-three days, except for fourteen days. Suellen sensed my wistfulness. "How does it feel not to have to walk tomorrow?" she patted my bare swollen feet, which I'd stretched out across the dashboard.

"Oh, yeah, that's right. I don't have to walk tomorrow, do I? Sorta sad, well, kinda I guess," I murmured trying to believe the journey was really over and I didn't have to walk anymore. "I guess it hasn't sunk in yet," I smiled. My feet hurt as much as they had for days. My body ached as usual, and I had on the same clothes I had worn for weeks. Nothing had changed. Slacking with Suellen had gotten to be such a routine that having her pick me up was not out of character. Maybe tomorrow, when the early light of dawn eased under the window shade and I realized there was no reason to pull on a green shirt, duct-taped shorts, and Uncle George's socks the reality would sink.

Sitting perfectly still and letting Suellen make all the decisions felt right. It hadn't fully occurred to me until that moment what a problem-solving, decision-making ordeal I had been through. Support from home had been phenomenal, and Trail Magic occurred whenever I needed it; but interacting with the raw wildness of life had been my responsibility. For the moment I needed to sit, just sit, and not deal with anything.

"They're back; here she comes!" I heard Jen call from the porch as we pulled into the Big Moose Inn. Jen hurried down the steps to greet me. After meeting her mom and Carol, I slumped in a wicker rocking chair. Jen served iced tea. Jody and Carol gave me big hugs and wanted to hear everything.

"I don't know what to say. I did it. It was fantastic. I'm glad it's over. I never dared believe I could do it until I was safely off the mountain. That mountain is fantastic," I stuttered, trying to find words. I felt overwhelmed. It was impossible to capture the essence of the journey in a few sentences. I felt like a newscaster trying to report on a major event in five-second media bites. I let the women do most of the talking. I answered their questions as gracefully as I could. The details had escaped me. Carol handed me a wrapped gift. I slowly removed the tissue paper. In my hands lay a beautiful framed color picture of Mt. Katahdin. "How perfect. Thank you so much." I sat and stared at the photograph. "What a paradox that I sit here and hold in my hands a picture of what took me five months to reach. This photograph symbolizes how short our life is and how important it is to fulfill our dreams." I could still hear the sound of creeks, the birds in the trees, and the wind in the tall pine trees. The Appalachian Trail still moved through my soul. I was very sad there would be no more Trail tomorrow; but Katahdin, the great mountain, would always be in my dreams.

Suellen sensed my need to regroup and suggested I shower and get ready for dinner. Like a child, I let her lead me to our room. She handed me clean shorts and a tee-shirt. I'd seen the clothes before but didn't recognize them. I went through the motions of showering and dressing. An hour later, in clean clothes, with my hair on my shoulders instead of in a matted braid, I made my way down the stairs. I felt very confused and out of place. Dinner was delicious, cordial, and comfortable. Jody's humor, Carol's gracious spirit, Jen's sweet nature, and Suellen's perceptive character created a delightful blend of women for my celebratory gathering. The spontaneous natural way the dinner plans had come together were my last examples of Trail Magic, at least for this chapter of my life.

The following day Suellen and I started on our way back down south. A mutual friend had suggested that Suellen give Ann and Helen in Saco, Maine a call for a place to stay on her way to meet me. She had done so and enjoyed her visit with them so much that we stopped on the way back. Ann and Helen welcomed me like family. A year later Ann became a trusted advisor responding to the first raw drafts of this book. Their house made a perfect base while I visited with my mom at her RV in Wells Harbor.

"Now I can finally sleep!" Mom gasped, as she threw her arms around me. "You did it! You really walked the whole thing." Settled in the camper, she wanted to hear everything; but I felt tongue-tied. It was hard to think of anything specific to say. One minute I talked about how hard it had been, and the next minute I referred to whole trip as easy. My stories revolved around the wonderful people. The more questions Mom asked the harder it was to find words to express the experience. The journey seemed like a dream. It was; a dream come true.

For three days Suellen and I visited with my mom while staying with Ann and Helen. As the waves moved in and out on the white sandy beach, I felt waves of peace. The beach and the rocky coastline were the same as they'd been every time I'd visited. Nature offered a sense of stability. For weeks rocks, land, and water had been my home. On the Trail, each day was unfamiliar, but here on the beach I recognized patterns. Fantasizing about this very spot had brought order to the rocks, mud, flowers, and rain I'd walked through. The stability of nature's familiar spaces gave life continuity. Nature had been my solace in the woods as a child, it had offered a healthy learning environment in which to raise my children, and now it gently coaxed me back into reality

Adjusting to civilization was difficult. Everything seemed complicated, everyone moved too fast, and every day seemed alien from the life I had known for nearly five months. The longer I was off the Trail, the more I wanted to return. Reacclimating came slowly and in spurts. I was relieved to hear from a student in sports psychology in Northampton, Massachusetts that disorientation or post traumatic stress disorder is common after a long rigorous journey. The warning brought me comfort as I struggled to live in a world that felt foreign. Reality checks helped. When I opened up the back of the van and saw my backpack lying among our belongings I'd ask, "What is the pack doing in here? We didn't need to bring it to the beach." Suellen was near with gentle words to put my life back in perspective.

Touching me, she softly said, "Ellen, you just finishing hiking the Appalachian Trail. You carried your backpack on the Trail. I came and picked you up."

"Oh, oh yeah," was all I could utter. The Trail was another world. As we wound our way down the interstate, the memory lapses continued to occur. Once at a rest stop while waiting for Suellen I crossed my arms across my chest and felt my ribs protruding. "Oh, no! I hope I'm not sick. I can feel my ribs," I exploded when Suellen returned.

"You're not sick, you've just lost weight."

"But, I've not been on a diet," I said struggling to make sense of the changes in my body.

"You've been on the Trail and you've burned more calories than you've eaten for months. Your body will be normal again," Suellen gently tried to ease my anxiety.

"I guess so," I mumbled. "But I don't want to gain my weight back."

Diet, exercise, and weight loss had been an on-going battle all of my life. I already felt heavy. My legs and thighs were so big I could hardly pull my pants up over them, but once up around my waist they bagged way out and looked ridiculous. My fat had turned to muscle. My body had changed in such a peculiar way I wasn't sure what to make of it. My left knee hurt all the time and I couldn't run.

When we got back home, I wanted to exercise but I couldn't walk even around the block. I was terrified I'd gain my weight back. I tried to eat less, but my metabolism was accustomed to enormous amounts of food. I stayed hungry. I felt like I was in relapse from an addiction or that my body was in detox. Time and again when I looked down at my feet I couldn't remember why my toes nails were gone, why my feet were so sore, or why the tops of my toes were numb. Over and over Suellen reminded me I had just finished hiking 2,160 miles.

In Cookeville my surroundings were as unfamiliar as my body. My first trip to the Wal-mart resulted in a major anxiety attack as I wandered around panic-stricken looking for white blazes. Overwhelmed and disoriented, I found an exit, and left without making a purchase. The store was too crowded, too big, and far too busy. The house felt crowded, my study crammed, and my closet packed. I rearranged the house, threw clothes away, and purged my files. As I sat pulling weeds under a dogwood tree in the front yard, I gazed across the street and didn't know where I was. The neighborhood didn't look familiar. I didn't have a clue why I was weeding flowers. It took weeks of reality checks to focus on a culture I once took for granted. However, adjustment had to come quickly.

We returned to Cookeville on August 4th, and my new anthropology teaching job began on August 18th. Two weeks after that, my job with Cumberland Career Equity Center started. I began weaving my Trail experiences into the presentations in the schools. My world began to make sense again. Developing teaching material about my experiences kept the Trail alive.

Bob Grimac, my free-lance educator friend in Knoxville, asked me to talk and show slides at a Vegetarian Society meeting in January. He provided me with Knoxville public school contacts. I began receiving invitations to speak. Denis Kiely and Dana Girard from the Equity Center at Tennessee Tech. University helped me develop a brochure. I used Tuesdays to do free lance lectures. I spoke to nearly a hundred Tennessee Boy Scout leaders, members of a Sierra Club in Knoxville, residents in a Master's Health Care, the P E O, and the V.F.W in Cookeville. The program took on a slant to fit the needs of the audience. I spoke to kindergarten students enthralled with the animal slides, adults interested in the equipment, adolescents in rehabilitation centers, and to my own anthropology students struggling to select their own life goals. My experiences on the Appalachian Trail touched people's basic needs. From five-year-old girls to retired gentlemen, the positive comments I received answered the question as to why I had walked 2,160 miles. "I'm going to hike that when I turn 100," declared 86-year-old Aunt Myrtle, after seeing the slides at Master's Health Care. "Now I understand how to use the steps of recovery," confided an adolescent female in a treatment facility. "Knowing which stove thru-hikers most often use will help us when we make decisions on equipment," smiled a Boy Scout leader. "Having a goal like hiking the Trail encourages me to find a purpose in my own life," reflected a twenty-year-old female sophomore. "You look younger in that picture than you do now. Is climbing easier than teaching?" piped up a kindergarten girl pointing to a slide of me smiling on a rock ledge.

From sincere appreciation to childlike observations, the presentations had a positive impact on the very young to the very old. The significance of the experience put the goal in perspective for me too. I settled into a hectic teaching and presenting schedule, and spent the evenings at the computer, writing out my story while my knee healed enough to exercise again. As my mind shifted to a stable place, my body went out of control. I'd left with the attitude that walking all day for five months would conquer my weight problem once and for all. Before I left I'd been pigging out on carbohydrates and not watching my fat consumption. I assumed I'd lose the added pounds on the Trail. Two hundred and seventy miles into the trip, I got on scales in Hot Springs and was surprised to be ten pounds heavier than I was when I left. By the time I got to Auntie Sue's, I'd lost the ten pounds. Muscular and very lean, I gingerly climbed on scales after climbing Katahdin and was very surprised I'd not lost or gained a single pound. I'd lost all my fat and become very muscular, but the scales hadn't budged. I weighed the same when I got off the Trail as I had when I began.

Within days my muscles began to diminish and my fat started to return. It was preposterous to expect the journey to be a permanent solution to my weight problem. Physical changes in my body after the Trail were as much as part of the experience as was doing the Trail. I accepted changing weather, terrain, and companions, but was not willing to admit my body would change also. Ingrained since childhood, the mind-set that nothing lasts forever had given me strength to walk through rain, over mountains, and across rocky ridges. I needed to commit to a healthy balance between food and exercise, and be honest. As the pounds returned, my friend Judy and I discussed at length our problems with finding a healthy balance between food and exercise.

"I'm embarrassed to be giving presentations, as fat as I am. I'm afraid people won't believe I climbed Katahdin," I plunked myself down on the living room couch.

"Let's concentrate on getting control and not on what people think," Judy understood my struggles. "One small, slow step at a time you made it from one shelter to the next. Day after day you succeeded the same way alcoholics put together weeks of sobriety. The same slow, steady, determined behavior can give us success over food. Don't you see, this experience was like going on a five-month diet. You and I know that doesn't work, but you learned the value of a consistency." I'd never seen Judy so excited discussing food. She was right. I could use the same determination I had on the Trail to get control over a food addiction. By winter, after several bottles of Glucosamine Sulfate and Brome-lain, I was running a four-mile loop four days a week and swimming a mile. The Trail had a beginning and an end, but it's impact was far reaching.

When March 1, 1998 approached I felt nostalgic. A whole year had passed. An appreciation for the sacredness of time created a need to make quality use of my life. A quotation I'd had since undergraduate school finally made sense. "This is the true joy in life, being used for a purpose recognized by yourself as a mighty one; being a force of nature instead of a feverish, selfish little clod of ailments and grievances, complaining that the world will not devote itself to making you happy . . . My life belongs to the whole community, and as long as I live, it is my privilege to do for it whatever I can. I want to be thoroughly used up when I die, for the harder I work the more I live. I rejoice in life for it's own sake. Life is no 'brief candle' to me, it is a sort of splendid torch that I have got hold of for the moment, and I want to make it burn as brightly as possible" Shaw (xxxii). I wanted a balanced global life that didn't judge life in opposites of either good or bad. Women connect so naturally with nature, but fear often denies them wilderness experiences. Perhaps the magic of my dream would encourage other women to step to their own Trailing dreams.

I recognized the "common bond" Wendell Barry speaks of in *Unknown Wilderness*: "Always in big woods, when you leave familiar ground and step off alone to a new place, there will be, along with feelings of curiosity and excitement, a little nagging of dread. It is the ancient fear of the unknown, and it is your first bond with the wilderness you are going into. What you are doing is exploring. You are understanding the first experience, not of the place, but of yourself in that place. It is the experience of our essential loneliness, for nobody can discover the world for anybody else. It is only after we have discovered it for ourselves that it becomes common ground, and a common bond, and we cease to be alone" (34). I was tired of being alone.

After rising shakily through the 1970's, leaning on my introvert nature, and clinging to abandonment issues, I'd lived as an individualistic nonconformer with little need for community. My weeks in nature showed me I no longer wanted to be a loner. By moving through my fears and oppressions I'd become empowered. I'd dared to claim that power. Fear, without facades or false fronts, had moved me all the way to Katahdin. Fear of my limitations had been more powerful then fearing predators. But focusing on my vision, I'd found strength in the power of the white blazes. The symbol of their strength carried me through all physical, mental, emotional, and spiritual fears. I'd walked home, I would return home, and I was at home all in one majestic moment. My thru-hike was a success because I trusted in symbols: Daddy's spirit, simplicity, my soul, and the sign on the summit of Katahdin.

My thirty-five year dream had come to fruition. I recalled the words from the final chapters of *Walden*. "We can never have enough of Nature. We must be refreshed by the sight of her inexhaustible vigor, vast, and Titanic features." I had walked my dream.

*****

### 1997 My  Maildrop Schedule - March 1 through July 23   145  days

Springer Mountain,  GA

Maildrop 1  Hiawassee, GA  30546

Maildrop 2  Fontana Dam, NC 28733

Maildrop 3  Newfound Gap, Gatlinburg, TN 37738

Maildrop 4  Hot Springs, NC  28743

Maildrop 5  Elk Park, NC 37687

Maildrop 6  Damascus, VA 24236

Maildrop 7  Bland, VA 24315 *

Maildrop 8  Catawba, VA 24070

Maildrop 9  Montebello, VA 24464*

Maildrop 10  Auntie Sue- call from Loft Mt. Campground  *

Maildrop 11  Harper's Ferry, WV 25425

Maildrop 12  Boiling Springs, PA 17007

Maildrop 13  Port Clinton, PA 19549

Maildrop 14  Delaware Water Gap, PA 18327

Maildrop 15  Bear Mountain, NY 10911

Maildrop 16  Falls Village,  CT 06031

Maildrop 17  Dalton, MA  01226

Maildrop 18  Bennington, VT  05201 *

Maildrop 19  Sherburne Pass, Killington, VT 05751

Maildrop 20  Glencliff, NH  03238

Maildrop 21  Gorham, NH 03581

Maildrop 22  Rangley, ME  94870

Maildrop 23  Monson, ME  04464

Baxter State Park     Mt. Katahdin, Maine

*not recommended: too far off the Trail or stops where I stayed with a relative.*

# Items carried to Katahdin

Items I picked up along the journey *

| | | |
|---|---|---|
| walking sticks* | sleeping bag | cell mat* |
| camera and film | one pan | one spoon |
| rainbow bandana | pan handle | gaiters |
| plastic cup* | wool socks * | mini-flashlight |
| Mace | 2 pair of underwear | 2 water bottles |
| The Handbook | clothes bag | Teva sandals |
| A Data Book | toothbrush | water bag |
| food | tooth paste | duck tape |
| 1 supplex shirt | pens | pants |
| 2 tee-shirts* | journal | salt |
| WhisperLite stove | Polar Pure* | small gas bottle |
| Dr. Brommer's soap | One Sport boots (2pair)* | Lowe backpack |
| sock liners | 6 Tampax | aspirin |
| one lighter | toilet paper | tiny mirror |
| mole skin and tape | waist pack | Swiss army knife |
| tiny hair brush | one hair elastic | small pac towel |
| rain jacket | whistle | 2 pair of supplex |
| DEET bug spray* | plastic ground cover | |

# Items I left Springer with, but sent home

Items I sent priority mail, maildrop after mail drop, from VA to Monson.*

| | | |
|---|---|---|
| space blanket | peanut butter tubes | batteries* |
| large knife | toothbrush cover | large pac towel |
| Fold-a-cup | body lotion | sunscreen* |
| Vaseline | Band-Aids * | rope |
| sleeping bag liner | iodine tablets * | water filter in VA |
| extra paper | rain pants | tent in VA |
| tape recorder | tapes | trail maps |
| extra pads* | sweater | matches |
| Bungi cords | surveys | jumbo cup |
| extra spoon* | extra lighters * | therm-a-rest in VA |
| 1 pan | 1 supplex shirt * | poncho |
| food * | bug spray* | itch balm |
| fork | water bag liner | pens* |
| medical supplies* | | |

223

# Seasonal Items sent in mail drops boxes

| | | |
|---|---|---|
| long-sleeve shirt | tee-shirts | insect repellent |
| fleece hat | gloves | halter top |
| sunscreen | fleece pullover | long underwear |

## In mail drops boxes

| | | |
|---|---|---|
| traveler's checks | tooth paste | plastic bags |
| stamped post cards | trail maps | soap |
| toilet paper | plastic bags | food |
| vitamins | Bic lighters | Tampax |
| laundry soap | small baggies | shampoo |
| 2 rolls of film for camera | socks every 500 miles | paper |
| stamped envelopes | hand lotion | aspirin |

# Food for a Vegetarian Diet

### Breakfast

Hot cereals (oatmeal, wheat germ, wheatena, quinoa, cream of rice, quinoa flakes, multi-grain cereal, bulger wheat, and couscous).

Nuts, dried fruit, peanut butter, almond butter, tahini, and humus on bagles.

### Lunches

Energy bars, peanut butter and crackers, pemmican bars, balance bars, power bars, granola bars, health cookies, soy nuts, natura pastries, and date bars. Nut spreads and bagels. I did not cook at lunch.

### Dinners

Precooked dried black and pinto bean flakes. Ramen noodles. Fantastic and Lipton soups. Noodles, pasta, rice, Prima-vera pasta, whole wheat vegetarian pasta, instant mashed potatoes, macaroni cheese, and vegetable noodles with sauces such as: pasta garden, black olive, pesto, parmesan cheese, gyro, and Tahini sauces. Polenta, humus, and vegetarian pate. Donna's dehydrated vegetables.

Nuts and beans were my main protein.

I drank only water, herb tea, and decaf coffee.

# Bibliography

Berry, Wendell. *The Unknown Wilderness: An Essay on Kentucky's Red River Gorge.* Lexington: University of Kentucky, 1971.

Bruce, "Wingfoot," Dan. *The Thru-hiker Handbook.* Hot Springs, North Carolina: Center for Appalachian Trail Studies, 1996.

Chazin, Daniel. *Appalachian Trail Data Book.* Harper's Ferry, West Virginia: The Appalachian Trail Conference, 1995.

Chopra, Deepak. *The Seven Spiritual Laws of Success.* San Rafael, CA: Amber-Allen, 1994.

Estes, Clarissa Pinkola. *Women Who Run with the Wolves.* New York: Ballantine, 1992.

Frost, Robert. "Stopping by the Woods on a Snowy Evening." In *Favorite Poems Old and New,* Helen Ferris, ed. Garden City, NY: Doubleday, 1957, p. 67.

Jung, C. G. *Collected Works of C.G.* Jung. 2nd ed. Princeton: Princeton University Press, 1972.

Marshall, Ian. *Story Line: Exploring the Literature of the Appalachian Trail.* Charlottesville, Virginia: University Of Virginia Press, 1998.

*Mind Walk.* Film based on the book *The Turning Point* by Fritjof Capra. The Atlas Production Company, produced by Adianna A. J. Cohen, 1990.

Rich, Adrienne. *Of Woman Born.* New York: W. W. Norton & Company, 1986.

Roe Betty, Suellen Alfred, and Sandy Smith. *Teaching Through Stories, Yours, Mine and Theirs.* Norwood, Massachusetts: Christopher-Gordon, 1998.

Rogers, Richard & Oscar Hammerstein. "You'll Never Walk Alone."from the musical *Carousel*, 1945.

Shakespeare, William. *Romeo and Juliet.* In *The Plays and Sonnets of William Shakespeare (Act II, Scene 2).*Volume One. William George Clarke and William Aldis Wright, eds. Chicago: Encyclopedia Britannica, 1952.

Shaw, George Bernard. *Man and Superman: A Comedy and a Philosophy.* Cambridge, MA. The Univerisity Press, 1903.

Snyder, Gary. *A Place in Space.* Washington D C: Counterpoint, 1995.

Snyder, Gary. *Practice of the Wild.* New York: North Point Press, 1990.

Thoreau, Henry David. *The Correspondence Of Henry David Thoreau.* Walter Harding and Carl Bode, eds. New York: New York University Press, 1958.

Thoreau, Henry David. *Walden.* J. Lyndon Shanley, ed. Princeton University Press, 1971.

Thoreau, Henry David. *Walden.* New York: Penguin Books, 1984.

Thoreau, Henry David. "Walking," in *The Appalachian Trail Reader.* David Emblidge, ed. New York: Oxford University Press, 1996.

Toor, Djohariah. *The Road by the River.* New York: St. Martin's Press, 1987.

# Walking the Dream

Telephone Orders: (931) 526-1974
Mail Orders: One Step Press,
c/o Ellen Wolfe
3623 Bartlett Dr., East Lake Estates
Cookeville, TN 38506
Email: ewolfe@usit.net

*Ship to:*

Name: _____

Address: _____

City: _____ State: _____ ZIP: _____

Telephone: (_____) _____
*Write checks to: Ellen Wolfe*

*Please send:*

_____ book(s) at $15.00                                          $_____
Sales Tax (Tennessee residents add $1.24 per book)    $_____
Shipping and Handling                                              $_____
*(add $2.00 for first book, $.75 per additional book)*
                                                            TOTAL   $_____

Ellen continues to do presentations about her journey on the
Appalachian Trail. For more information, call 931-526-1974.

Website: http://gemini.tntech.edu/~ewolfe/index.html

One Step Press  ·  3623 Bartlett Dr.  ·  East Lake Estates  ·  Cookeville, TN 38506